CIRCUS
MAXIMUS

CIRCUS MAXIMUS

The Economic Gamble Behind Hosting
the Olympics and the World Cup

2ND EDITION

ANDREW ZIMBALIST

BROOKINGS INSTITUTION PRESS
Washington, D.C.

Library of Congress Cataloging-in-Publication data
Names: Zimbalist, Andrew S., author.
Title: Circus maximus : the economic gamble behind hosting the
    Olympics and the World Cup / Andrew Zimbalist.
Description: 2nd edition. | Washington, D.C. : Brookings Insti-
    tution Press, 2016. | Includes bibliographical references and
    index. | Description based on print version record and CIP
    data provided by publisher; resource not viewed.
Identifiers: LCCN 2016001501 (print) | LCCN 2015040704 (ebook)
    | ISBN 9780815727279 (epub) | ISBN 9780815727286 (pdf)
    | ISBN 9780815727248 (paperback) | ISBN 9780815727279
    (ebook)
Subjects: LCSH: Hosting of sporting events—Economic aspects.
    | Olympics—Economic aspects. | World Cup (Soccer)—Eco-
    nomic aspects. | BISAC: BUSINESS & ECONOMICS / International
    / Economics. | POLITICAL SCIENCE / Public Policy / Economic
    Policy. | SPORTS & RECREATION / Olympics. | SPORTS & REC-
    REATION / Soccer.
Classification: LCC GV721 (print) | LCC GV721 .Z56 2016 (ebook)
    | DDC 796.48—dc23
LC record available at http://lccn.loc.gov/2016001501

Typeset in Sabon and Gotham Narrow

9 8 7 6 5 4 3 2

To the memory of
Ellie Abend (1924–2014),
my loving mother-in-law
and intrepid copy editor

Contents

	Preface to the Second Edition	ix
	Preface to the First Edition	xv
1	What's Wrong with the Olympics and the World Cup?	1
2	Setting the Stage	9
3	The Short-Run Economic Impact	35
4	The Long-Run Economic Impact	57
5	Barcelona and Sochi	75
6	Rio-Brazil and London	95
7	Bread or Circuses?	127
	Postscript	145
	Notes	165
	Index	197

Preface to the Second Edition

It's been an active year for the Olympics and the World Cup since the publication of the hardback edition of this book: an ugly scandal broke out at FIFA; the IOC passed its Agenda 2020 reform program; Rio stuttered its way toward the 2016 Olympics; Tokyo threw out its $2.5 billion plans for a new Olympic Stadium; Boston bidders bumbled their way to extinction; and the Russian government seems to have engaged in a massive cover-up and bribery scheme to promote extensive doping among its track-and-field athletes.

The first edition of *Circus Maximus* was published shortly after the U.S. Olympic Committee chose Boston to represent the United States in the international competition to host the 2024 Summer Games. Living in Massachusetts, I was immediately insinuated into the public discussion on the desirability of Boston hosting the Olympics: writing op-eds in the *Boston Globe*, giving public lectures, appearing on radio and television talk shows, testifying before the Boston Finance Committee, the NAACP executive committee, and the state senate, working with Chris Dempsey at No Boston Olympics, receiving a request from Boston 2024 to work with it, debating Steve Pagliuca and Dan Doctoroff on prime time television, and more. Mostly it was stimulating, edifying, and fun, though I got called a few names along the way—which I came to appreciate as badges of honor.

This paperback edition contains a postscript that discusses the Boston bid at greater length along with other salient events surrounding the World Cup and Olympics over the past twelve months. The text from the first edition is also updated and expanded.

Special thanks to Chris Dempsey from No Boston Olympics with whom I have had numerous conversations about the follies of Boston 2024 over the past year and to Jim Braude and Margery Eagan who have asked me all the tough questions. Thanks too to Andy Larkin, Enno Gerdes, Liam Kerr, Kelly Gossett, Lisa Genasci, Ted Cartselos, Dan Gardner, Stan Rosenberg, Bill Straus, Elizabeth Warren, John Henry, Malcolm McNee, Arthur MacEwan, Doug Rubin, and Peter Kwass for their conversations and insights. Bill Finan and Valentina Kalk at Brookings Institution Press have been supportive and an utter delight. Finally, big gratitude and love as always go to Shelley, Alex, Ella, Jeff, and Mike for being so supportive and interested in my work.

Preface to the First Edition

When I received a call from Gerry Schoenfeld, chairman of the Shubert Organization, Broadway's oldest show producer, in 2003, I had been working in the field of sports economics for over a decade. Some of my work had explored the economic impact of sports teams on cities.[1] Independent scholarly investigation was virtually unanimous: stadiums and teams could not be expected to have a positive impact on a city's employment or output. Part of this conclusion rested on the fact that most of the money fans spent at an arena or stadium was leisure budget money that they would otherwise spend at other entertainment venues within the city. Hence, spectator sport spending substituted for spending elsewhere in the local economy.

It seemed plausible that mega-sporting events (such as the Olympics, World Cup, or Super Bowl) would have a more positive impact. After all, a large share of the attendees came from out of the area or out of the country. They must be bringing new money, rather than recycled money, to town. Moreover, cities and countries were clamoring to host these events.

As it turns out, the substitution effect operates in a different way with mega-events, but it is still operative. Other factors as well conspire to render mega-events a dubious instrument to promote the local economy—except in special cases, with certain preconditions, and with very effective planning and implementation.

I wasn't fully aware of the lay of the mega-eventland when Gerry Schoenfeld called in 2003. I did know that it was two years after the events of September 11, 2001, and that New York City had an urge to rebuild. Under the leadership of Dan Doctoroff, the city's deputy mayor for economic development under Mayor Michael Bloomberg, and with the support of the city's major construction companies and unions, a committee had already formed to bid for the right to host the 2012 Summer Olympic Games.

Schoenfeld and the Shubert Organization didn't like the Olympic plan. In part, they thought it was a waste of the city's thin financial resources and not the most rational way to use its scarce land, but in larger part they were concerned with the impact that hosting the Games would have on Broadway. The keystone of the city's plan was a new Olympic stadium, to be built on land bounded by 31st and 33rd Streets and 10th and 11th Avenues. This six-square-block area houses the open train yards for the Long Island Railroad. Building an Olympic stadium on top of these yards would have first required putting a concrete slab over the yards. This six-square-block concrete slab alone would have cost an estimated $400 million (the construction of the stadium itself would have been an additional half billion dollars or more). The stadium would have had heavy use for the seventeen days of the Games, and then, after some costly refitting renovations, it would have served as the home field for the NFL's New York Jets. The Jets would have played ten home games there each year (including two exhibition games). There may also have been a few concerts and a perhaps a college football game, but it is not likely that the stadium would have been in use more than fifteen days a year. The slab and the stadium would have been paid for by the taxpayers.

I may not have fully understood mega-event economics at the time, but it was obvious to me that once a concrete slab covered six square blocks on the west side of mid-Manhattan overlooking the Hudson

River, it would be one of the most valuable pieces of real estate in the country, if not the world. Using it for fewer than 5 percent of the days of the year made no sense whatsoever.

And it made even less sense to the Shubert Organization. The stadium would have been a few blocks away from Broadway's theaters. The Jets play most of their home games on Sunday afternoons—that's major traffic jamming the streets for Sunday matinees. A few evening contests wouldn't help either. If public funds were to be employed to spiff up mid-Manhattan entertainment options, the Shubert Organization wanted to ask, how about some money to help maintain and renovate Manhattan's most venerable entertainment, the theaters of Broadway?

Schoenfeld wanted me to do some economic analysis, some writing, and some public speaking. I gave myself a crash course in Olympic economics and decided that Dan Doctoroff was pushing an unrealistic plan. Fortunately for New York City, the International Olympic Committee (IOC) agreed. In 2005 the IOC announced its choice of London to host the 2012 Summer Games.

In the years that followed, I continued to study the economics of mega-events and was asked to consult for a few cities as they contemplated bidding and hosting. In 2012 I edited a book with the German economist and Olympic gold medalist Wolfgang Maennig, the *International Handbook on the Economics of Mega Sporting Events*, which provided a more academic, discursive, and technical treatment of the subject.

In February 2013, the United States Olympic Committee (USOC) sent out a letter to fifty U.S. cities inviting them to bid to host the 2024 Summer Olympic Games. Boston was one of the cities to receive the invitation. It was not until several months later, however, that Mitt Romney suggested to Massachusetts governor Deval Patrick that Boston bid to be the host city. Patrick took the matter to the state legislature, which in turn appropriated funds for a study to be performed by a ten-member commission to be appointed by the governor.

After passing the appropriation, Massachusetts state senator and majority leader Stan Rosenberg e-mailed me to ask if I would be interested in serving on the commission. I responded affirmatively, depending on the timing and volume of the work involved. Senator Rosenberg thanked me and asked me to send him a résumé. He then sent my résumé with a cover letter to Deval Patrick, urging my appointment to the commission. Apparently, a similar interaction occurred between Victor Matheson, an economist at College of the Holy Cross in Worcester, Massachusetts, and an expert on mega-event economics, and another state legislator. I also pointed out to Senator Rosenberg that Judith Grant Long, a well-respected expert on the effect of the Olympics and other sports mega-events on urban economies, taught at Harvard University.

As it turned out, Governor Patrick did not appoint any of us to the commission. Instead, he appointed several executives, largely from the hospitality and construction industries—the latter industry having the most to gain if Boston were to host the Games. After several months the commission concluded that the matter warranted further study. While neither the state legislature nor the Boston city council voted to endorse the city's Olympic bid, the USOC selected Boston as the U.S. representative in the international competition to host the 2024 Olympics.

With Governor Patrick's maneuver, my cynicism about our political process and what interests it serves reached an all-time high. Perhaps you can't fool all the people all the time, but many politicians certainly seemed to be trying. I decided it was time to take a cold, hard look at the economics of hosting the Olympics and World Cup that would be accessible to noneconomists. That is what I have set out to do with this book.

The book's title, *Circus Maximus*, refers to an ancient Roman chariot racing stadium and mass entertainment venue. The word "circus" today refers either to the traveling show of animals, high-wire acts, and clowns or, metaphorically, to a chaotic and busy situation. "Maximus," of course, means greatest or largest. I don't think there are better terms to describe what the Olympics and World Cup represented in 2014.

The *New York Times* editorial board member Serge Schmemann has referred to the World Cup as "the battle for global primacy in what Americans insist upon calling soccer." As an American and an avid *New York Times* reader, I cannot make a liar out of Mr. Schmemann. Throughout this book I use the word "soccer" to denote "Association Football," to give the game its full title.[2] While "football" is the more common term used in the United Kingdom and most of the world, so as not to confuse it with American football, I demur. It is sometimes thought that the word "soccer" is an American invention for precisely this reason, but that is not the case. According to the *Oxford English Dictionary,* the first recorded use of the word "soccer" was in 1889 by an English writer (although using a variant spelling, "socca"). The word has been commonplace in England and elsewhere ever since. It is thought to be an abbreviation of "association," used originally to distinguish it from the game of "rugby football," also popular in England.[3] The Fédération Internationale de Football Association, or FIFA, is the governing body for international play in this arena.

I am indebted to many people who have assisted and supported me in researching and writing this book. First, I thank my colleagues Victor Matheson and Rob Baade. Initially our plan was to write jointly, but scheduling conflicts got in the way. We have discussed and shared a lot with each other. Second, I have learned much from the many colleagues I have worked with over the years on related projects, including Wolfgang Maennig, Roger Noll, John Siegfried, Allen Sanderson, Brad Humphreys, Dennis Coates, and Stefan Szymanski. Third, several individuals were directly useful in sharing materials and their expertise and time with me: Luis Fernandes, Gavin Poynter, Paulo Esteves, Fernan Brunet, Ricardo Guerra, Don Fehr, Denis Oswald, Anita DeFrantz, Michael Leeds, Nancy Hogshead-Makar, Anne Power, Martin Church, Derek Shearer, David Goldblatt, Jules

Boykoff, David Eades, Judith Grant Long, Sunil Gulati, James Easton, Phil Porter, Martin Müller, and Chris Gaffney. Finally, big gratitude and love to my family, Shelley, Alex, Ella, and Jeff and Mike for supporting me throughout.

1

What's Wrong with the Olympics and the World Cup?

No city wanted to host the 1984 Olympic Games. Mexico City's games in 1968 were marred by violence and political protest. Munich's games in 1972 ended in wrenching tragedy as eleven Israeli athletes were killed by terrorists. Montreal's games in 1976 cost 9.2 times more than initially budgeted and yielded a debt that took the city thirty years to pay down.

There was no glory associated with hosting the Olympics back then, and the International Olympic Committee (IOC) was desperate to find a venue. With no competition, Los Angeles stepped forward and made a deal. Los Angeles would not have to provide the typical financial guarantee, and the city could basically get by with its existing sports infrastructure, part of which came from having hosted the 1932 Olympics.[1] This favorable deal, together with some clever and aggressive marketing of corporate sponsorships by Peter Ueberroth, led the L.A. Organizing Committee to realize a modest profit of $215 million.

The Los Angeles experience turned the tide. Shown the alluring path to possible profits, cities and countries now lined up for the honor of hosting the games. The competition to host the games became almost as intense as the athletic competition itself. Would-be hosts lavished more and more money on their bids; today, spending upward of $100 million on the bidding process alone is not unusual.

With each bidder trying to outdo all the others, expenditures on hosting the games rose to over $40 billion for the Beijing Summer Games in 2008 and reportedly topped $50 billion for the 2014 Sochi Winter Games. Developing economies have jumped into the bidding in recent years. They require more substantial investments owing to inadequate transportation, communications, energy, hospitality, and sporting infrastructure. Other sports mega-events have experienced similar cost escalations. The cost of hosting the FIFA World Cup, soccer's quadrennial showcase event, has risen from several hundred million in 1994, when the United States hosted the event, to $5–$6 billion in 2010 in South Africa and $15–$20 billion in Brazil in 2014. Qatar could shatter all records when it hosts the event in 2022, with some estimating the final price tag will come in at an eye-popping $220 billion or more.

But history might be repeating itself. Just as forces conspired to eliminate bidders in the late 1970s, by 2014 escalating costs had imposed a major financial burden on countries with meager resources and deficient public services. While promoters of the games made lofty claims about the economic benefits to be gained from hosting these sporting extravaganzas, the local populations seemed unimpressed. Not only were there no evident economic gains, there were social dislocations and resource diversions away from meeting basic needs. The games may benefit their wealthy promoters, but those at the middle and bottom of the income ladder appear to be picking up the tab—and increasingly, they don't like it.

In June 2013, before and during the Confederations Cup (a quadrennial international soccer competition that precedes the World Cup in the host country), more than a million Brazilians across the country took to the streets to protest the government's spending $15–$20 billion on new stadiums and infrastructure (much of which was never finished) to host the 2014 World Cup. Meanwhile, the Brazil-

ian population faced woeful public transportation ser
fares, deficient medical care, poor schools, and insuf
Popular protests continued throughout 2013 and ther
scendo as the World Cup approached in June 2014. St
teachers, and transport and airport workers erupted ın ıany cities,
and street demonstrations, though heavily repressed, accompanied
the soccer competition.

Brazil is not alone in protesting government policies and priorities.
People worldwide, from the United States (Occupy Wall Street) to the
Middle East (the Arab Spring), Russia, Pakistan, Ukraine, Istanbul,
South Africa, Chile, Bolivia, and China, have risen up to protest what
they perceive to be unequal and unfair outcomes that are being aided
and abetted by government policy. Globalization and the march of
technology, together with market forces and a skewed distribution
of market power, have conspired to widen economic inequality both
among and within countries.

Of course, the members of the executive boards of FIFA and the
IOC themselves belong to the economic elite. They travel first class,
stay in the finest hotels, and rub elbows with the political and business leaders in the cities they visit. Sepp Blatter, the FIFA president,
earns a salary in excess of $1 million on top of what seems like an un-
limited expense account. Other FIFA executives earn compensation
packages well into six figures.[2] Blatter had been giving the twenty-
five members of the FIFA Executive Committee annual bonuses
ranging from $75,000 to $200,000 a year on top of their salary of
$100,000 for very part-time work. For appearances' sake, the prac-
tice of annual bonuses was ended in 2014, but FIFA's Sub-Committee
on Compensation (an appointed body of Executive Committee members[3]) made up for the loss of bonuses by secretly voting to double
their annual pay to $200,000, according to documents uncovered
by London's *Sunday Times*. The *Times* also reported that Executive Committee members received a $700 per diem while doing FIFA
work, traveled business class, and stayed in five-star hotels.[4] According to the FIFA ethics code, the twenty-seven Executive Committee

members are not supposed to receive gifts that have more than symbolic value. In September 2014, however, it was revealed that in the hotel gift bags in Brazil for the 2014 World Cup there was a luxury Swiss Parmigiani watch worth $25,000. Twenty-four members of the Executive Committee, including Sepp Blatter, did not report this gift; three members, U.S. member Sunil Gulati, Australian member Moya Dodd, and Jordanian member Prince Ali bin Al Hussein, reported the violation to FIFA's Ethics Committee. Apparently, the plan was to gift two more watches, each worth over $42,000, to each Executive Committee member, until the first transgression was reported.[5] After this news became public in early September, FIFA's Ethics Committee took a stand and ordered the Executive Committee members to return their watches.[6] These excesses are only the tip of the iceberg of corruption and opulence at Blatter's FIFA.[7]

The members of the IOC are unpaid, although they benefit from lavish expense accounts and the organization is populated by the rich, the famous, and others who seem as if they would be as comfortable in a ballroom or boardroom as on an athletic field.[8] Royalty on the IOC include Prince Feisal bin Al Hussein of Jordan; Frederik, Crown Prince of Denmark; Princess Haya bint Al Hussein of Jordan (and sheikha of Dubai); Sheikh Tamim Bin Hamad Al Thani, emir of Qatar; Prince Nawaf Faisal Fahd Abdulaziz of Saudi Arabia;[9] Prince Ahmad Al-Fahad Al-Sabah of Kuwait; Anne, Princess Royal of Britain; and Prince Albert II and Princess Nora of Liechtenstein.[10]

Distributional concerns inevitably are more pressing in countries at earlier stages of economic development. In light of the recent trend for developing countries, in particular the BRICS (Brazil, Russia, India, China, and South Africa), to host the Olympics and World Cup—countries where resources are scarcer, the fiscal balance is more fragile, hosting costs are far greater, and the income distribution is more lopsided—the potential for explosive protests seems imminent. While hosting a sport mega-event is hardly a seminal force behind a country's inequality, there is little question that it contributes to and reinforces existing patterns of inequality. That the Olympics and

World Cup are so heavily publicized and so visible only increases the likelihood that wasteful spending will catch the attention and scorn of the population.

With Olympics bidding, the typical pattern is for a country's National Olympic Committee (NOC) to call for bids from prospective host cities eleven years before the games. There ensues a competition among the interested cities to win their country's nod, which occurs nine years prior to the games. The selected cities at this stage are known as "applicants," and each pays the IOC $150,000 to be considered. The applicant cities are then whittled down to a group of usually three to five finalist or "candidate" cities. Each candidate city pays the IOC an additional $500,000 for the privilege of being considered as an Olympic host. (The IOC collapsed these two phases into one during the summer of 2015.)

The bids by cities are driven by major private economic interests within the city's political economy, such as construction companies, construction unions, insurance companies, architectural firms, hotels, local media companies, investment bankers (who will float the bonds), and the lawyers who work for these groups.[11] These groups in turn hire a public relations firm and a consulting firm to generate interest and excitement around the hosting prospect and to make elaborate claims of the potential economic benefits to the city.

Except in special cases, however, the promised benefits are not forthcoming. Equally troublesome, to prepare for the games the host city often must clear land, which frequently means relocating communities and jobs; hire migrant labor; divert resources away from important social services; and borrow billions, encumbering future tax dollars. Along the way, local communities experience congestion and pollution in the name of constructing venues and infrastructure that may have little or no effective use after the games and that may charge admission prices well beyond the reach of the common person's budget.

Seven years before the games, after two years of competition among the candidate cities aimed to convince the IOC that they are the most worthy of the hosting honor, the IOC anoints a winner. A similar selection process occurs for the World Cup. With multiple bidders from around the globe and only one seller (the IOC or FIFA), it is almost unavoidable that the winning city or country will have overbid. This outcome is made even more likely because the groups pushing each city's bid are representing their own private interests, not the city's. And these groups will not have to pay the construction bills; rather, they will be the ones on the receiving end, getting the lucrative contracts. Economists believe the outcome of such a bidding process is likely to result in a "winner's curse"—an outcome in which the winner has bid above the object's true worth.

The problem for the IOC and FIFA is that rising popular protests are alerting politicians to the fact that hosting the Olympics and World Cup may not be such a good deal economically or politically. Fewer cities and countries are entering the bidding. Voters in St. Moritz and Davos, Switzerland, in March 2013; in Munich, Germany, in November 2013; in Stockholm, Sweden, in January 2014; and, in Krakow, Poland, in May 2014 went to the polls and rejected their cities' entering the bidding competition to host the 2022 Winter Games.[12] In October 2014 the Norwegian government decided not to back Oslo's bid to host the 2022 Olympics, stating that it was offended by the "insane demands that the IOC be treated like the king of Saudi Arabia." Norway's withdrawal placed the IOC in an embarrassing position: it was left to choose between cities in two authoritarian countries, Almaty, Kazakhstan and Beijing, China, each environmentally, financially, and human-rights challenged.

The new IOC president, Thomas Bach, spent much of December 2013 and January 2014 attempting to convince cities to bid for the 2024 Summer Games. At the pre–Olympic Games meeting in Sochi, Russia, in February 2014, trying to avert another downward bidding cycle similar to the late 1970s, Bach called for new approaches to the bidding process. Then, in December 2014, the IOC passed Bach's Agenda 2020 reform. (Whether Agenda 2020 will constitute real reform or is just new optics will be discussed in the book's postscript.)

The chapters that follow take a closer look at all these issues. The next chapter considers the evolution of both the Olympics and the World Cup, how each came to be the Circus Maximus it is today, and the challenges each confronts. Chapter 3 discusses the short-term costs and benefits of hosting the Olympics and World Cup. Chapter 4 analyzes the long-run or legacy impacts of hosting. Chapter 5 presents the experiences of Barcelona with the 1992 Summer Games and Sochi with the 2014 Winter Games, while chapter 6 explores the experiences of Rio de Janeiro and Brazil with the 2014 World Cup and the upcoming 2016 Summer Olympics, and of London with the 2012 Summer Games. Chapter 7 offers an assessment of what works and what doesn't for host cities and countries, what problems FIFA and the IOC are facing, and what reforms they are considering or should consider. The postcript considers the major developments between September 2014 and September 2015 that have impacted the hosting of the Olympics and the World Cup and what these developments may mean for the future of both events.

2

Setting the Stage

The modern Olympic Games began in Athens in 1896. They bear little resemblance to the ancient Greek games of more than two millennia ago.

The Era of Amateurism

The nineteenth-century French aristocrat, intellectual, and writer Pierre de Frédy, baron de Coubertin, studied the program of physical education at the Rugby School in England. Coubertin believed that the incorporation of physical education into the British educational system promoted the balanced development of mind and body and was a major reason for the expansion of British power during the nineteenth century. France, in contrast, was still reeling from its humiliating defeat in the Franco-Prussian War, and Coubertin saw educational reform as a key element in nation building.

Coubertin's effort at educational reform, however, found little success, and he soon turned his attentions to a new plan, also founded on some notion of the benefits of physical activity and athleticism: reviving the ancient Olympic Games of Greece.[1] Coubertin was wedded to two basic principles that he saw embodied in the ancient games: first, the competitors should be amateurs,[2] and second, the games should be a way to bring different cultures and antagonistic nations together, promoting better understanding and peace.

Historians question whether the ancient games were in fact characterized by amateurism and peace, as Coubertin imagined. While some historians hold that competitors in the Greek Olympics were always directly or indirectly paid, others maintain that the ancient games only became professionalized after 480 BCE. Whatever the reality, all historians understand that there was a class component to the notion of amateurism: only the upper class had the leisure time available to engage in sport. Coubertin's insistence on the modern games being for amateur athletes only was tantamount, in the late nineteenth century, to limiting participants to the upper class.

Coubertin's belief that the ancient games promoted peace was also suspect. The only recognizable peace ensued from an agreement among warring regions to allow athletes and religious pilgrims to pass safely through territories on their way to the games at Olympia. There appears to be no evidence that the games either ended existing hostilities or prevented new ones from arising.

The New Olympic Movement

When the modern games began in Athens in the summer of 1896, however, it mattered not whether Coubertin had his history right or whether he was perpetrating myths. The intentions of the new Olympic Movement were enshrined in its charter, including these principles:

> Olympism is a philosophy of life, exalting and combining in a balanced whole the qualities of body, will and mind. Blending sport with culture and education. . . . The goal of Olympism is to place everywhere sport at the service of the harmonious development of man, with a view to encouraging the establishment of a peaceful society concerned with the preservation of human dignity. . . . Any form of discrimination with regard to a

country or person on grounds of race, religion, politics, gender or otherwise is incompatible with belonging to the Olympic Movement.[3]

The nondiscrimination principle was violated at the outset. No women athletes participated in the 1896 Athens Games. These first modern games were diminutive by current standards: 295 athletes from fourteen nations participated, competing in forty-three events. The Athens organizers had expected soccer teams from four countries to compete, but none showed up. The Athens games were funded jointly by private and public funds.

The next two Olympic Games were staged in Paris, in 1900, and St. Louis, in 1904, but were overshadowed by the coincident Paris Exposition in the former and the World's Fair in the latter. Nonetheless, the Paris games were notable because they marked the first time women participated, as well as the introduction of soccer competition. To be sure, the representation of women athletes was modest, but at least it was a start: Paris featured 1,066 male athletes but only eleven women. The St. Louis games were marked by the near absence of foreign participation—of the 650 athletes, 580 were from the United States.

London hosted the games in 1908, and Stockholm in 1912. The Stockholm Olympics are remembered for the legendary performance by the Native American Jim Thorpe, who won the gold medals in both the pentathlon and the decathlon competitions (and defeated the future IOC president Avery Brundage in each event).[4] After Thorpe admitted to playing a summer of professional baseball while a student at Carlisle Indian School, the IOC stripped him of his medals. Some critics raised questions about whether the IOC's action may have been tainted by racism.

Following a hiatus in 1916, when the Olympics were canceled because of World War I, the 1920 Games were held in Antwerp, Belgium. Although the Olympics were intended to be apolitical and to promote world peace, the Allied powers of World War I were not interested in having the Germans participate in the games, and Germany was unceremoniously excluded. The number of female athletes grew to 64, versus 2,527 male athletes.

Money, Politics, and the Olympic Brand

The Belgian games exhibited a characteristic that was to become a hallmark for future hosting cities. In Antwerp, a group of wealthy sportsmen and businessmen initiated the drive to host the 1920 Games, along with a world's fair. They agreed to contribute 1 million Belgian francs, and asked for a contribution from the city of 800,000 francs. The intervention of World War I discombobulated the plans and prevented the original design from being implemented. Nonetheless, the promoters persisted, and a new plan emerged. The games were finally awarded to Antwerp in 1919, just sixteen months prior to the opening ceremony—which helps explain the unfinished stadium, the poor condition of the athletic tracks, and the inadequate accommodations.[5] The organizing committee ran commercial events for months leading up to the games to promote local businesses. In the end, the financial record showed the following: (1) the 1-million-franc private contribution had turned into a 1-million-franc loan, at 4 percent interest; (2) the public contribution from federal, provincial, and city coffers rose to 2.5 million francs; and (3) a bottom-line deficit of 626,000 francs remained at the end of the games. Meanwhile, the promoters from the local sporting and business elite benefited from new business and the modernization of the facilities of their sports club. Two Belgian historians concluded, "What is clear is that a small group of prominent citizens of large fortune had succeeded in using the Olympic Games for their own financial advantage and social prestige."[6]

The strict requirement of amateurism led to festering disagreements within the IOC. The IOC organized a special congress to debate the issue in Prague in May 1925. Was amateurism necessary? If so, could athletes' expenses be paid? Could an athlete receive "broken-time payments" to compensate for lost days of work? With some dissension, the policy going forward would be that athletes could receive expense reimbursement for up to fifteen days, but no compensation beyond that. The international soccer federation, however, broke ranks and declared it would allow its athletes to receive broken-time payments.[7]

Coubertin's intentions and exhortations to the contrary, political disputes were never far from the modern Olympics. If idealists did not acknowledge this before the 1930s, the staging of the 1936 Winter and Summer Games in Germany must have convinced even the most recalcitrant. Germany was awarded host status for the 1936 Games in May 1931, when Heinrich Bruning's centrist coalition was still in power. Hitler's rule was not to commence until January 1933, six days after the organizing committee for the games was formed.

Yet FIFA's new tournament, the World Cup, beat the IOC to the table in having its international competition hosted by a fascist government. FIFA was founded in 1904. By 1914, FIFA had been put in charge of organizing the soccer competition at the Olympics. But FIFA always regarded the Olympics as a second-rate soccer tournament because of the IOC's insistence on amateurism. FIFA had more clout than any other Olympic sport organizing body because soccer was an established and globally popular sport. In 1928 FIFA decided to have its own competition, unfettered by IOC rules. The first World Cup competition was held in Uruguay in 1930. Only thirteen countries sent teams to participate—seven from South America, four from Europe, and two from North America.[8] The rift between FIFA and the IOC grew deeper when the organizing committee for the 1932 Olympics, held in Los Angeles, opted not to include soccer, on the pretext that it was not a popular sport in the United States.[9]

The 1934 World Cup was hosted in Mussolini's Italy. Italy was selected over Sweden in 1932, primarily because of the impressive budget that Mussolini had proposed for new stadiums and infrastructure. Just as Germany saw the 1936 Olympics as a way to showcase its new government, Mussolini saw the World Cup as an opportunity to promote Italian fascism, but, unencumbered by the athletic embarrassments and eligibility battles that were to preoccupy the Germans, Mussolini's Italian team won the competition.

There was a strong lobbying effort in several countries to boycott the 1936 German Games. The primary concern was that Hitler would not allow Jews to participate on the German team. Based on nothing more than verbal assurances from the German government, Avery Brundage, a key figure on the American Olympics Committee and a future president of the IOC, persuaded the United States to participate.[10] In the end, no Jews were on the German team.[11] Brundage took his fawning one step further. So as not to irritate Hitler, Brundage seems also to have arranged for the only two Jews on the U.S. track and field team to be pulled from the relay race.[12]

The standout athlete at the games was the black American athlete Jesse Owens who, among other things, set the world record of 10.3 seconds in the 100-meter sprint, winning three gold medals and putting a dent in the claim of Aryan superiority. When the Korean Kitei Son won the marathon and Japanese swimmers took home four gold, two silver, and five bronze medals, Hitler's propaganda machine had to work overtime to claim victory.[13]

The 1936 Games were the first televised Olympics, though on a limited basis and only within Germany, and this pattern of limited transmission remained in place for a time. After the 1940 and 1944 Games were derailed by World War II, the next games took place in London in 1948 and were televised only within England. Similarly, the Melbourne Games of 1956 were broadcast only in Australia.[14] The 1960 Summer Games in Rome were the first televised live throughout Western Europe, with the broadcasts reaching a total of twenty-one countries.[15] CBS paid $660,000 for the right to fly film back to the United States for prime-time telecasts. Of this modest sum, the IOC kept only 5 percent, with 95 percent going to Italy's National Olympic Committee (NOC). The 1964 Summer Games in Tokyo were the first to be carried by satellite transmission and to be broadcast live around the world.[16]

For the 1968 Games, U.S. television rights jumped to $4.5 million. As the money became more substantial, conflict emerged among the IOC, the NOCs, the International Federations (IFs) of each sport, and the local organizing committees for the Olympic Games (OCOGs) over how to divide the loot.[17] A compromise was reached for the 1968 Games: the first million dollars would be divided equally among the IOC, the NOCs, and the IFs. Of the second million, one-third would go to the OCOGs and two-thirds would be split equally among the IOC, the NOCs, and the IFs; and the third million would go two-thirds to the OCOGs and one-third to the IOC, the NOCs, and the IFs.[18] The formula would be continually tweaked as the television rights fee grew and political tensions found new expression.[19] IOC money continues to be shared with the NOCs and IFs. The evolution of the division of television money between the IOC and the OCOGs is depicted in table 2-1.

The percentages given in table 2-1 functioned more as guidelines than as rules. As IOC television policy was being devised in the 1970s and 1980s, there were continual disputes between the OCOGs and the IOC, as well as among the IOC, the NOCs, and the IFs, over the distribution of revenues. One of the most contentious items was how to distinguish between the cash payments made by a network and the money the network would spend on "technical services" (for

TABLE 2-1. Division of Television Rights Fees for Olympic Games, 1948–2010

Period	International Olympic Committee (%)	Organizing Committees for Olympic Games (%)
1948–68	1–4	96–99
1972–80	10	90
1984–92	33	67
1996–2004	40	60
2006–2010	51	49

Source: Data kindly provided by Denis Oswald of the IOC Executive Committee.

example, cameras, studios, technicians, telecommunications equipment, and so on). For instance, for the 1984 Summer Olympics in Los Angeles, ABC committed to $225 million for U.S. television rights. Of that sum, $100 million was paid in cash and the remaining $125 million was attributed to technical services. After much dickering and several international trips, the L.A. Organizing Committee was obligated to share one-third of the cash payment only, or $33 million, as opposed to one-third of the entire $225 million.[20] Disagreements also emerged over the split of television broadcasting rights payments from other continents (which were much lower, mostly owing to the presence of state television monopolies or negotiating cartels), and in those cases the IOC garnered closer to 25 percent.[21]

The 1968 Summer Games in Mexico City—the first Olympics to be held in a developing country—also introduced a new type of Olympian politics. There was the quadrennial squabble about whether or not apartheid South Africa should be allowed to participate. IOC president Avery Brundage (1952–72) stood again on the less moralistic side and espoused inviting the South African team. The IOC membership, however, voted not to invite the South Africans. Shortly after the vote, the UN Security Council condemned the white supremacist government of newly independent Rhodesia, and Mexico, ignoring instructions from Brundage, refused to grant entrance visas to the Rhodesian team.

Meanwhile, Mexican students were protesting the domestic policies of the hegemonic PRI (Partido Revolucionario Institucional) government.[22] The students saw an opportunity to attract world attention to their cause and established a theme that was to be repeated elsewhere, most recently in Brazil. When countries beset with social problems host the Olympics or World Cup, protesters seek to capitalize on the worldwide attention focused on their country.

The PRI government had other ideas. A few weeks before the games were to begin, the Mexican army was summoned to squash the student movement. According to some reports, more than 200 demonstrators were killed.

But other trouble was brewing. The IOC's waffling position on South Africa and Rhodesia and the assassination of Martin Luther King on April 4, 1968, almost led U.S. black athletes to boycott the Mexico City games. When black U.S. athlete Tommie Smith won the 200-meter race in a world-record time of 19.83 seconds and his teammate John Carlos finished third, they each wore a black glove on their right hand on the medals podium and raised their fists in a Black Power salute during the playing of the U.S. national anthem. Smith and Carlos were summarily sent home.[23]

The 1972 Summer Games in Munich are infamous for a different political reason. Just after 4 a.m. on September 5, a group of Palestinian terrorists scaled the fence at the Olympic Village and entered the quarters of the Israeli squad.[24] The terrorists held the Israelis captive and demanded the release of 234 Palestinians detained in Israeli prisons. When the assault and negotiations ended, eleven Israelis lay dead, along with five terrorists and one German policeman. The Munich games, like those in Mexico City, are a vivid illustration of how the image of a host city can be tarnished rather than burnished. The brand of the Olympics also began to suffer.

IOC optics worsened once more in November 1972. At its Amsterdam meeting in 1970, the IOC awarded Denver the right to host the 1976 Winter Olympics. However, following a grassroots campaign that focused on escalating costs and environmental degradation, 60 percent of the voters in a public referendum objected to the use of public funds to finance the 1976 games. Denver had to withdraw as host city.

The Olympic brand took another hit with the 1976 Summer Games in Montreal. Several African nations boycotted the games over the IOC's refusal to ban New Zealand, whose rugby team had been touring in South Africa, and Canada's government, having recognized the People's Republic of China in 1970, refused to grant entrance visas to members of the Taiwanese team.

Montreal, with a bid estimate of C$120 million, had been awarded the games in May 1970 over rival bids from Moscow and Los Angeles. Not atypically, with poor management, industrial disputes, and problematic stadium and airport design, construction fell considerably behind schedule, and the provincial government of Quebec took over the Olympics works project.[25] Notwithstanding the notorious boast of Montreal's mayor, Jean Drapeau, that "the Olympics can no more have a deficit than a man can have a baby," the final tab exceeded C$1.6 billion, creating a debt that Montreal did not pay off for thirty years.[26]

The Montreal games were notable for one other feature—the rising dominance of East Germany's swimmers and track and field athletes. East Germany's Kornelia Ender set Olympic records in the 100-meter and 200-meter freestyle swimming events and the 100-meter butterfly, and then earned a fourth gold medal in the medley.[27] In track and field, East German women won nine events and finished first, second, and third in the pentathlon. Few observers were persuaded by East German denials about the use of anabolic steroids, and the IOC, which set up a drug commission in 1966, began to ban certain drugs in 1972, aggressively ramping up its enforcement against artificial performance enhancers. Under an IOC initiative and with IOC funding, the World Anti-Doping Agency (WADA) was eventually established in 1999.

In its bid to host the 1980 Summer Games, the Soviet Union showed some capitalist marketing flair. Beginning in 1970, Moscow set out to court the IOC. In 1973, thirty-two IOC members were invited to Moscow to be wined and dined. A year later all eighty members were VIP guests in Moscow, and in October 1974 the IOC anointed Moscow as the 1980 host. Although the ongoing cold war raised suspicions about the prospects for the Moscow games, all was progressing relatively smoothly until the Soviet Union invaded Afghanistan in December 1979. U.S. president Jimmy Carter issued an ultimatum three weeks later: if the Soviet Union did not withdraw from Afghanistan, the United States would boycott the Moscow Olympics. The Soviet Union stayed in Afghanistan for ten years, and first the U.S. Congress, and then, threatened with the loss of gov-

ernment financial support, the USOC, supported Car'
boycott.[28] Carter then leaned on Prime Minister Ma'
to have England join the boycott. Thatcher agreed and p.
the House of Commons to support the plan, which it did. The Briu.
NOC, however, in keeping with its tradition of political independence, voted 18-5 to send its athletes to Moscow. Over the ensuing
months, the question of skipping the Moscow games was entertained
by one country after another: West Germany chose to boycott, the
rest of Europe opted to participate; Japan and China joined the boycott, and so it went. In the end, the athletes of sixty-two nations
stayed home and those of eighty-one nations participated.

Following the political debacle in Mexico City, the horrific terrorist acts in Munich, the financial catastrophe in Montreal, and the
extensive boycott of Moscow,[29] the Olympic brand was markedly diminished. The only candidate city to host the 1984 Summer Games
was Los Angeles, and the L.A. bid did not come from the city but
from a private group.[30] IOC president Killanin at first insisted that,
in accordance with the Olympic Charter, the bid come from the city
and the city assume full financial responsibility. L.A. mayor Thomas
Bradley responded that the city was not interested. Moreover, the
L.A. city charter had recently been amended to prohibit public funding of the Olympic Games.[31] The executive board of the IOC relented
and waived Rule 4, leaving Los Angeles without financial responsibility in the event of any operating losses.

It is noteworthy that despite the L.A. charter amendment pro-
scribing the use of public funds, the city of Los Angeles agreed to
collect a 0.5 percent hotel tax when the games were first awarded,
and also to levy a municipal tax on tickets to Olympic competitions.
The collected funds of approximately $19.3 million would go to help
fund the games and their security. Of that sum, $15 million was bud-
geted for the Los Angeles Police Department, to be used as part of
the games' security budget.[32] The notion that levying a tax on hotels
or car rentals produces a free good for the local population has been
promulgated by many cities when seeking to fund sports facilities.

It makes little sense. The higher "tourist tax" will either discourage business travelers and leisure tourists by the higher prices or it won't.[33] To the extent it reduces tourism, it lowers demand and hurts the local economy. To the extent that it doesn't discourage travel (because tourists are not sensitive to a small increase in the price of visiting the city), then the tax could be levied even if the city did not host the Olympics, and then used to improve public services or to fund tax reductions. In either case, the local residents are paying.

In any event, the stop-loss precaution in L.A.'s agreement with the IOC proved to be unnecessary. Four ingredients made the L.A. games a financial success: one, television rights grew by almost $200 million above the fees paid for the Moscow games (and L.A.'s share grew accordingly); two, Peter Ueberroth, head of the L.A. Organizing Committee, followed an energetic and innovative marketing strategy, creating exclusive product categories[34] and raising another $130 million in corporate sponsorships; three, most of the athletic, transportation, and communications infrastructure was already in place; and four, the few new, smaller facilities that were built for the games were privately funded. In the end, it mattered little that the Soviet Union and most of its allies, along with the steroid-pumped athletes from the GDR, boycotted the games.

The Rise of Commercialization and the End of Amateurism

The L.A. games marked a watershed for the Olympic Games. After sixteen years of a weakening reputation, the financial success of the L.A. games (which produced a $215 million operating surplus[35]) turned the IOC's fortunes around. That the L.A. games coincided with an explosion in television rights, a new corporate sponsorship strategy, and IOC president Juan Antonio Samaranch's move to professionalize the Olympics only made the uptick more pronounced. Despite all the positives that the L.A. games had going for them, Ueberroth still thinks that the surplus could have been a deficit had it not been for a run of good fortune: "We were lucky: Nothing happened—no massive security problems, no labor strikes, no transportation breakdowns, and no natural catastrophes."[36]

Table 2-2 depicts the remarkable escalation in television rights fees. The largest percentage increase occurred between the Moscow and the Los Angeles games (and their Winter games counterparts, in Lake Placid and Sarajevo).[37] There was also a sizable jump in the number of countries receiving television coverage of the Olympics: from 111 countries for the Moscow games and 40 for Lake Placid in 1980 to 156 for Los Angeles and 100 for Sarajevo in 1984. In both 2010 and 2012, 220 nations received television distribution of the games.

TABLE 2-2. Television Rights Fees for Olympic Games, 1960–2012

Olympic Games	Broadcast revenue (millions of USD)	Olympic Games	Broadcast revenue (millions of USD)
Summer Games		*Winter Games*	
1960 Rome	1.2	1960 Squaw Valley	0.05
1964 Tokyo	1.6	1964 Innsbruck	0.94
1968 Mexico City	9.8	1968 Grenoble	2.6
1972 Munich	17.8	1972 Sapporo	8.5
1976 Montreal	34.9	1976 Innsbruck	11.6
1980 Moscow	88.0	1980 Lake Placid	20.7
1984 Los Angeles	286.9	1984 Sarajevo	102.7
1988 Seoul	402.6	1988 Calgary	324.9
1992 Barcelona	636.1	1992 Albertville	291.9
1996 Atlanta	898.3	1994 Lillehammer	352.9
2000 Sydney	1,330.0	1998 Nagano	513.5
2004 Athens	1,490.0	2002 Salt Lake City	738.0
2008 Beijing	1,740.0	2006 Turin	831.0
2012 London	2,600.0	2010 Vancouver	1,280.0

Source: IOC, *Olympic Marketing File*, 2014, p. 26. The figures apply to the total worldwide network commitment of rights fees, both the cash and the technical service components. In recent years the technical service component has been largely defrayed by the host city and the equipment has been paid for by the network and not included in the rights fee payments. The figures also do not distinguish the timing of the payments, parts of which can vary by months or by years.

The other substantial transformation that occurred at the time was the jettisoning of amateurism. Unlike his predecessors, the new IOC president, Juan Antonio Samaranch (1980–2001) sought to realize the Olympics' full commercial potential.[38] If that required allowing professional athletes to participate in the games, then so be it. Samaranch believed that the games should showcase the world's best and most famous athletes. Of course, the games' television partners saw matters exactly the same way, and this convergence of views helps explain the inflation of television rights fees with the L.A. games. The full sponsorship by the state of Olympic athletes in the communist countries was another motivating force behind professionalization.

In 1984 the IOC voted to allow the IFs to set the eligibility rules for their sport, within some limits. In 1987 the IOC voted to permit professional tennis players to participate in the games, and in 1989 the IOC extended the welcome to all professional athletes. Finally, in 1991 the IOC lifted all restrictions on professionalism, a decision that was heralded by the U.S. Dream Team's competing in the 1992 Barcelona Games.[39] The Dream Team, which included Michael Jordan, Magic Johnson, Larry Bird, David Robinson, and Patrick Ewing, to no one's surprise, took the gold medal in basketball.

A final step toward commercialization was taken in 1992, when the IOC decided not to have the Winter and Summer Olympics in the same year. This way the take from business advertising expenditures could be maximized by not having to stretch corporate promotional budgets to cover two large competitions in the same year.[40] Henceforth the games would alternate every two years, commencing with the Winter Games in Lillehammer in 1994.

The Olympics were ascendant again, and aspiring host cities were springing up around the globe. The number of applicants went from one in the case of Los Angeles (to which the games were awarded in May 1978) and two in the case of Seoul (awarded in September 1981) to six in the case of Barcelona (awarded in October 1986), six in Atlanta (awarded in September 1990), eight in Sydney (awarded in September 1993), and eleven in Athens (awarded in September 1997).[41]

Thus, everything was turning up roses for the IOC—perhaps too many roses. All the media and corporate money and all the competition among bidding cities led to temptation. And IOC president Juan Antonio Samaranch enjoyed every bit of what high demand had to offer. Samaranch, the son of a wealthy factory owner from Barcelona and longtime Francoist, set a new tone for the IOC when he began his reign in 1980. He insisted on being referred to as "His Excellency" and being treated like a head of state. Before Samaranch became president, IOC members had to pay their own way to cities bidding for the games. Within a few years they were getting not one but two first-class tickets, plus all expenses and lavish entertainment. Samaranch himself always insisted on limo service and the best suite in the fanciest hotel in any city. In Lausanne he had the IOC rent for his use a massive penthouse suite at the Palace Hotel for $500,000 a year. IOC members followed Samaranch's lead, and payoffs grew by leaps and bounds.[42]

Although isolated innuendos concerning payoffs and abuse of the IOC bidding process had reached the media before, the flood began on November 24, 1998.[43] The Salt Lake City television station KTVX reported that a 1996 letter in its possession revealed that the Salt Lake City bid committee had offered a college scholarship to the daughter of the IOC member from Cameroon. At the time, IOC regulations permitted members to receive gifts from bid committees, but only up to $150 in value. Subsequent testimony and written evidence showed that this limit was surpassed in spades. Relatives of IOC members had received approximately $400,000 in financial aid or scholarships in a program that began after 1991, when Salt Lake City lost its bid to host the 1998 Winter Olympics. Further evidence revealed that IOC members and their relatives had benefited from lavish gifts, hospitality, escort services, medical treatment, employment, shopping trips, holiday travel, and opulent accommodations.[44]

As the news about the Salt Lake City scandal was breaking, reporters approached the Nagano (1998 Winter Games host) bid committee to see its records. The journalists were told that the Nagano committee had ordered its ninety-volume accounting books to be burned.[45] A senior official with the bid committee, Sumikazu Ya- maguchi, explained that the books were destroyed because they contained "secret information." There were many stories circulat- ing about the unsavory, behind-the-scenes maneuvering during the Nagano bid. One concerns Samaranch's close adviser Artur Takacs's son, who was a lobbyist for Nagano's organizing committee and was being paid a salary of $363,000, plus a bonus if Nagano won the games. A consortium of Japanese businessmen promised $20 million for the construction of an Olympic museum in Lausanne if Nagano got the games. Nagano hosted the games, and the museum was built. Salt Lake City lost out, but learned a lesson.[46]

Joining the chorus, on January 22, 1999, John Coates, president of the Australian Olympic Committee and the point man in Sydney's bid to host the 2000 Summer Olympics, released various documents to the press. Among other things, these revealed that the day before Sydney's election, the Australian bid committee had offered $50,000 scholarships to the children of the Ugandan and Kenyan members of the IOC. Sydney won its selection by two votes.[47]

Sharing the Spoils

As drama over payoffs was erupting between the IOC and the Olympic bid committees, a financial drama of a different sort was unfolding within the Olympic Movement. The rapidly growing tele- vision rights fees were not divided equally among the NOCs. Since broadcast rights in the United States went for much higher sums than those in other countries, the U.S. Olympic Committee (USOC) felt that it was entitled to a larger share of Olympic revenues than other NOCs. And for a while, the IOC seemed to agree.[48] During 1986–98, U.S. rights fees accounted for 83 percent of total Olympics television revenues. The U.S. share fell to 60 percent during 2001–04 and to 53 percent during 2005–08. Meanwhile, the United States received 12.75 percent of the IOC's total television distributions to the NOCs (and 20 percent of the IOC's sponsorship distributions) during 1985–2012.[49]

The NOCs felt this unequal distribution both violated the Olympic spirit and was inappropriate in light of the enormous resources available to support athletics in the United States. The NOCs also made an economic argument, to wit, much of the revenue earned by U.S. sponsors and television advertisers, such as Coca-Cola, is generated outside the United States.

When the IOC voted in 2005 to drop baseball and softball as Olympic sports and to select London over New York City to host the 2012 Summer Games, many observers interpreted this decision as a reaction to the financially privileged position of the USOC in the Olympic Movement. The same was said when the IOC selected Rio de Janeiro over Chicago to host the 2016 Olympics. In 2012, the USOC and the IOC negotiated a new agreement whereby, beginning in 2020, the USOC share of revenues from television broadcasting rights would fall to 7 percent and its share of global sponsorship revenues would fall to 10 percent, with the USOC guaranteed a minimum of $410 million per quadrennium (adjusted for inflation).[50]

Enter the BRICS

With the exceptions of Mexico City in 1968 and Moscow in 1980, the Winter and Summer Olympics were always held in Western Europe, North America, Japan, or South Korea until the Beijing games in 2008. "BRICS" is an acronym that refers to five large and erstwhile rapidly growing countries, Brazil, Russia, India, China, and South Africa. Since 2008, each of the BRICS countries has hosted either the Olympics or the World Cup or the Commonwealth Games. Each has made it clear that it perceives these mega-events as a sort of coming-out party signaling that it is now a modernized economy, ready to make its presence felt in world trade and politics.

One of the problems facing developing economies when they host mega-events is that their existing transportation, communications, lodging, entertainment, and sports infrastructure is lacking. Thus, the amount of investment necessary to properly host a mega-event is extraordinary. Beijing spent more than $40 billion in preparation for the 2008 Summer Games. Brazil reportedly spent between $15 billion and $20 billion to host the 2014 World Cup. Sochi spent more than $50 billion to host the 2014 Winter Games.[51] And Rio's cost to host the 2016 Summer Olympics is expected to approach $20 billion.[52] Compounding these escalating infrastructure, venue, and operating expenses, all hosts of mega-events face astronomical security costs, often rising to $1 billion or $2 billion.

At these investment levels, a positive economic return to hosting in the short run is improbable. Any justification for the investment would have to lie in a transformative long-run impact—or "legacy," in the PR vernacular of the IOC. The situation for the BRICS is, of course, only exacerbated where the planners do not have to be responsive to the populace, where the planning is incomplete or shortsighted, and where kickbacks and corruption are rampant.

The massive and disappointing outcomes of these recent events have given the IOC's new president, Thomas Bach, pause. All but two applicant cities dropped out of the bidding for the 2022 Winter Games. More generally, as shown in table 2-3, there has been a steady decline in the number of applicant and candidate cities over the last five bidding cycles.

Bach does not want the Olympics to price itself out of the hosting market and experience a return to the conditions of the early 1980s. Accordingly, Bach spent the first months of his tenure (which began on September 10, 2013) globetrotting to instigate more interest in bidding. At the IOC meeting prior to the Sochi games, Bach signaled his interest in reforming the bidding process, and in December 2014 the IOC passed the so-called Agenda 2020 to introduce some new policies. I discuss Agenda 2020 and other proposals for reform in chapter 7 and the postscript.

TABLE 2-3. Decline in Number of Cities Bidding for Olympic Games

Bid year	Year of games	Host city	No. of applicant cities	No. of candidate cities
Summer Games				
1997	2004	Athens	12	5
2001	2008	Beijing	10	5
2005	2012	London	9	5
2009	2016	Rio de Janeiro	7	4
2013	2020	Tokyo	5	3
Winter Games				
1995	2002	Salt Lake City	9	4
1999	2006	Turin	6	2
2003	2010	Vancouver	7	3
2007	2014	Sochi	7	3
2011	2018	Pyeongchang	3	3
2015	2022	Beijing	5	2

Source: Arne Feddersen and Wolfgang Maennig, "Determinants of Successful Bidding for Mega Events: The Case of the Olympic Winter Games," in *International Handbook of the Economics of Mega Sporting Events,* ed. Wolfgang Maennig and Andrew S. Zimbalist (Cheltenham, U.K.: Edward Elgar, 2012), p. 72.

Financing the Olympics

Table 2-4 shows the sources of revenue generated from the Winter and Summer Olympics during the last two quadrennia. Television revenue is the largest source, accounting for 47.8 percent of revenue during the Vancouver games and the London games. Of the $3.85 billion from television rights, 56 percent came from U.S. rights fees.

It is worth noting that the total revenue from both the Vancouver games and the London games was just over $8 billion. Of this, $5.2 billion came from London and $2.8 billion from Vancouver. The Beijing Summer Games generated approximately $3.6 billion. That one-time revenue of $3.6 billion is less than 10 percent of China's $40 billion-plus in investments and operating expenses. Making the contrast even more striking, the IOC does not share a large portion of

TABLE 2-4. Sources of Olympic Revenue

Source	2005–08 (millions of current USD)	2009–12 (millions of current USD)
Television	2,570	3,850
International sponsorships	866	950
Domestic sponsorships	1,555	1,838
Ticket sales	274	1,238
Licensing	185	170
Total	**5,450**	**8,046**

Source: IOC, *Olympic Marketing Fact File,* 2014, p. 6.

the generated revenue with the OCOG. For instance, in the latest cycle less than 30 percent of the TV revenue is shared with the OCOG.[53]

The new policy is to share a fixed amount, not a percentage, of worldwide television revenue with the host city. As television rights have skyrocketed, the IOC has kept payments to the host basically flat. Today the host's share of the total revenue from the games is at its lowest level ever. The IOC received a total of $2.569 billion in broadcasting revenue for the 2012 London Games; of this, it shared $713 million, or 27.8 percent, with the London OCOG.[54] Referring to all revenue sources, IOC president Thomas Bach announced in July 2014 that the IOC "will contribute $1.5 billion to the [2016] games, which will leave a huge sporting, economic and social legacy."[55] Yet the 2016 Rio Games will generate well in excess of $5 billion in revenue. Bach has thus given a magnanimous spin to an increasingly parsimonious policy.

Of course, the local economy of the host city will also benefit from lodging and food expenditures by the visitors to the games, but the sum of money involved here is almost certainly less than $500 million; further, most or all of this money is not a net addition to the local economy because sports tourists replace regular tourists and a good portion of this spending leaks out of the local economy, a topic I take up in the next chapter.

FIFA and the World Cup

FIFA—the Fédération Internationale de Football Association—was established in 1904, and the World Cup competition started in 1930. FIFA's mission has always been to promote soccer. Although FIFA's rhetoric has connected the growth of soccer worldwide to the promotion of a better world, it has never embraced political goals. The World Cup has not been a target of political movements and has never been boycotted by countries for political reasons.[56] Part of the explanation for the reduced political turmoil around the World Cup compared with the Olympics may lie in the fact that fewer countries participate (thirty-two today) than in the Olympics (204 in the Summer Games, eighty-eight in the Winter Games).

Nevertheless, by bringing countries together and having them confine their battles to the soccer pitch, the implicit promise is that tournaments like the World Cup can only lead to a more harmonious political environment. For those who had hoped that the World Cup would promote world peace, the events in Honduras and El Salvador in the summer of 1969 leading up to the finals in Mexico came as a bitter disappointment.

To set the context, El Salvador at the time had a population density eight times that of Honduras, and increasing numbers of emigrants from El Salvador were living in Honduras. The Honduran economy was struggling, and unemployment was high. Many Hondurans believed that the 300,000-odd Salvadoran immigrants were taking their jobs.

A three-game playoff between the two countries began in Tegucigalpa, Honduras, with the Honduran team prevailing 1-0 on a last-minute goal. The second game was played in San Salvador, El Salvador. The night before the game, the hotel where the Honduran team was staying was set on fire. The team was transferred to a new hotel, only to be greeted by all-night serenaders beneath their windows. It is little wonder that the Salvador team took the second game, but Hondurans took out their frustrations on some of the Salvadoran immigrants living in Tegucigalpa.

The rubber match was played in Mexico City. The Salvadoran team went ahead in the game's last moments to win. A violent riot ensued on the streets of Mexico City, and military skirmishes broke out on the El Salvador–Honduran border. Soon Salvadoran troops penetrated into Honduras, and four days of heavy fighting followed. The Organization of American States persuaded each side to sign a cease-fire agreement, but not before 2,000 to 3,000 people had been killed and more than twice as many wounded. Over 100,000 Salvadorans were expelled from Honduras, the border was shut, and hostilities lingered on. Unfortunately, soccer contests spilling over into violence on the streets have not been a rare occurrence.[57]

As shown in table 2-5, participation in and the popularity of the World Cup have grown gradually over the years. Today, FIFA has a larger membership of nations than the IOC and considerably outdraws the Olympics in international television ratings.

FIFA's Internal Struggles

While FIFA has not reflected the drama of world politics to the same degree as the Olympic Games have, the organization has been filled with internal leadership struggles and has seen more than its share of corruption scandals.[58] On multiple occasions there have been allegations of payoffs to individuals on the twenty-five-member Executive Committee prior to a hosting decision. Sometimes the charges have gone as high as the president or general secretary, and sometimes member nations have been sanctioned. As will be discussed in the postscript, 2015 brought the indictment of several top FIFA officials and the promised resignation of its president since 1998, Sepp Blatter.

One internal struggle within FIFA has concerned equity among its six continental subdivisions with regard to hosting the quadrennial World Cup finals. The basic pattern had been to alternate host nations between Europe and the Americas. This pattern was broken in 2002 with the World Cup's first Asian finals, and again in May 2004, when the rights to host the 2010 finals went to the first African host.

TABLE 2-5. World Cup Attendance since 1930

Year	Host country	No. of teams	Total attendance	No. of matches	Average attendance
1930	Uruguay	13	590,549	18	32,808
1934	Italy	16	363,000	17	21,353
1938	France	16	375,700	18	20,872
1950	Brazil	16	1,045,246	22	47,511
1954	Switzerland	16	768,607	26	29,562
1958	Sweden	16	819,810	35	23,423
1962	Chile	16	893,172	32	27,912
1966	England	16	1,563,135	32	48,848
1970	Mexico	16	1,603,975	32	50,124
1974	West Germany	16	1,865,753	38	49,099
1978	Argentina	16	1,545,791	38	40,679
1982	Spain	24	2,109,723	52	40,572
1986	Mexico	24	2,394,031	52	46,039
1990	Italy	24	2,516,215	52	48,389
1994	United States	24	3,587,538	52	68,991
1998	France	32	2,785,100	64	43,517
2002	South Korea/Japan	32	2,705,197	64	42,269
2006	Germany	32	3,359,439	64	52,491
2010	South Africa	32	3,178,856	64	49,670

The new policy was to rotate the hosting rights among the six continents represented in FIFA. It was South America's turn to host the 2014 finals, but when the World Cup was awarded in October 2007, there was only one bidder from the continent, Brazil.

Without competition among potential hosts, FIFA would lose its leverage. So FIFA changed its policy of continental rotation. Henceforth the new policy held that countries that were members of the same continental confederation as either of the last two World Cup hosts would be ineligible. This way, rather than identifying a single continent that could bid to host the tournament, countries from four continental confederations would be eligible to bid.

The new policy seems to have engendered a desirable level of competition from FIFA's perspective. Eleven bids to host the 2018 finals were submitted to the FIFA Executive Committee in March 2009. After a couple of withdrawals and a deal that only European countries would compete for the 2018 tournament, the number of bidders was whittled down to four: Belgium–the Netherlands, Spain–Portugal, England, and Russia. Many considered England to be the favorite. As the tournament's birthplace, not having hosted the finals since 1966, boasting a superb infrastructure with modern stadiums, and the bid committee having spent more than $33 million in preparing and publicizing its plan, England seemed like the logical choice. Yet Vladimir Putin was able not only to push Russia's bid within his country, he was somehow able to successfully promote it with FIFA's Executive Committee.

On December 2, 2010, Sepp Blatter announced both that Russia would be the 2018 host and that Qatar would be the 2022 host. This was the first time that two consecutive hosts were selected at the same time. Many suspected that this unique practice was designed by Blatter to allow Executive Committee members to trade votes for their favored country. The latter selection also raised some eyebrows. Qatar was competing against Australia, Japan, South Korea, and the United States. Not only were the 1994 U.S. games the most heavily attended in World Cup history, the United States had the best infrastructure and was in the process of developing soccer as a leading professional sport. Further development of U.S. soccer would have been a great boost to the game internationally and to FIFA. Qatar, a nation the size of the Falkland Islands and lacking a football history or an enticing trajectory, and without the proper infrastructure or a suitable climate, was awarded the games. Worse still, analysts projected a high-level security concern in Qatar.

Some were left scratching their heads over the selection of Qatar; others were left cursing. According to a news report in London's *Sunday Times* in early June 2014, the Qatari vice president of FIFA, Mohamed bin Hammam, "used secret slush funds to make dozens of payments" totaling more than $5 million to senior officials "to create a groundswell of support for Qatar's plan to take world football by storm." The *Sunday Times* based its allegations on a cache of millions of e-mails and other documents. FIFA at first refused to comment. Then, following a subsequent report that a gambling syndicate had paid off field referees to fix games during the South African World Cup in 2010, FIFA president Sepp Blatter quixotically delivered "a tirade" in which he called the British newspaper racist.[59] Further evidence came to light in 2015 suggesting that Qatar was able to buy several European votes—including that of Michel Platini, president of the European Soccer Federation (UEFA)—by offering to place a large order for jets from Airbus.

Meanwhile, politics within FIFA continue to fester, with the seventy-eight-year-old Blatter declaring his candidacy to remain for another term as president and Platini refusing to support him. In an attempt to round up votes for his candidacy, at the FIFA meeting in Brazil before the 2014 opening match Blatter opportunistically announced that he was tripling FIFA's annual distribution to its member countries' soccer federations. Subsequent to that came the decision to double the salaries of Executive Committee members. Blatter was to win election to another four-year term in May 2015. A few days later, following the implication of Blatter's chief lieutenant, FIFA General Secretary Jerome Valcke, in a kickback scheme to award the 2010 Cup to South Africa and UEFA's threat to organize a parallel competition to the 2018 World Cup in Russia, Blatter announced his plan to resign after a new election for president in February 2016.

Financing the World Cup

FIFA has altered its approach to sharing revenue with the host country over the years. Until 2010, FIFA and the host country had split broadcast, sponsorship, licensing, and ticketing revenues according to varying formulas. In 2002, when there were two cohosts, Japan and South Korea, FIFA made an additional lump sum payment to each country to compensate them for the fact that each bore practically full administrative costs but received only half the revenue. In both South Africa (2010) and Brazil (2014), a new system was introduced. The host country now produces an operating budget, which is subject to FIFA's approval, and then FIFA covers virtually all of the operating expenses. FIFA also retains all of the revenue. The stated purpose of the new system is to ensure that the host country does not experience an operating deficit. FIFA also provided a legacy fund of $42 million to South Africa and intends to provide a similar amount to Brazil. The catch, of course, is that all infrastructure spending on transportation, communications, stadiums, and so forth is the responsibility of the host country. Such spending is several times greater than the operating costs of the games.

For the World Cup four-year cycle ending in 2014, FIFA took in $5.72 billion in revenue. FIFA's expenses over the same time period were $5.38 billion, leaving a surplus of $338 million. At the end of 2014, FIFA had an accumulated surplus of $1.52 billion.[60]

In addition to appropriate infrastructure, tax preferences, and various hospitality services, FIFA requires the host country to have eight modern stadiums, each with a minimum capacity of 40,000, to include one stadium for the opening match with at least 60,000 seats and another for the finals of 80,000 capacity.[61] Without the proper -stadium infrastructure, South Africa was obligated to build eight new or renovated stadiums, but ended up building ten and spending $5–$6 billion to host the World Cup matches. In 2002, South Korea reportedly spent $2.5 billion and Japan $5 billion. In contrast, with adequate facilities already in place, Germany (2006), the United States (1994), and France (1998) each spent under $1 billion.[62] As we shall see, the same countries that have to invest substantial sums in modern, new stadiums are also likely to be the ones that find little economically viable use for these facilities after the World Cup is over. In both the short and the long run, hosting a mega-sports event is likely to prove a present and future burden rather than a benefit to the host country's economy.

3

The Short-Run Economic Impact

The claims are impressive. World Cup and Olympic Games organizers and their hired consultants would have us believe that hosting those events is one of the best tools of economic development since the steam engine. According to InterVISTAS Consulting, the 2010 Vancouver Games lifted output by $10.7 billion and created 244,000 jobs. The Dentsu Institute for Human Studies estimated that the part of the 2002 World Cup held in Japan raised that country's output by $24.8 billion. A 2010 study by the consultancy Grant Thornton projected that the World Cup that year in South Africa would attract 483,000 overseas visitors and generate $12 billion in output, and another Grant Thornton report estimated that the London Olympics in 2012 increased output by at least $17 billion and created 31,000 new jobs.

Different Assumptions, Different Results

Making Predictions—Ex Ante Studies

The studies cited above are promotional in nature and share a common method of estimating costs and outcomes.[1] Rather than looking at the economic results of the event and comparing them to preexisting trends, these studies made assumptions, or predictions, about the number of visitors and the amount of spending connected to the games—an approach known as the ex ante method—and then ran them through an input-output model of the country's economy.[2] (In other words, nothing specific to the event has yet happened that can be measured.) The input-output model describes the purported relationships among sectors of the economy in such a way that when one sector expands, it has a predetermined impact on a connected sector, which in turn has a predetermined impact on a third sector, and so on. For instance, let us say a tourist buys a $100 meal at a local restaurant. To produce that meal, the restaurant must buy some local vegetables, fish, and bread, as well as some tables, chairs, and plates, and so on. So the purchase of the meal helps not only the restaurant business but also businesses in other sectors of the economy. The owners and workers at these businesses earn additional income, a portion of which they spend on the services and products of still other businesses.

The purpose of the input-output model in these studies is to generate a multiplier. The multiplier is supposed to tell us when a visitor buys a $100 meal at a restaurant and, as the $100 works its way through the rest of the economy, how much new output has been created. Depending on the model, the multipliers employed in these promotional reports tend to be in the range of 1.7 to 3.5. Thus, $100 of spending to buy a meal would increase output by between $170 and $350.

There are lots of issues with this methodology. The first set of issues is that the input-output models generally are based on inter-sectoral relationships that evolve over a period of years, involve fixed coefficients, assume constant returns to scale, and are highly aggregated. For instance, the fact that restaurants need tables does not mean that if, during a mega-sporting event, a restaurant experiences a 10 percent increase in its sales revenue, it will buy 10 percent more tables. It could rather mean that the restaurant makes fuller use of its existing capacity, or that it has the same number of customers but has raised its prices 10 percent. Further, if it raises its prices 10 percent, then the relationship (coefficient), measured in dollars (or the local currency), between sectors of the economy will change (decrease). So, because the input-output model (1) is based on longer-term patterns of trade and (2) assumes fixed coefficients, it will misrepresent what is happening in the local economy.[3] Another problem is that input-output models operate at highly aggregated levels, such as textiles, sports, and food, rather than at the level of individual products, such as blue denim jeans, tennis balls, or cheese enchiladas. A common model of the U.S. economy has only 144 branches, but there are tens of millions of products in the economy. This high level of aggregation renders the model less accurate in projecting the effect of an increased demand for a particular product.

An important aspect of how a multiplier functions is related to the fact that most economies depend significantly on trade. Thus, a restaurant in Vancouver may buy its potatoes from Idaho, its silverware from France, and its tables from Sweden. To the extent that Vancouver's restaurants or hotels buy their inputs from outside Vancouver or outside Canada, visitors' expenditures locally will have less impact on the Vancouver economy.[4]

Macroeconomic models of the entire U.S. economy have multipliers around 1.3. Since the U.S. economy is less open (depends less on trade) than most of the world's economies, the national multipliers in other economies are bound to be smaller. Further, when the economic impact of a mega-event on a single city is being considered, the multiplier must be still smaller: cities must import (from outside the city) a much higher proportion of the labor, materials, and goods that they use because of the large volume of construction in a short period of time. Thus, the input-output models producing multipliers greater than 1.3 are simply not credible. City sports multipliers are more reliably between 0.7 and 1.1.[5]

Still another problem is that when a foreign soccer fan spends $100 at a Brazilian restaurant during the World Cup competition, it might not be a net gain for the Brazilian economy. This is because between

June 12 and July 13, 2014, there may have been tens or hundreds of thousands of people (tourists or businesspeople) who would otherwise have traveled to Brazil but instead chose to avoid the congestion, tight security, and high prices during the World Cup and either went elsewhere or stayed home. This plays out in real life: tourism in Beijing fell during the 2008 Summer Games, as it did in London during the 2012 Olympics. That is, even counting the athletes, the media, the administrators, and the Olympic tourists, the total number of visitors to these cities fell during the month of the Olympic Games. Further, some local residents may have the same impulse that foreigners have: they believe their city or country will be excessively crowded and expensive during the mega-event and that the period of the competition would be a good time to take a vacation outside the country. The amount of outbound tourism from China grew by 12 percent in 2008, the year China hosted the Summer Olympics.[6]

Yet another issue is that profits earned by local businesses during the competition may not stay in the city or the country. If an international hotel chain owns a hotel in London and its typical price for a room for one night in late July is $400 but during the 2012 Olympics it is $800, then the hotel will reap an additional profit of $400 per room per night during the games (assuming the hotel has the same occupancy rate in both instances.) The hotel does not have to hire any additional desk clerks, chambermaids, or concierges during the games, so there is no gain to local employment or to employment income. Indeed, it is likely that the entire $400 extra profit will be repatriated back to the hotel's home office in another country. The standard procedure for an ex ante, input-output study would be to take the $800 and multiply it by an inflated multiplier (1.7 to 3.5) and come up with an economic impact of $1,360 to $2,800 for the hotel spending alone from that one-night stay. The reality, in this hypothetical case, is that the impact would be zero if the Olympic fan were simply replacing a normal tourist, or it would be closer to $400 × (0.7 to 1.1) ($280 to $440) if the Olympic fan did not displace a normal tourist. In either case, the ex ante economic impact study produces a vastly inflated and unrealistic estimate.

Another major leakage from the local economy occurs when a local resident buys tickets to an Olympic or World Cup event. For instance, a good majority of the attendees at the 2014 World Cup were Brazilians. When Brazilians paid for tickets to the tournament, this money went to FIFA—it left the local economy. Total ticket sales for the 2014 World Cup competition were around $350 million, suggesting that over $200 million that would otherwise have contributed to domestic demand in Brazil did not do so.

There are still other reasons why the typical ex ante report might overstate any impact. Someone in the host city for a reason other than the competition (for example, normal tourism, visiting relatives, conducting business) may decide for an evening's entertainment to go to a competition rather than to the theater or a fine restaurant. No money is added to the local economy, but that individual will be classified as an Olympic tourist and deemed to be adding to the area's economy.

Yet another possibility is that an individual or family may have been planning a normal tourist visit to the host city for later in the year but instead moved up the vacation to take advantage of the games. Here too there is no added tourism, just a different timing of the tourist visits.

Finally, ex ante promotional studies leave out a vital economic element—how the games are paid for. If a government borrows $10 billion at 5 percent over a thirty-year period, then its yearly costs of financing that loan are $651 million for thirty years.[7] To pay for this debt service, the government must either raise taxes or reduce government services, either of which would introduce a drag on the local economy. This drag too must be seen as part of the cost of the games. (Of course, if politically palatable, the government could also choose to borrow more money to pay back the first debt, but this just pushes these costs further down the road.)

Looking at Results—Ex Post Studies

In contrast to the ex ante studies, which have largely been performed by consulting firms hired by interested parties and have been marred by the use of an inappropriate methodology and unrealistic assumptions, a growing number of disinterested, scholarly studies have attempted to gauge the economic impact of hosting the Olympics and World Cup. These studies use an ex post methodology: the authors wait until the tournament is over, then examine the actual economic data generated before, during, and after the event. The common approach is to use econometrics and to attempt to control for all the other relevant variables that could have affected output or employment over the period of the study. Generally, the month or year of the competition is treated as a binary (dummy) variable. Table 3-1 summarizes the findings of major studies on the economic impact of hosting the Olympics or World Cup.[8]

The results of these studies can be summarized as follows (some studies cover more than one mega-event): in sixteen cases, the games were found to have no statistically significant effect on employment or income, in seven cases a modest positive effect on income or short-run employment was found, and in three cases a negative effect on income was found.[9] Where there was a modest short-term positive employment effect, it was in each case a fraction of the officially projected effect and must be measured against the large public investment in all cases, except Los Angeles in 1984, where public funding was diminutive. Later I consider the conditions under which a positive effect might be created; here I attempt to explain the much more common outcome of no positive effect.

The first step is to grasp that, despite the enormous cultural penumbra of the World Cup and the Olympics, the events are really quite small quantitatively in relation to the economy of the host country. If one adds up all the sources of World Cup revenue in 2014 (from ticket sales, sponsorships, international television rights, and so forth), the sum is likely to approach $4.5 billion. FIFA does not share any of

TABLE 3-1. Studies on the Economic Impact of Hosting the Olympics and the World Cup

1. Feddersen, Grötzinger, and Maennig (2009). FIFA World Cup 2006. The games had no significant impact on employment or income in urban areas where new stadium construction took place compared to other urban areas.

2. Baade and Matheson (2004). FIFA World Cup 1994. Comparing income across the thirteen host cities, the authors found the average income was $712 million below trend, versus boosters' claims of $300 million gains.

3. Du Plessis and Maennig (2011). FIFA World Cup 2011. International tourists numbered 40,000–90,000, versus ex ante forecasts of approximately 400,000.

4. Hagn and Maennig (2008). FIFA World Cup 1974. The authors found no significant positive impact on long-run employment in the host cities through 1988.

5. Hagn and Maennig (2009). FIFA World Cup 2006. The authors found no significant employment impact on the cities that hosted games compared to other German cities that did not host the games.

6. Allmers and Maennig (2009). FIFA World Cup 1998, 2006, 2010. The authors found no significant impacts on hotel stays, income, or retail sales in France (1998). Significant positive impacts on hotel stays and income were found in Germany (2006).

7. Szymanski (2002). World Cup, various. Hosts experienced slower growth during year of event, amounting to a loss of 2.4 percent of nominal GDP in the host country.

8. Du Plessis and Venter (2010). FIFA World Cup 2010. The authors estimate that the World Cup lifted GDP by 0.1 percent in South Africa.

9. Jasmand and Maennig (2008). Summer Olympic Games 1972. The authors found a significantly positive impact on income in some host regions but an insignificant impact on employment in host regions.

10. Porter and Fletcher (2008). Summer Olympic Games 1996, Winter Olympic Games 2002. The authors found no significant impacts on taxable sales, hotel occupancy, or airport usage.

11. Feddersen and Maennig (2013). Summer Olympic Games 1996. The authors were unable to reject the null hypothesis that the games provided no employment boost in the U.S. state of Georgia.

12. Feddersen and Maennig (2012). FIFA World Cup 2006. The authors found no statistically significant general economic impact but did identify a small, short-run impact on employment in the hospitality sector.

13. Giesecke and Madden (2011). Summer Olympic Games 2000. The effect of Sydney hosting was to reduce Australian household consumption by $2.1 billion.

(continued)

TABLE 3-1 (*continued*)

14. Billings and Holladay (2012). Olympics, multiple years. The authors developed a difference-in-difference estimator for all Olympic host cities between 1950 and 2005 and found no long-term impact on real GDP or trade openness.

15. Von Rekowsky (2013). Olympics and World Cup, various years. Based on a study of Olympic and World Cup Games between 1990 and 2010, the author concludes these mega-events offered no meaningful lasting economic benefits.

16. Baumann and others (2012). Winter Olympics 2002. The authors found a short-term impact on the leisure industry amounting to an increase of between 4,000 and 7,000 jobs in Salt Lake City, but no effect on employment after twelve months.

17. Baumann and Engelhardt (2012). World Cup 1994. The authors found no statistically significant increase in employment in the nine cities that hosted this World Cup, no impact on the leisure and hospitality sectors, and a negative impact on the retail sector.

18. Baade and Matheson (2002). Summer Olympics 1984 and 1996. The authors found a modest short-run employment effect in Los Angeles amounting to an increase of 5,043 jobs and in Atlanta of between 4,500 and 42,500 jobs, but no long-run effect in Los Angeles.

19. Hotchkiss, Moore, and Zobay (2003). Summer Olympics 1996. Using difference-in-difference methodology, the authors found employment gains, but not wage gains, in counties hosting Olympic venues and counties nearby Olympic venues, when contrasting the economic performance of 1985–93 and 1994–2000.

Sources: See note 8 on p. 174.

this revenue with Brazil, but it does pay for local operating expenses during the World Cup. Let's assume that these expenses come to $2 billion, and that all of that amount goes to buying goods and services only from Brazil. The GDP in Brazil is approximately $2.5 trillion, so the amount of World Cup money staying in the country, optimistically gauged, is about one-twelfth of 1 percent of Brazil's GDP in the year of the competition.

It might be objected that the foregoing does not include the revenue generated through hotels, meals, local transport, and so on by visitors attending the games. Here it is important to recall the displacement and substitution effects considered earlier. It is quite possible that there will be no net increase in tourist spending during the competitions, and that if there is an increase, it is bound to be considerably smaller than that projected by the event organizers. For example, the organizers of the 2010 World Cup in South Africa initially projected 400,000 international tourists would come to the games; subsequent academic research found that the actual numbers were between 40,000 and 220,000.[10]

But let us be optimistic and assume that a country experiences a net increase of 300,000 international tourists, that each spends $300 a day (and all on goods and services produced in the host country, excluding event tickets), and that each spends five days in the country.[11] The sum total of expenditures in this circumstance would be $450 million. So, if this hopeful figure is added to the $2 billion of revenue staying in the country from the World Cup, the total would now be almost $2.5 billion.[12]

We can now compare the $2.5 billion with how much World Cup or Olympic budgets have been in recent years: for Athens in 2004, $16 billion; for London in 2012, $18 billion plus; for Beijing in 2008, $40 billion plus; for Brazil in 2014, $15–$20 billion; for Sochi, $51–$70 billion, and so on. Two points need to be made. First, a good chunk of these costs relates to nonsports infrastructure (transportation, telecommunications, energy), and much of this investment may be beneficial to the country going forward. Hence, any fair appraisal of the economic impact of the games would have to include an assessment of how appropriate these investments were in relation to the city's or country's long-term development needs. Second, and complementing the first, since the short-run benefits are extremely unlikely to offset the costs, any economic justification for hosting the competition must be found in the long-run or legacy benefits. I consider legacy benefits in the next chapter. First we must take a closer look at the costs.

Hosting Costs

Bidding

The first cost, and one that applies not only to the city eventually selected as host but to all those cities that would be hosts, is the bidding expense. There are the upfront payments to the IOC or FIFA for being considered in the preliminary applicant stage and then again in the final candidate stage. For the IOC, these payments are $150,000 and $500,000, respectively. (In the summer of 2015, the IOC joined these two phases, meaning fewer would-be host cities are eliminated during the final two years of competition.) Well beyond these costs are those required to put together a plan, to hire consultants, to make fancy brochures and videos, to host IOC and FIFA executives, to travel to IOC and FIFA meetings, and so on. Chicago spent more than $100 million in its failed bid to host the 2016 Summer Olympics. Other cities and countries have reported similar sums, or more. Tokyo reportedly spent $150 million in its failed bid to host the 2016 Summer Games.

The Netherlands considered a bid to host the 2028 Summer Games. According to a study by RTLnews, the largest commercial broadcaster in the country, as of 2012 the Dutch had already spent $105 million in direct costs to study the feasibility of hosting, draw up preliminary plans, mobilize relevant parties, and organize events "to entice IOC members to vote for us."[13] Based on the burdensome anticipated expense detailed in two consulting studies, the Netherlands decided not to bid for the 2028 games.[14]

Opening and Closing Ceremonies

Another, often underappreciated expense for Olympics hosts is producing the opening and closing ceremonies. Cities and countries frequently see these ceremonies as their big opportunity to promote local history, culture, and beauty—their main shot at creating an enticing image of their city or country and attracting worldwide tourism for years to come. Accordingly, they spend lavishly. China, for instance, reportedly spent $343 million (in 2014 prices) on its opening ceremony.[15]

Sports Venues and Nonsport Infrastructure

The most obvious costs are those associated with building sports venues (which number more than thirty for the Summer Olympics) and nonsport infrastructure. Depending on the material conditions of the country (its level of economic and sport development), either a modest or a substantial investment will be required—these days running between roughly $5 billion and $50 billion (although the strange case of the 2022 World Cup in Qatar is on track to go over $220 billion). And, of course, sometimes we don't know the true costs, because either (1) the host engages in dissimulation or cover-ups, or (2) the host committee has the financial records destroyed (as was the case with Nagano in 1998 and Salt Lake City in 2002), or (3) there is disagreement about what infrastructure spending should be attributed to the sporting event and what should be considered to be independent of the event.

Business Disruption

A related cost is that the intense period of construction for the games may disrupt local business. Retail businesses from London, Sochi, Athens, Capetown, and elsewhere tell of high expectations, investments to expand their operations, and then slumps in sales as surrounding streets are cordoned off to foot traffic or become too noisy to attract customers.

Another disruption is the IOC's brand protection policy which requires the host to take control of all billboard advertising in the city from a month before the games to one week after. The city, in turn, loses advertising revenues on its buses, trains, and airport, and must compensate private billboard owners for lost income, as well as absorb the costs of taking down and putting up the promotional material.

Security

There are also increasing costs for security. Ever since the events of September 11, 2001, security expenses have escalated rapidly. Athens in 2004 was the first post-9/11 host of the Summer Games. Athens initially forecasted a security budget of $400 million. The European Tour Operators Association (ETOA) put Athens's final security cost at $1.5 billion.[16] More recent competition hosts have reported security costs in the $1 billion to $2 billion range.

Cost Overruns

One of the more interesting and important dilemmas facing host cities and countries is the phenomenon of cost overruns. Overruns are ubiquitous, and most are massive, as reflected in table 3-2. What is notable about these numbers is that in each case, the overrun is not of a normal order of magnitude but instead is fourfold to tenfold (or more) than the initial estimate.

A 2012 study by the Said Business School at Oxford University, considering only operating and venue costs (excluding infrastructure costs), found that every Olympic Games since 1960 for which reliable records are available has experienced cost overruns. According to the study, the average cost overrun for the summer Olympics since 1976 is 252 percent after adjusting for inflation.[17]

How can we explain the consistency and the degree of these cost overruns? First and foremost, a significant part of the story is deliberate deception. The main promoters of hosting are the economic interests that stand to gain the most, such as construction companies and their unions, insurance companies, real estate interests, architectural firms, the investment bankers who will float the loans and their lawyers, and perhaps some local media companies, hotels, and restaurants. It is in their interest to convince the relevant government body or bodies to support the bid effort. If a realistic estimate of costs were provided, the probability of getting a political green light would diminish substantially. The clear strategy is to lowball the cost esti-

TABLE 3-2. Cost Overruns

Host city or country	Year of games	Initial bid (billions of USD)	Estimated final cost (billions of USD)
Athens	2004	1.6	16
South Africa	2010	0.3	5–6
London	2012	4.0	15–20
Sochi	2014	12.0	51–70
Brazil (stadiums only)	2014	1.1	5

Sources: E. Cottle, ed., *South Africa's World Cup: A Legacy for Whom?* (University of KwaZulu-Natal Press, 2011), and P. Alegi and C. Bolsmann, eds., *Africa's World Cup* (University of Michigan Press, 2013). Interestingly, the Commonwealth Games in India in 2010 were initially budgeted at $250 million. *Business Today* magazine estimated the final cost at $9.2 billion. If these numbers are accurate, then the overrun was on the order of 36 times! See Nalin Mehta and Boria Majumdar, "For a Monsoon Wedding: Delhi and the Commonwealth Games," in *International Handbook on the Economics of Mega Sporting Events,* ed. Wolfgang Maennig and Andrew S. Zimbalist (Cheltenham, U.K.: Edward Elgar, 2012).

mates with a bare-bones plan, and then, once it is approved, to add the bells and whistles.

Second, it is important to remember that prospective hosts are involved in an eleven-year (or longer) process, facing first domestic competitors and then international ones. Along the way there is constant and strong pressure to outdo other competitors' designs, extravagance, amenities, and security features. An eleven-year process of one-upmanship, along with meeting direct demands made by the IOC or FIFA, leads to ever more elaborate and expensive plans.

Third, the long lag time between the initial plan and the competition itself means there are many years of intervening inflation. Especially when a lot of production is concentrated in a few areas, the increasing demand for construction materials, engineers, and manual labor pushes up the prices of all the inputs.

Fourth, cities and countries invariably fall behind in their construction schedule—because of political encumbrances, or environmental challenges, or deficient planning or sloppy administration, or bad weather, or labor disputes. As hosts fall behind their timetable, construction must be rushed. This leads to relaxed bidding rules, which raises prices, and to premium prices demanded by construction companies for quick delivery (which often also leads to inferior workmanship and higher maintenance costs down the road).

Fifth, along with higher construction prices, it is common for real estate prices to rise in the run-up to the games, and, in anticipation of wealthy foreign tourists, prices tend to rise more rapidly throughout the local economy. The generalized price increases in turn feed protests coalescing around the games. The *Los Angeles Times* aptly described this dynamic in Rio de Janeiro prior to the 2014 World Cup competition:

> Fed-up Rio residents have taken to social media to share photos of price tags, receipts and menu items so pricey, it almost seems they could only have been dreamed up by the Spanish surrealist artist.
>
> There is a shrimp omelet, now famous, that costs $41 at a simple bar and beachside restaurant in the Copacabana neighborhood. At a nearby snack stand, a side of fries goes for $13. A fruit salad at another beach kiosk is $17, and one establishment charges passersby $1.75 to use the bathroom.
>
> Normally laid-back *cariocas,* as Rio inhabitants are known, are getting steamed, said George Patino, a spokesman for the Technological Park of Rio who hosts a Facebook page dubbed Rio Surreal.
>
> In that online forum, locals gripe daily about the prices of taxi rides, color copies, liquor, produce and more. Some have organized "cooler" parties outside popular bars, drinking their own beer on the streets rather than paying steep tabs inside.
>
> "We've been seeing price increases in all sectors in Rio for a long time. But things have gotten worse, and people are now really upset," Patino said. "With the World Cup and other big events coming, it seems everyone has lost their sense of perspective. Everyone is trying to make money as if this was their last chance ever to do so."[18]

Other Costs

Then there are the rest of the operating costs of the games: the PR and advertising campaign, the provision of sumptuous food and lodging for IOC and FIFA executives, the transporting of athletes and executives, the underwriting of at least a portion of the food and lodging for the athletes, the costs of maintaining the sports venues and practice fields, and covering the expenses of administration, sanitation, utilities, traffic control, ticket sales, forgone tax revenues, ushers, and so on.

There are also indirect costs. The IOC requires the host city to clear all its advertising billboards in the city for use by Olympic sponsors. It also demands that all athletes, sponsors, and IOC personnel be exempt from all forms of taxation. To the extent that private land is used for Olympic venues, the city loses the property tax revenue. Normal business activity may be curtailed during the games.

Next, there is the cost of payoffs and corruption. Government officials in charge of doling out contracts tend to be large beneficiaries of considerations from construction companies. Stories of this behavior are legion and are sprinkled later into the text.

There is also the opportunity cost of the human capital invested by engineers, planners, and politicians in the preparation for and implementation of the games. Their skills and time could have been dedicated to other, perhaps more beneficial activities.

Finally, there are the human costs, which may appear in the form of heavily exploited migrant labor, human rights violations, construction-related deaths, environmental degradation, architectural anomalies, and eviction and community destruction.[19] Examples of these problems are discussed in chapters 5 and 6.

All told, the direct financial costs of hosting the Olympics are usually divided into three buckets: the operating budget (the costs of running the games for seventeen days plus the construction of any temporary venues); the venue budget (including the construction costs of permanent sporting venues, plus the Athletes' Village and the Broadcasting and Media Center); and the infrastructure budget (for roads, parking lots, bridges, landscaping, trains, and other facilities connected to the hosting). When it is publicly reported that an Olympic Games balances its budget or has a surplus, it invariably refers *only* to the operating budget. More often than not, the operating budget is reported to be balanced, but this leaves out not only the venue and infrastructure costs, but also the usual, and substantial, subsidy from the local host government as well as various indirect costs.[20]

Hosting Benefits

Several short-run benefits are commonly touted in connection with hosting the Olympics or the World Cup. An evaluation of the key benefits mentioned in this regard suggests that the vast majority do not play out in reality.

Overcoming Political Gridlock

A common and often sensible claim made by mega-event boosters is that without the pressure that comes with being thrust onto the world stage and a firm deadline, the local political system would be incapable of appropriating money for sorely needed infrastructure. For instance, in 2004, when New York City was bidding to host the 2012 Summer Olympics, it was frequently argued that a major benefit was that the Javits Convention Center on the west side would finally be expanded and modernized. Various funding proposals had been presented to the state legislature in Albany over the years, but the Republicans and Democrats could not agree. While there may be some validity to this reasoning, it might also be argued that the planned investment in the expansion of the Javits Center was ill conceived in the first place.

A similar argument was made for Brazil being the host of the World Cup: it would create enough urgency for infrastructure investment and pacifying the favelas that it would finally get done. The question here is whether the Brazilian political morass was actually overcome or whether the morass precluded the effective installation of needed infrastructure and constructive development.

In general, if the political system is so ineffective, it is questionable whether it is desirable to entrust it with planning and implementing a mega sporting event. In the end, government must learn to effectively plan and administer policy without the pressure of a mega-event.

Higher Real Estate Prices

Higher land prices are often cited as a benefit of hosting mega-events. Land prices do tend to rise where infrastructure and facility construction is taking place. Such price increases undoubtedly benefit landowners, real estate agents, and speculators, but they are also likely to hurt lower-income families, who are evicted or unable to afford rising rents. These families are often obliged to relocate miles away, disrupting travel to work and to school for their children, as well as compelling a social and emotional adjustment to a new community.

Feel-Good Effects

Being at the center of the world stage creates excitement, as does the buildup to the several weeks of fame and glory. Survey work in host cities confirms that, with some exceptions, the mood and spirit of the local population tend to be uplifted. (Brazil 2014 is arguably an exception to the rule.) Host committees organize thousands of local residents to do volunteer work for the games, and this engenders a greater sense of community and cooperation. To the extent that this effect takes hold, however, it tends to be ephemeral. When the planet's attention disappears, life and spirits return to normal.[21]

Construction

Most promotional studies for mega-events include a section that estimates the employment and output gains from the period of construction leading up to the games. These studies generally do not take into account two crucial factors: the future effect of the debt incurred to finance the construction and the macroeconomic (and labor market) conditions during the construction phase.

Other than in Los Angeles (where public spending was minimal), there has been a significant financial contribution from the public sector. Such a contribution must be financed in one of three ways: (1) by cutting back on other public services, (2) by raising taxes, or (3) by government borrowing. The first two methods reduce income, output, and employment, tending to offset any gains from spending for games-related construction. The third method (assuming away the rational expectations and complete crowding-out positions) will have a positive short-run effect on output, but it will require debt service going forward, and this debt service (other things being equal) will entail either future reductions in public services or increases in taxes, or both.

If increases in public construction spending did not have to be funded eventually, maintaining full employment would be trivial. Each city could simply hire a thousand workers to dig a big hole every week, and then hire another thousand to fill it up. Too bad economics is not so simple. If the object being built has no or little value, then it is a bad investment for the city. A good investment would return enough value not only to retire the relevant debt service but also to cover the return on the next best available public investment at the time (the opportunity cost).

Another consideration is the state of the economy and the labor market at the time the investments for the games are made. If the economy is booming and labor markets are tight, then the most likely outcome will not be additional output but a reallocation of output toward the sports and nonsports facilities for the games and away from existing areas of investment. Moreover, since there will be excess demand on the scarce resources of building materials and construction labor, the prices of these inputs are bound to rise, creating inflationary pressure. This pressure in turn may lead to contractionary macropolicy and eventually to lower output.

Alternatively, if the economy is weak and the labor market slack, then the games-related investments may lower unemployment and lead to output growth. The question in this case is whether there are other investments that would have the same salutary short-run impact but would also be more likely to raise productivity in the longer run. Because public debt is being incurred, it is important to evaluate the long-run effect of public spending.

Beyond these considerations, it is necessary to keep in mind that the bidding process for the Olympics or the World Cup is not synchronized with a country's business cycle. When a city or country bids, it bids on the IOC's or FIFA's timetable. It would be a fool's errand to bid to host either the Olympics or the World Cup on the assumption that when the bulk of construction took place, the local labor markets would be slack.

Finally, the sheer volume of sport and infrastructure construction for a host of the games usually results in a shortage of construction labor. It becomes necessary to import migrant labor, either from other areas of the country or from other countries. Under these circumstances, migrant labor is generally mistreated and underpaid. For instance, early reports out of Qatar are horrifying: the Qataris have confirmed that during 2012 and 2013, over a thousand migrant laborers died as a result of the unsafe working conditions and dismal living conditions at construction sites for the 2022 World Cup.[22] According to a report in London's *Guardian,* pay slips revealed that workers building the first stadium for the 2022 Cup were paid as little as $0.76 an hour.[23]

Tourism

The evidence for a boost in tourism during the Olympics or the World Cup is uneven. The so-called Olympic and World Cup communities (the athletes, the coaches, the judges or referees, the media, the families, the sponsors and their guests, the administrators from FIFA or the IOC) are large and, depending on the event, run in the 10,000 to 25,000 range. These visitors alone would seem to guarantee additional tourist income for the host city or country during the games.

But it is not always so. Some hosts have experienced a modest increase in tourist revenue, while others have had a decrease or no appreciable change. For instance, an econometric study of the Atlanta Summer Olympics in 1996 that examined monthly data found that when other factors were controlled for, there was no statistically significant change in retail sales, hotel occupancy, and airport traffic during the Olympics. The only indicator that increased was hotel rates, and, not surprisingly, most of the additional revenue from this source went to the headquarters of hotel chains in other cities.[24]

In another example, the number of foreign tourists visiting China in 2008 was 24.3 million, or 6.8 percent fewer than the 26.1 million who visited in 2007. Beijing received 30 percent fewer foreign arrivals in August 2008 than in August 2007, and the number of hotel bed nights in the city dropped 39 percent during the games compared to a year earlier. Beijing had anticipated 400,000 foreign visitors per night during the Olympics, but the actual number was 235,000.[25]

China is not the only host country to forecast the number of foreign tourists overly optimistically. Sydney anticipated 132,000 foreign visitors daily but received only 97,000. Athens expected 105,000 per night but received only 14,000.[26] According to the European Tour Operators Association, the problem is universal: "No city has yet predicted with any accuracy the number of people who attend."[27]

For the London games, the U.K.'s Office for National Statistics reported that in July and August 2012, there was a net decrease in overseas visitors to the United Kingdom of 6.1 percent relative to the number in July and August 2011 (from 6.57 million visitors in 2011 to 6.17 million in 2012). In Salt Lake City, the number of visitor skier days in Utah during the Olympic year of 2001–02 was 2.98 million, 9.9 percent below the 3.28 million in 2000–01 (and 5.3 percent below the 3.14 million in 2002–03). Foreign tourism during the 2002 World Cup in South Korea equaled 403,406, which was 37 percent below the forecasted level and 12.4 percent below the number for the same month in 2001.[28]

In contrast, the number of foreign visitors to Sydney increased modestly, from 2.5 million in 1999 to 2.7 million in 2000, the year the city hosted the Summer Games. That was the good news for Sydney. The bad news was that the city anticipated 27 percent more visitors than it received, and the number of tourists fell steadily over the next three years, to 2.3 million in 2003, as neighboring New Zealand's numbers soared. Moreover, Sydney hoteliers imprudently expanded room capacity by 30 percent for the games, which led to a fall in the occupancy rate to a reported 57 percent during the Olympics.[29]

British Columbia also experienced a modest increase in tourism in 2010, the year that Vancouver hosted the Winter Olympics. The hotel occupancy rate rose from 58.8 percent in 2009 to 60.1 percent in 2010 and tourist entries increased from 5.61 million in 2009 to 6.19 million in 2010—still well below the annual average during 2005–07 of 6.88 million.[30] Employment in tourism-related industries (air transport, accommodations, food and beverage, arts and entertainment), however, after growing at 3.2 percent annually between 2005 and 2009, fell by 1.1 percent in 2010.[31] The drop in employment is all the more notable because the North American economy had begun to recover from the 2007–08 financial crisis.

Brazil's 2014 World Cup also appears to have increased foreign tourism. According to preliminary estimates, although the government projected that the Cup would bring 600,000 international tourists to Brazil, the Ministry of Tourism released a report in mid-July claiming 1 million foreign visitors between May 23 and July 13. (The first game of the Cup was on June 10.) This figure did not jibe with that issued by the Brazilian Airline Association, which projected in the middle of the competition that total air travel would fall between 11 and 15 percent during the Cup.[32]

The Brazilian Ministry of Tourism also increased its projected tourist revenue from the Cup from R$1 billion (Brazilian reales; the real was worth approximately 45 cents in July 2014) to R$4.4 billion. The revenue figures are based on survey work done by consulting groups.[33] The 67 percent increase in number of foreign tourists, according to the ministry's figures, in conjunction with the 4.4-fold increase in revenue from tourists' spending implies that the average spending per tourist was 2.65 times above what was originally projected. Something appears to be significantly off in these estimates. The disparity becomes more glaring when it is considered that most of the foreign tourists came from the neighboring countries of Argentina, Uruguay, Colombia, and Chile, all of which had teams in the final sixteen. In Rio, for instance, which enjoyed the largest influx of foreigners, Argentine tourists led the way, with 77,000, Chile was second, with 45,000, and Colombia was third, with 31,000. The United States had 24,000 visitors in Rio, while France had 16,000 and England and Germany each had 10,000. According to various anecdotal reports, the tourists from nearby South American countries in large numbers slept on the beach or in trailers and used public restrooms.[34] Their spending was minimal. Thus, the special geographic and competitive circumstances of the Brazilian games helped to raise the number of international visitors but probably did very little to raise foreign exchange earnings for the economy.

In any event, it is problematic to simply look at the change in number of tourists from one year to the next because so many other factors could be moving the needle. As an example, the background trajectory of tourist numbers could well mask a drop during the Olympic year. Most countries that host the Olympics are in a growth phase for their economy and for their tourism industry. If tourism numbers had been growing at 4 percent per year prior to a country's hosting the World Cup and then grew at 2 percent per year afterward, it would be difficult to make the case that hosting lifted tourism, even though the numbers grew on a year-over-year basis after the games.[35] Changes in the world economy or political factors also come into play. The point is simply that the notion that hosting the Olympics or the World Cup is an automatic plus for the tourism industry is misleading. The long-run changes in tourism, discussed in the next chapter, also do not bear out the rosy picture painted by the organizing bodies' PR efforts.

4

The Long-Run Economic Impact

As the costs for hosting the Olympics and the World Cup have skyrocketed over the past thirty years, rising into the tens of billions of dollars, the potential short-run increase in economic activity of between $2 billion and $5 billion has paled in comparison. To justify the enormous expense of hosting the competitions, the IOC has introduced the term "legacy" to refer to the presumed long-run benefits. "Legacy" was introduced into IOC parlance after the 2000 Games in Sydney and has become a broad, encompassing concept, seemingly limited only by the imagination of the employees in the IOC's PR office in Lausanne.[1] FIFA has been happy to adopt the legacy argument.

Here is a noninclusive list of what the IOC has asserted are potential legacy benefits for the host city and country:[2]

—Construction of sports venues

—Construction of transportation, communications, and energy infrastructure

—Construction of accommodations

—Boost for tourism

—Increased trade and investment

—Improved management practices; better coordination among government agencies

—Improved national spirit and mood

—Educational benefits

—Public health benefits—more exercise and sports participation and better standards of cleanliness in restaurant food preparation

—Greater accessibility for handicapped persons

—Improved sustainability policies and standards

—More effective cultural preservation

—Lower crime rates

—Higher real estate prices

—Reduced racism

—Greater social inclusion[3]

Several observations can be made about this list. First, since the changes enumerated all represent putative long-run benefits, the host city or country potentially must wait years to decades before experiencing the full gains. Second, since many other variables intervene in the long run, it is more difficult to tie any changes to the impact of the games themselves. Third, many of the envisaged benefits are intangible and not quantifiable. Fourth, the calculus for political leaders or members of the organizing committee of the games shifts dramatically. Those who promised economic and other advantages from hosting become basically unaccountable. If there are no apparent gains, the politicians can always proclaim that the benefits are on their way. Thus, in the short run the games' boosters can appeal to the promise of long-run legacy benefits, while in the long run the boosters can appeal to the expectation of still longer-run benefits down the road. By this time the politicians who originally appropriated public funds to finance the games may be long gone.

Let us turn to consider the evidence from multiple studies on the alleged legacy benefits.

Long-Term Benefits

Tourism

In the last chapter we considered the effect of the games on tourism in the short run; namely, whether tourism grows in the run-up to and during the games themselves. Here we consider the possibility of a branding effect that might increase the number of tourists in the years following the games.

One of the most frequently heard and stridently claimed benefits is that hosting the games provides wonderful advertising value and a unique opportunity to develop the host country's brand. Both the World Cup and the Olympics are watched on television and the Internet by billions of people worldwide, and there is no better occasion to trumpet the touristic glories and appetizing business opportunities of your city or country, runs the PR.

Here is Jacques Rogge (IOC head from 2001 to 2013) extolling the television reach of the 2004 Athens Games: "The Athens Olympics broke global TV viewing records, with nearly 4 billion tuning in . . . beating the previous record of 3.6 billion viewers for the 2000 Sydney Olympics."[4] The European Tour Operators Association (ETOA) mounted a biting response to Rogge's claims: "There are roughly 6.5 billion people on the planet. Of these, 1.6 billion have no access to electricity. A further 300 million may have access to electricity, but are under five years old."[5] That leaves 4.6 billion people who could have watched the Athens Olympics. So, Rogge was claiming that 87 percent of those who could have watched the games actually watched them. What Rogge's numbers seem to represent in reality is the number of people who could have *potentially* watched the Olympics, rather than a reliable tally of those actually watching.

Even if the IOC and FIFA exaggerate the number of eyeballs watching their competitions, it is true that the worldwide audience is enormous. The larger issue is not whether there are half a billion or 4 billion viewers, it is whether the actual viewers and television cameras are focused on the tourist attractions of the hosting country or on the outcomes of the sporting competitions. To the extent that viewers who are in an economic position to travel to or invest in the host country focus on the qualities of the country, there is the question of whether the viewers' take-away is positive or negative. Did viewers have a better impression of Mexico after the 1968 Summer Games, which were preceded by the killing of more than 200 student demonstrators by the military, followed by the political protests of U.S. black athletes—and all of this occurring against the background of broadcasters' repeated assertions of terrible air pollution? Similar questions could be asked about Munich in 1972, Montreal in 1976, Moscow in 1980, Atlanta in 1996, Athens in 2004, Beijing in 2008, Sochi in 2014, or Brazil in 2014. A 1991 study by J. R. Brent Ritchie and Brian H. Smith on awareness of the 1988 Calgary Winter Games found that the most common characteristic identified with Calgary among U.S. and European viewers was the cold. Moreover, Ritchie and Smith found that while there was strong awareness of Calgary as the host in 1988, there was also a rapid drop-off in awareness by 1989, just one year later. The authors concluded that the hosting impact "on levels of top-of-mind awareness decreases measurably after a short period of time."[6]

No matter how inherently charming and appealing a city or country may be, then, it seems that hosting always involves uncertainties and risks: the weather may be bad, popular protests may arise, terrorism may surface, or traffic snarls may infuriate. For countries with widespread poverty, problematic pollution, variable weather, a repressive political apparatus, rampant corruption, or an underdeveloped infrastructure, the risks are magnified.

The ETOA has conducted several studies on the impact of the Olympics on tourism. In each case the conclusion was pessimistic. One of the more telling arguments made by the ETOA is that Olympic and World Cup fans visit the host country to watch the sporting competitions rather than to enjoy the country's lasting tourist attractions. When sports fans went to London in 2012, for instance, they didn't go to the theater, to concert venues, to the Tate Gallery, to the

British Museum, to Buckingham Palace, or to Hyde Park. They went to East London for the competitions. When they returned home, they might have described the excitement of the games to their friends, relatives, and neighbors, but the games are ephemeral, and no future tourist will go to London in 2016 because there were exciting games in 2012. And while Olympic fans may have had little or nothing to say about the enduring virtues of visiting London, they likely did have something to say about high-priced hotels and restaurants and endless traffic jams.

The ETOA claims that the most effective way to advertise tourism is by word of mouth. With mega-event tourists, the value of word of mouth is largely lost, and indeed, to the extent that the mega-event tourist chases away the traditional tourist who touts the enduring attractions of a city, the impact of the games on future tourism may be negative. In its 2010 report, the ETOA put the matter this way:

> The post Olympic blight was common to all the cities that hosted the Games since Seoul. As was pointed out in 2006, every Olympics displaces tourists: Olympic visitors do not behave like normal guests. Their presence is determined by their interest in sport. They do not come to sightsee, attend the theatre or recreate themselves on a beach. They come to attend a sporting event.
>
> This removal of visitors has a detrimental effect on subsequent demand. The most important motivator for visitors is example and word of mouth: this sales mechanism loses momentum as visitors are deterred. Their very absence is a suppression of marketing. This failure far outweighs any gains derived from the television audience, an audience whose size and propensity to travel is exaggerated.[7]

The dichotomy between normal and sports tourists may be sharper for the Olympics than for the World Cup. The World Cup takes place over roughly twice as many days, leaving more time for the sports tourist to visit traditional tourist sites. Thus, Brazil's Ministry of Tourism reported healthy increases in the number of visitors to the Christ the Redeemer statue, as well as to Sugarloaf Mountain.

Assessing the long-run impact of the World Cup or Olympics on a country's tourism is not an easy matter. One must parse the preexisting trend in tourism, the growth of the regional and world economy, changing transportation and hotel prices, visa regulations and costs, other domestic investments in promoting tourism, and so on. In a few cases, such as Barcelona in 1992, it appears that the games did provide a fillip to the tourism industry—though many other factors were also at work in Barcelona contributing to this effect. In other cases it is difficult to identify any clear impact, and in yet other cases the effect appears to have been negative.

The impact of the 2000 Sydney Olympics on tourism offers a cautionary example. An Australian tourism industry report based on detailed survey evidence offered a plausible explanation for the crucial American market's reluctance to see Australia as a newly desirable destination for tourism and investment:

> Given that the Sydney Olympics were considered as global entertainment, U.S. media-coverage of the Games and Australia, for the most part, simply reinforces the already-held imagery of Australia as a far-away exotic location peopled by friendly folk who seemed almost American. Given that there was no Sydney 2000 media coverage that served to fundamentally challenge already-held images and attitudes, American perceptions, not surprisingly, remained largely constant before and after the Sydney Olympics.[8]

In another study, *The Sydney Olympics: Seven Years On,* James Giesecke and John Madden of Monash University's Centre of Policy Studies concluded, "In terms of purely measurable economic variables the Sydney Olympics had a negative effect on New South Wales and Australia as a whole."[9]

Sydney increased its stock of hotel rooms by 30 percent to accommodate expected Olympic travelers. By the end of 2004, ten of the city's major hotels had closed.[10] David Mazitelli of the Australian Tourism Export Council put the matter bluntly:

> The Sydney Olympics had few long term positive impacts beyond 2000 on the growth of Australian tourism. . . . The forecast of a strong impact for the four years following the Games did not eventuate. As soon as the Olympics finished, we started to see a fall away in inbound activity. Australia went into three years of negative growth (2001, 2002 and 2003).[11]

International arrivals in Sydney went from 2.7 million visitors in 2000 to 2.6 million in 2001, 2.4 million in 2002, and 2.3 million in 2003.[12] While some attributed the decline to changes in the international political and economic environment, it is notable that foreign arrivals to New Zealand grew each year, increasing by 17 percent between 2000 and 2003.[13]

Jon Teigland, in an October 1996 study on the 1994 Lillehammer Winter Olympic Games and the two prior Winter Olympic Games, in Calgary, Canada, in 1988 and in Albertville, France, in 1992, found that the long-term impact on tourism was between nonexistent and very modest after what appeared to be about a "three-year" novelty effect. The impact on tourism after the Winter Olympic Games in Innsbruck, Austria, in 1976 was similar.

There is little to indicate that, even in the best of cases, the Olympics or World Cup boosted tourism beyond a couple of years, if at all. On tourism growth following the games, Teigland opined with regard to Lillehammer's experience:

> The tourism developments so far in the Norwegian host town and region are in many ways lower than expected by both private investors and public authorities. One effect of the too high expectations is a clear overcapacity of commercial accommo-

dation supply afterwards. Another effect is serious economical problems in the host town, which now has decided to reduce its public budget by 12–15% from 1997 on. The recent sale of the major facility for 1 (one) U.S. dollar to prevent bankruptcy reflects also that the realities have been different from local expectations (and forecast by more or less serious advisers).[14]

Athens 2004 presents a somewhat more positive and complicated story. First, Athens was prudent to be more cautious in expanding its hotel capacity for the seventeen-day event. Hotel capacity was expanded by only 8 percent, less than one-third of Sydney's expansion. Second, a significant part of Athens's Olympic budget went into modernizing its airport, roads, public transportation, and communications system. Although Athens's tourism fell by 6 percent in the Olympic year of 2004, the improved infrastructure, together with the city's strong tourist reputation prior to the games, seems to have contributed to a healthy growth in foreign arrivals in 2005 and 2006.[15] After 2006, tourism suffered, but the decline was likely the result of external and domestic economic weakness. It is also notable, however, that despite its post-Olympic growth during 2004–06, Greek tourism growth was outpaced in those years by tourism to both Turkey and Croatia.

It seems clear that the post-Olympic or post–World Cup tourist trajectory will vary by country, depending on characteristics of the country, its previous tourist experience, and economic conditions, among other things. There is little evidence, however, that the world media exposure from the games will by itself launch the city or country onto a higher growth path. Each prospective host would do well to ask the question, if we have $10 billion or $20 billion or more to spend on promoting tourism, what is the most effective use of those resources?

Trade and Investment

If there is advertising value from hosting, then presumably it might appeal not only to potential tourists but also to people interested in doing business with the host city or country. It is not surprising, then, that event promoters frequently trumpet increases in international trade and investment as a potential benefit. Until a 2011 study by Andrew K. Rose and Mark M. Spiegel, however, there was no independent scholarly study that attested to such a positive effect.[16] Rose and Spiegel found that Olympic host countries experience substantial and lasting increases in their exports.[17] They attributed this effect not to the actual hosting of the games but to the bidding to host the games. That is, the positive effect they identified holds equally for countries that bid to host and are not selected by the IOC to host and for countries that bid and are selected to host. Rose and Spiegel suggest that the causal effect is through each country's signaling an openness to commerce, as well as an interest and competitiveness in trade, by bidding to host the games.

A subsequent study by Wolfgang Maennig and Felix Richter, however, effectively critiqued Rose and Spiegel on the grounds that their sample of countries was not representative:

> We challenge the empirical findings of Rose and Spiegel because they compare Olympic nations such as the United States, Japan, Germany, Canada, Italy, Spain, and Australia, which have been among the leading export nations for centuries, to all other nations. Their comparison of structurally different, nonmatching groups might suffer from a selection bias.[18]

When Maennig and Richter corrected for this bias by using only structurally similar countries, they found that the positive trade-signaling effect completely disappeared. Thus, we are left without any empirical evidence to confirm the touted benefit.

Qualitative and Other Benefits

The list of alleged qualitative benefits associated with hosting the Olympics is long and reaches in many directions: improved management practices and business culture, uplifted mood, reduced crime, higher real estate values, increased exercise and participation in sports, better sustainability practices, and improved values. Here, too, independent corroborative evidence is lacking. While there have doubtless been improvements in some of these areas for some hosts, such improvements would likely have occurred with or without hosting. Other so-called benefits, when they do occur, can be a mixed blessing. Higher real estate prices, as noted, are good for current property owners in the affected areas, but they are not good for current tenants or people and businesses hoping to move into the area. Nor are they good for the people who were evicted.

Still other claimed benefits do not appear to be benefits at all. A 2012 study that estimated the impact of sporting events and professional sports teams on local crime rates found that while franchises do not have a statistically significant impact on crime rates, the Olympics are associated with a 10 percent *increase* in crime rates.[19] Other research has found that the Olympics and World Cup are associated with increases in prostitution and sex trafficking.[20]

Sustainability is another area in which results may be mixed to poor, despite the IOC's recent rhetorical focus on this issue. Following pushback after the ecological losses sustained during and after the Albertville, France, Winter Games in 1992, the IOC announced its "Agenda 21"—henceforth to promote sustainable games—at the Earth Summit in Rio. At the Olympic Congress in 1994, the IOC stressed that environmental preservation was "an essential component of Olympism," and in 1995 it inserted mention of the environment into Rule 2 of the Olympic Charter, requiring that the IOC see that "the Olympic Games are held in conditions which demonstrate a responsible concern for environmental issues."

The example of South Africa, which hosted the 2010 World Cup, suggests the difficulty of making a net improvement on this dimension. There were advances in wastewater treatment, and technological knowledge was gained regarding more efficient energy use. However, there was also increased pollution from construction materials, as well as a massive carbon footprint from international air travel to and from the competition (more than 80 percent of the 2010 Cup's carbon footprint came from jet travel). While jet travel to games anywhere will leave a significant carbon footprint, when the host country is located in the southern part of the Southern Hemisphere and isolated from population centers longitudinally, the footprint grows measurably.

In the case of Brazil in 2014, the government's PR boasted of the BRT transportation system that was created in several cities. This system consisted of special lanes for rapid transit buses. At best, BRT connected airports with World Cup (or future Olympic) venues, but it did little or nothing to ameliorate the woeful inadequacy of public transportation for the Brazilian people in Rio, São Paulo, and other cities.[21] The main BRT line in Rio runs 39 kilometers from the airport to the upscale residential suburb of Barra da Tijuca (where the main Olympic cluster for 2016 lies) and rips through a dozen lower-income neighborhoods. From the perspective of sustainability, Brazil is a country without passenger train service and in desperate need of an effective light rail system. The commitment of billions of dollars to infrastructure for the World Cup and Olympics was an opportunity to address the glaring deficiencies in public transportation; instead, there was investment in the BRT bus system and airport expansion promoting the use of fossil fuels.[22]

Equally troubling is Brazil's plan to build a golf course in a low-lying, environmentally fragile area of Barra da Tijuca. Golf is returning to the 2016 Olympics for the first time since 1900. In Brazil, golf is exclusively the domain of the wealthy. Of Rio's two golf courses, neither is open to the public. Rather than preserving the natural beauty of the coastal land, the Olympics will yield a legacy of a third golf course for the city's elite. Christopher Gaffney, a mega-event and urban planning expert at Rio's Federal Fluminense University, concludes: "One of the few remaining areas of environmental protection in the Barra da Tijuca region has been appropriated by the government, opened up for toxic land use patterns and handed over to a private development firm for recreational and real-estate purposes."[23] In September 2014 a court in Rio de Janeiro ordered the local organizing body to make changes in its plans for the golf course. Citing potential ecological damage, the judge called for the course to be moved away from the lagoon and to the north. If the relocation occurred, it would have interfered with a planned high-end residential development.[24]

Interestingly, while the IOC mentions promoting sustainability as one of its main goals (although it provides no metric or standard against which to assess any progress), FIFA's position is more modest. FIFA's goal is "minimizing negative impacts," thereby acknowledging implicitly that there will be environmental damage from hosting a World Cup.[25]

Brazilian communications have improved modestly through the investment in coordinating emergency services across sectors of the government and through installations in and around stadiums (although most of the twelve World Cup venues did not have the promised functioning wireless systems). In contrast, there was no broad-based expansion of communications technology across the Brazilian economy.

Brazil also listed combating racial prejudice as one of the gains to be expected from hosting the World Cup. This claim was no doubt ironic to the people of the Aldeia Maracanã indigenous community, who were violently removed from their land next to the Maracanã Stadium in Rio by shock troops. The head of the state agency responsible for the Maracanã complex at the time of the eviction commented, "The place for Indians is in the forest; that's why we're preserving the Amazon."[26]

To the extent that hosting the Olympics or World Cup brought benefits in any of these areas, the benefits must be weighed against the costs of providing them, and the opportunities forgone to devote resources to other areas. It is inevitable that any hosting experience will leave a positive residue of at least a handful of constructive infrastructure investments. Mega-event boosters will always be able to point to these, and some will claim that they justify the hosting of the event. The question is not whether there is a trace element of pro-development activity. Rather, the questions are: why couldn't these positive investments have been made without hosting the games, and why was it necessary to spend tens of billions of dollars to host the event in order to get several hundred million dollars, or even a billion or more dollars, of worthwhile infrastructural investments?

Long-Term Costs

When specialized facilities are built for an event that lasts seventeen to thirty-four days, it is perhaps unavoidable that some of these facilities will not be effectively used when the event is over. When they are not utilized or are underutilized, they will still cost money to maintain and operate. The long-term costs in these cases involve the operating and maintenance fees going forward, the debt service on the loans that were issued to finance the original construction, and the opportunity cost of the land on which the facility sits. Such under- or unutilized facilities are commonly referred to as white elephants.[27] They seem to pop up ubiquitously after sport mega-events.

White Elephants

The Bird's Nest in Beijing, which served as the Olympic Stadium for the 2008 Games, cost a reported $460 million to build. It had a capacity of 90,000 for the Olympics, with 140 luxury suites. One plan was for the Beijing Guo'an soccer team to play in the stadium after the Olympics, but the team backed out, afraid of the embarrassment of drawing its standard 10,000 fans to a venue with eight or nine times that capacity. Today it costs some $10 million a year to maintain, hosts an occasional event, and serves as a tourist stop for visitors to Beijing. According to a *CBS News* report from February 2014, "Few tourists are willing to pay more than $8 to tour the facility as enthusiasm for the 2008 Games fades, and the venue has struggled to fill its space with events."[28] The CBS report goes on to note: "But other venues have withered in neglect. A rowing park in the city's suburbs that cost $55 million has fallen into disuse, and visitors to this paid facility are few and far between. The cycling race tracks in another outlying district are covered in weeds, and the sand volleyball courts have been largely closed off to the public."[29]

While the Bird's Nest may be the best known of the white elephants, the Athens games seem to have spawned the largest number of them. Writing in the Toronto *Globe and Mail* in May 2014, Doug Saunders shared his impressions of the aftermath of the 2004 Athens Olympics:

> If you spend some time wandering the fields and hillsides outside of Athens, as I've done, you will see rising from the scrub a very different sort of Greek ruin. There's a crumbling volleyball stadium with nomadic families living in its stands. There's a 20,000-seat softball park largely reclaimed by trees. A barren, grass-covered hillside resembling a huge abandoned amphitheater turns out to have been a kayaking venue. All were built for the 2004 Olympic Games.[30]

According to one researcher, "Twenty-one out of 22 of the stadiums, arenas, sports halls and swimming pools built for the games are either derelict, in a state of disrepair, boarded up or unable to find a buyer and underused. As the Beijing games opened four years later Athens faced a bill estimated at $784 million simply to maintain this ghost town of Olympian extravagance."[31] Half of the 2,300 apartments in Athens's Olympic Village were still unoccupied in 2011, and most of the commercial properties on the site had closed, while promised schools were never finished. A 2011 article in the *The Telegraph* of London related some aspects of the depressing story:

> Despite grand plans for an Olympic legacy, municipalities ran out of money and the political will to maintain them.
>
> "We had some very good plans, well-laid plans," said Athanasios Alevras, a socialist MP from the ruling PASOK party and former deputy minister of culture in the run-up to the Games. "The idea was to build sites that could be then converted to benefit the lives of Atheneans afterwards. The Olympic Village was a great plan to regenerate an area."
>
> But, he admits, it went wrong. "We promised infrastructure and facilities that then weren't delivered. The plans were not respected. Basically, it's a disaster."
>
> He blames a change in the government and a lack of vision. "It isn't just that we ran out of money but that the administrative system just wasn't prepared to do what was needed," said Mr. Alevras.
>
> Many on the streets of Athens see state overspending on the Olympics as a major contributor to Greece's runaway financial problems. Sofia Sakorafa, an MP thrown out of George Papandreou's ruling PASOK party after voting against the bailout package a year ago, estimates the Games cost Greece €27bn, vastly over the given €5.5bn budget. She added that no official figure for the cost has ever been published.
>
> "It was a hugely wasted opportunity and one that sticks in the throat of many people. We are left with installations that are rotting away because we don't even have the money to maintain them. A lot of entrepreneurs and property developers got rich very quickly," said Ms. Sakorafa.

Other former hosts have also had a hard time finding long-term uses for Olympic venues. In Nagano, five large structures from the

1998 Winter Games remain, but many complain that they are too costly for a town of less than 400,000 to maintain. Nagano's Olympic Stadium was converted into a baseball stadium, but there are no teams in Nippon Professional Baseball that play in Nagano. Atlanta's Olympic Stadium was converted into the Atlanta Braves' home park in 1997, but in 2013 the Braves announced that they would move to a suburb north of the city. Barcelona's Olympic Stadium from 1992 still lacks a primary tenant.[32]

Of the twenty stadiums that were built or remodeled for the 2002 World Cup, held jointly in Japan and South Korea, a majority have fallen into disuse.[33] Vancouver's Olympic Village was taken over by the city because the developer defaulted on its loans. A large number of its units remained unsold in early 2014, and the city projected a loss of $300 million on the project.[34]

The South African Premier Soccer League averages only 7,500 fans per match. The Cape Town stadium for the 2010 World Cup was originally to be built in the working-class community of Athlone, with plans for extensive investment to modernize the area's infrastructure. At FIFA's insistence, the new stadium was moved to Green Point, a white, affluent community on the waterfront, at a huge cost. Juliet Macur described her 2013 visit to the Cape Town stadium in the *New York Times:*

> Last fall, I paid about $4 to tour Cape Town Stadium, which was built for the 2010 World Cup in South Africa but had turned into a cavernous ghost town. Maybe 100 people a week buy tickets to get a close look at the Cup-generated waste. The space can be rented for weddings or other events, like the small fashion show that I saw there.
>
> Suites that once held World Cup parties were dusty and silent. The state-of-the-art locker rooms, with tiny safes at each stall and rows of sinks to wash dirt off cleats, remained untouched. Thousands of tiny lights glistened from the ceiling of a V.I.P. entrance.[35]

Of the ten stadiums employed for the 2010 Cup, five were newly constructed, with renovations at the others. One of the new stadiums was built in Polokwane, South Africa, just east of the existing Pietersburg Stadium. The latter was originally going to be updated for the Cup, but FIFA was not satisfied, and the decision was made to build the Peter Mokaba Stadium. The Mokaba Stadium has a capacity of 41,733, but it is rarely used by either professional soccer or rugby teams. Another new facility in Nelspruit, South Africa, is the Mbombela Stadium, with 40,929 seats. There were five worker strikes during the construction. After the last strike, the workers were fired and the project was completed with subcontractors. Serious corruption charges were made, and at least three persons were murdered in connection with the allegations. Many more received death threats. Mbombela is also rarely used, and both Mokaba and Mbombela may have to be demolished to avoid the crippling operating and maintenance costs. Green Point Stadium in Cape Town has yearly maintenance costs of $6.2 million. The Nelson Mandela Bay Stadium is still looking for an anchor tenant and will cost an estimated $8.7 million a year to run.[36]

FIFA has a 420-page stadium manual that explains that a new stadium "provides many benefits for the local community" and enhances community pride. In too many cases, this is fanciful nonsense, but either the executives at FIFA are willfully ignorant or they just don't want any facts getting in the way of their PR machine. The manual doesn't contain a section that elaborates the long-term costs and how to avoid building white elephants.

If finding long-term tenants for soccer stadiums and residential units is difficult, then one can only imagine the challenge in finding uses for lesser-used and more obscure venues such as velodromes, whitewater canoe/kayak runs, beach volleyball stadiums, speedskating ovals, and bobsled tracks. The list of underutilized, vacant, and demolished facilities is long. Some of them are discussed in chapters 5 and 6, which look in detail at specific host cities' experiences with mega-events.

Long-Term Debt and Opportunity Costs

Just as rollicking parties often leave heavy hangovers, Olympic and World Cup games leave massive debt. Governments borrow to finance their sports extravaganzas. The legacy is that the debt has to be paid back, usually over periods of ten, twenty, or thirty years.

The *New York Times* commented on the residue of heavy debt from the Vancouver Winter Olympics:

> The immediate legacy for this city of 580,000 is a nearly $1 billion debt from bailing out the Olympic Village development. Beyond that, people in Vancouver and British Columbia have already seen cuts in services like education, health care and arts financing from their provincial government.[37]

The Brazilian economy is in dire need of light rail, metros, intercity train transport, roads, bridges, ports, and airport improvements, yet it spends only 1.5 percent of its GDP on infrastructure, compared to the global average of 3.8 percent. Among other things, Brazil's deficient infrastructure puts its businesses at a competitive disadvantage internationally. For instance, a Brazilian soybean farmer in the state of Mato Grosso may spend 25 percent of the value of his product getting it to port, whereas a U.S. soybean farmer in Iowa spends 9 percent.

The money that services the billions of dollars of debt cannot be used for worthy infrastructure projects, for health care, for education, or for promoting sustainability. In fact, paying off the debt has to mean either cuts in public services or higher taxes. Such a financial legacy can be economically justified only if the original investments made with borrowed money have positive consequences for the city's or the country's long-term development. Parties are fun, but promoting jobs and economic development is a more complicated matter.

5

Barcelona and Sochi

Barcelona and Sochi stand at opposite ends of the spectrum in realizing gains from hosting the Olympics. The advance planning, the sources of funding, and the inherent potential based on cultural endowment and location dramatically separate the two cities' experiences and provide an illustrative and cautionary tale for prospective mega-event hosts.

Barcelona

Barcelona is the poster child of success for cities hosting the Olympic Games. Each new host city studies and seeks to emulate the experience of Barcelona in hosting the 1992 Summer Games. In many ways, the Barcelona case does indeed represent how to do it right, and there is good reason for other cities to try to learn from Barcelona. In other ways, however, the circumstances in Barcelona were unique, and will not be easy for other cities to duplicate.

Some historical background helps set the context for Barcelona's success. From 1939 until his death in 1975, Francisco Franco was the authoritarian ruler of Spain. The Catalonian region, where Barcelona is located, was relatively neglected during this period. Development in Barcelona was characterized by real estate speculation, inadequate investment in infrastructure, and little thought given to urban design. Despite Barcelona's desirable climate, location on the Mediterranean Sea, rich architectural heritage, and interesting culture, the city was well down the list of European tourist destinations and business centers.

With the end of Francoism, the city anxiously anticipated a new opportunity to reshape its development. A positive spirit of cooperation between capital and labor and among the municipal, regional, and national governments fostered a proactive approach. In 1976 the city produced the General Metropolitan Plan (PGM), which established a new spatial framework for the city. A significant part of this framework entailed opening the city to the sea. This involved relocating rail lines that separated the Pobleneu neighborhood from the beach and placing a roadway below-grade at the bottom of the famous street, Las Ramblas. It also meant that an area of mostly abandoned warehouses and factories in Pobleneu would be razed and become the eventual site of the Olympic Village, to be converted to residential housing after the games. Other parts of the plan related to improving the road network around the city, extending the metro system, redesigning the airport, renovating public spaces and museums, and modernizing the sewerage system.

Thus, an early plan for urban redevelopment was formulated by 1976 and then elaborated in the following years. It was not until 1986 that the IOC selected Barcelona to host the 1992 Games.

In 1983, city planners put out a preliminary report on the feasibility of hosting the Olympics and concluded that the refurbishment of the 1936 stadium in Montjuic (which became the Olympic Stadium) and the construction of the Sports Palace and Swimming facility would be undertaken whether or not the city was selected to host the games.[1] Of the thirty-seven sports facilities ultimately used during the 1992 Olympics, twenty-seven were already built and another five were under construction at the time Spain was selected to host the games in 1986.[2] Thus, a central feature of the Barcelona experience is that *the plan preceded the games,* and hence the games were put at the service of the preexisting plan, rather than the typical pattern of the city development plan being put at the service of the games.[3]

Several factors further contributed to the salutary role played by being host to the games. First, of the $11.5 billion total cost of the games (as measured in constant 2000 dollars), $6.9 billion (or 60 percent) came from private sources. Of the 40 percent that came from public sources, only $235 million (5 percent of all public funds) came from the Barcelona city budget.[4] Out of all the investments in urban improvements connected to the PGM and the games, 83 percent went into nonsports facilities.[5]

Second, the macroeconomic conditions in Spain were auspicious. After an annual average rate of GDP per capita growth of 6.1 percent during 1960–74, the next eleven years brought near stagnation, with annual per capita growth falling to 0.8 percent during 1974–85. The protracted period of slow growth meant that the large infrastructural and facility investments of the PGM would stimulate employment and output increases rather than provoke strong inflation. Stated differently, the Barcelona economy was ready to receive and benefit from stimulus spending.

Third, the favorable macroeconomic conditions were enhanced by Spain's entry into the European Economic Community (today known as the European Union) in 1986. Spain's membership facilitated finance, trade, and tourism.

Fourth, and quite important, Barcelona was a hidden jewel. Its location, climate, architecture, and history meant that the city had a tremendous potential for tourism and business that had been unexploited for decades. While many prospective host cities would like to believe that they can emulate Barcelona, few would be able to bring together the special features that characterized Barcelona in the 1980s.

Between November 1986 and July 1992, unemployment in Barcelona fell from 127,774 to 60,885, corresponding to a drop in the unemployment rate from 18.4 percent to 9.6 percent.[6] With a new airport terminal and forty new hotels in the city, the number of passengers at Barcelona's airport almost doubled, from 5.46 million in 1985 to 10.04 million in 1992. Barcelona's ranking as a tourist and business meeting destination among European cities improved from eleventh in 1990 to fourth in 2009.

Of course, although there is a temporal association, it is not necessarily the case that these gains can be attributed solely to hosting the Olympic Games. In fact, the ETOA did a study in which it questioned whether any significant improvement resulted from the 1992 Games. The following is an excerpt from that report:

> Hotel occupancy actually dropped from 70 percent in 1991 to 64 percent in 1992, the Olympic year. Fears of construction and overcrowding played a role in deterring visitors. Further decreases in hotel occupancy followed in the two years after the Olympics registering just 54%. It then took a further two years for Barcelona's occupancy rates to recover. Only in 1998 did they exceed the 80% mark.
>
> Whilst Barcelona has undoubtedly grown as a tourist destination, the extent to which this growth is due to the Olympic Games is by no means certain. If there is any benefit to tourism from hosting the Olympics, then the biggest benefit should be immediately afterwards. This, after all, is when the image of the city would be freshest in the minds of the audience.
>
> But if you plot Barcelona's tourism growth against that of Venice, Florence and Lisbon, its performance is below average.
>
> But Barcelona was, even before the Olympics, the byword for urban cool, feted by everyone from Freddy Mercury to Robert Hughes. The nearest match to a "Barcelona without the Olympics" would be Dublin and Prague, both medium sized national centres which blended hedonism with considerable cultural appeal. If you track Barcelona's visitor growth against these cities, then the "Olympic effect" disappears.[7]

Yet a closer look at Barcelona's tourism numbers suggests that the ETOA's critical analysis may have been overstated.

Table 5-1 shows the number of domestic and foreign tourist bed nights (the number of tourists multiplied by the average number of nights per tourist), which is a more complete measure of tourism's economic impact than simply the number of tourists. (Three of the columns provide ratios comparing bed nights between years to depict the growth over the period.) While the number of bed nights in Barcelona did decline in 1993, the year following the games, it grew handsomely thereafter. If we compare Barcelona's performance with that of Florence and Venice during the 1990/1991 through 1994 period, we find that Barcelona's tourism increased more than Florence's whether we use 1990 or 1991 as the base year, and increased more than Venice's when 1990 is used as the base year for comparison. Barcelona also outperformed the growth of all other major European cities during either time frame. More significant, since 1993 Barcelona's tourism growth has far outpaced that of all the other European cities in table 5-1. The city's tourism rise has been remarkable by any standards.

What accounted for Barcelona's take-off since 1993? A 2010 English study, seeking to garner lessons for the upcoming 2012 London Games, observed about the Barcelona games: "However, hotels that had an average annual occupancy of 80% before the Olympic Games, now found that they had less than 50% occupancy. This, in turn, caused prices to fall with the very real prospect that the city would fade back into obscurity."[8]

This interpretation is consistent with that of the ETOA: the games by themselves greatly expanded the supply of hotel rooms without automatically increasing the demand for hotel rooms commensurately. Hotel prices fell, the hospitality sector fretted, and the city took action.

In 1993, Barcelona established its Bureau of Tourism (Turisme de Barcelona), a combination of public and private interests. The bureau is presided over by the city's mayor, while its executive committee is

TABLE 5-1. European Tourism by City

City	Millions of bed nights, by year										
	1990	1991	1992	1993	1994	Ratio, 1994/1990	Ratio, 1994/1991	1995	2000	2010	Ratio, 2010/1991
London	91.300	84.400	84.100	85.782	92.100	1.01	1.09	103.300	124.440	114.636	1.36
Paris	31.166	28.269	30.976	26.453	26.984	0.87	0.95	24.813	33.547	35.790	1.27
Berlin	7.244	7.668	7.661	7.292	7.344	1.01	0.96	7.530	11.413	20.803	2.71
Rome	12.915	12.019	12.406	12.367	14.374	1.11	1.20	12.828	14.781	20.395	1.70
Barcelona	**3.796**	**4.090**	**4.333**	**4.257**	**4.705**	**1.24**	**1.15**	**5.675**	**9.276**	**15.342**	**3.75**
Madrid	9.482	8.728	7.717	7.186	8.056	0.85	0.92	8.372	12.655	15.193	1.74
Prague	4.524	4.700	4.363	3.515	4.556	1.01	0.97	5.104	8.155	12.090	2.57
Vienna	8.079	7.617	7.606	7.226	7.493	0.93	0.98	7.623	8.235	11.676	1.53
Munich	6.924	6.608	6.541	6.095	5.932	0.86	0.90	6.127	7.756	11.096	1.68
Amsterdam	5.721	5.364	5.850	5.414	5.912	1.03	1.10	6.214	7.766	9.725	1.81
Hamburg	3.962	4.072	4.044	3.960	4.115	1.04	1.01	4.165	4.845	8.877	2.18
Milan	5.791	5.574	5.590	5.352	5.764	1.00	1.03	6.005	5.035	8.420	1.51
Florence	5.671	5.468	5.756	5.647	6.202	1.09	1.13	6.455	6.874	6.008	1.10
Budapest	6.586	5.032	4.519	4.149	4.373	0.66	0.87	4.328	4.873	5.854	1.16
Venice	2.432	2.209	2.388	2.583	2.809	1.16	1.27	2.944	3.563	5.761	2.61

Source: Data compiled from TourismReview.com (www.tourism-review.com/bednight-figures-in-european-cities-reach-for-the-sky-in-the-european-cities-marketing-benchmarking-report-news2847), various years.

headed by the president of the Chamber of Commerce. The bureau undertook extensive market research and launched an aggressive promotional campaign. As well, new port facilities were exploited to develop a cruise market; today those facilities can accommodate more than 26,000 passengers daily. Serendipitously, the deregulation of European airlines in 1997 led to the emergence of new, private companies offering heavily discounted air service within Europe. Together, these factors, along with Barcelona's inherent attractions, catapulted the city onto its gilded path to tourism glory.

Thus, although hosting the games was hardly the only factor behind Barcelona's success, it appears to have been a catalyzing influence. It is not without reason that Barcelona has become a poster child of Olympic good fortune.

But Barcelona's hosting experience had some less appealing aspects, too. The development plan included the removal of old industrial and residential areas. Barcelona's widely published and well-known architectural critic Josep Maria Montaner leveled the following criticism at the changes to the city's urban landscape:

> [There was a] mistreatment of heritage, especially the industrial heritage in Poblenou. To understand this, one must understand that the underlying characteristic of the Spanish tradition, from dictatorship to democracy, was one of forgetting—wiping out the past and ignoring the responsibility of Francoism. . . . This programmed amnesia was similarly applied to urbanism. . . . The aim being to erase the city's working class memory, by demolishing popular and cooperative centers, old social housing and factories . . . and the total absence of any sustainability objectives. . . . In no building project . . . were any ecological criteria or sustainability standards implemented.[9]

Barcelona's new urban zones were redeveloped with improved public services and, in some cases, direct access to the sea. These parts of the city became gentrified, and hand in hand with gentrification came higher prices. Higher prices meant that lower-income people had to relocate, and, more generally, plans for public housing were underfulfilled.[10] One study noted the following impacts:

—Strong increases in the prices of housing for rent and for sale (from 1986 to 1993 the cumulative increase was 139 percent for home sale prices and nearly 145 percent in home rentals)

—A drastic decrease in the availability of public housing (from 1986 to 1992 there was a cumulative decrease of 5.9 percent)

—A gradual decrease in the availability of private houses for rent (from 1981 to 1991 the cumulative decrease was 23.7 percent)[11]

Thus, like the experience with mega-events elsewhere, hosting the games in Barcelona was accompanied by a redistribution of living standards to the detriment of lower-income groups.[12]

Finally, it is noteworthy that Barcelona made a major investment to host the 2004 Universal Forum of Cultures. The planning for this 141-day international event did not benefit from either the political euphoria of the 1980s or the cooperation of different sectors of the Barcelonan community. Indeed, there was vocal opposition from several NGOs, which argued the planning was controlled by big-business interests in the city. The cost of hosting the Forum was $2.3 billion, and the extended event was expected to draw more than 5 million visitors. The official attendance figure was 3.5 million, but various independent estimates were significantly lower.[13] According to one study, the physical legacy of the 2004 Forum had little to commend it:

> The coastal area built up around the forum district offers few amenities to pedestrians. What was left after the 2004 events are sprawling empty spaces on a scale useless for much else than future large events. The result, unsurprisingly, is a wasteland of plazas. Worse yet, the unpopularity of these plazas spreads to the parks and beaches that flank them (to the point where one feels unsafe in them).[14]

Barcelona, then, found it difficult to emulate its own experience, which should sound a strong cautionary note to would-be hosts of future Olympic and World Cup competitions.

Sochi, Russia

If Barcelona is the poster child for how to host the Olympics success-fully, then Sochi is the poster child for how to do it unsuccessfully. Plans to develop Sochi into a winter resort had existed since late Soviet times, and the bid for the 2014 Games was the third such visiting of the idea. The two previous ones in the 1990s failed owing to a lack of funds and the collapse of the economy after the fall of the Soviet Union.[15] Because of the 2014 Olympics, Sochi's "refurbishment" became much grander than it would have been otherwise. The initial plan was to spend $12 billion. For Vladimir Putin, the Winter Games were intended to elevate Russia's status worldwide to that of a superpower.

Sochi is a city of 350,000 inhabitants on the Black Sea. It has a subtropical climate, with warm summers and mild winters, and has long served as a summer retreat for Russia's elite. In addition to hosting the 2014 Winter Games, it will be one of the host cities for the 2018 World Cup.

Although the PR spin from Putin was that Sochi would become a stylish, year-round European resort, the evidence seems to suggest that not only will that not occur but that Sochi's historical draw as a summer resort may have been damaged. The price tag for this grandiose foray certainly exceeded $50 billion and may have reached above $65 billion.

Of course, the real cost of the Sochi games is a closely guarded state secret, and we will probably never know. Igor Nikolaev, director of the Strategic Analysis Department at FBK, one of Russia's most re-spected financial and accounting consulting firms, estimated the total cost at $66.7 billion.[16] But let us be conservative for the moment and use the figure most often cited by Russian officials and the media, $51 billion—still some $10 billion more than the previously most expensive games, in Beijing in 2008, and also more costly than all previous Winter Olympics combined. Even at $51 billion it repre-sents five times the initial Sochi bid documentation for total costs at $10.3 billion.[17]

How much money would have to be made from Sochi tourism

to justify an investment of $51 billion? A $51 billion loan financed over thirty years at an 8.25 percent interest rate, the Russian Central Bank's interest rate in late 2013, would require $4.7 billion in profits from Sochi tourism *a year* to make the annual debt payment. To put that tidy sum in perspective, the *total* annual personal income generated in Pitkin County, Colorado, home of the famous ski resorts of Aspen and Snowmass, in 2010 was under $700 million.

Now let's consider what we know about the "plan" for the Sochi games and its record investment. The ultimate goal of Putin in seeking the games was revealed by Deputy Prime Minister Alexander Zhukov in July 2007, when Russia was selected to host the 2014 Olympics. Zhukov declared, "This is international recognition of the new Russia." Boris Gryzlov, the leading Duma member, added, "Russia is once again becoming a world leader."[18]

Putin's vanity games involved little planning for the future. They were about proving that Russia could pull off this mega-construction project, in some ways similar to Stalin's superindustrialization project during the first Soviet Five-Year Plan of 1928–32. If enough resources were lavished on Sochi and sufficient payoffs made, then it could and would be done—or almost done. A lot went wrong.

The Oligarchs and Private Funding

Originally, the idea was to have the private sector cover about two-thirds of the construction costs, which were supposed to total $12 billion (the estimate was increased from the initial $10.3 billion bid presented to the IOC). Putin went to his oligarch friends, whom he had set up with sweetheart leases to Russia's mineral wealth, and called in his chips. The oligarchs, somewhat reluctantly, went along at first, expecting a controlled amount of funding and subsidies from the state. As the required investments grew, the hoped-for subsidies were not forthcoming and the necessary payoffs to get the work done ballooned.[19] The oligarchs grew weary. Two such oligarchs were Vladimir Potanin (nickel) and Oleg Deripaska (aluminum).

Putin had suggested that Potanin finance the building of one of four ski resorts, some thirty-eight miles from Sochi, while the two of them were on a ski vacation together. Deripaska, who borrowed $1 billion from the state bank VEB and later undertook projects on the port, roads, airport, and Olympic Village worth an estimated $2.4 billion, was told that it would be highly advisable for him to go along with projected Sochi investments if he wanted future Kremlin support for his business ventures.[20]

Both Potanin and Deripaska gave numerous interviews to express concern about their investments and to call for enhanced government subsidies, tax benefits, and low-interest credit. Potanin told Reuters in 2012 that he wanted to sell the hotels he was building before the games, but pressure from the Kremlin dissuaded him. A study by the Center for Security Analysis and Prevention in Prague similarly found that "the developers who build new hotel complexes [in Sochi] are losing interest in these projects." The report went on to state that "some of the private investors have realized the impossibility of achieving a return on realized buildings and they demand a percentage subsidy on loans from the state bank and want the state to buy a share in their companies."[21]

Mikhail Kasyanov, a former prime minister under Putin, suggested the private investments were coerced: "If you want to carry on doing business in Russia, here's the tax you need to pay—the kind of a tax that [Putin] wants you to pay." Nonetheless, as the magnitude of the Sochi expenses escalated, the share of the private financing, although huge to the individual investors, fell. By some estimates, although originally projected to cover roughly 67 percent of all costs, private funds probably accounted for less than 10 percent. Public monies and the Russian people covered the rest.

To be sure, what originally appeared as private funding may end up as public funding because some loans from the state bank won't be repaid and additional budgetary appropriations are slated to subsidize private losses on certain investments. A July 2014 article in *Around the Rings* reported the following:

Russia's development bank, the VEB, has asked for the federal government to cover losses related to Sochi Olympic construction—as much as $5 billion.

A report in the Kommersant says Prime Minster Dmitry Medvedev told the finance ministry to include the losses in its 2015 budget, which will fund the government in 2016 and 2017.

VEB chairman Vladimir Dmitriev said nine borrowers were at risk of missing payments on construction. Included in that group are developers behind the Rosa Khutor and Gorki venues, the Olympic Village, the Sochi 2014 headquarters, and a group of hotels built for the Games.[22]

Civil Rights, Worker Exploitation, and Forced Relocations

Human Rights Watch published a study in February 2013 that found extensive violations of Russian labor law. Investigators interviewed dozens of migrant workers—about 16,000 of whom came from outside Russia—at the various Olympic venues and transportation construction sites and found that it was common for workers to work seven days a week, more than ten hours a day, and to receive no overtime pay. The nominal pay range varied between $1.80 and $2.60 an hour, although some workers did not receive any pay, or received delayed or partial payments. The migrant workers were put in excessively crowded living conditions with inadequate nutrition. The report notes that this treatment is in direct contravention of the Olympic Charter, which pledges to promote and uphold human dignity.[23]

The report also notes that, as is common to Olympic construction sites, the investigators observed many instances of forced evictions and relocations, with below-market compensation to the displaced residents. Tatiana Skiba's new hillside home was ruined when vast amounts of concrete and rubble were dumped from an Olympic construction site. Skiba stated that while she was initially excited about the Olympics coming to Sochi, "Now the Olympics is hell for me and for everyone who lives along this street. It is hell and we are very bitter toward the government."[24]

Pollution

Environmentalists have argued that venue and infrastructure construction around Sochi has been damaging to the sensitive mountain landscape, has hurt biodiversity, and has dumped toxins into the Black Sea. Here is Jules Boykoff:

> By 2010, both Greenpeace and the World Wildlife Fund had severed ties with Russia's state-owned construction firm Olympstroi, which the NGOs blamed for dumping heavy metals and industrial waste. In 2009 the Russia-based group Environmental Watch on North Caucasus lodged a complaint that the natural gas giant Gazprom was illegally crossing into the Caucasus Strict Nature Reserve in order to build a road connecting to the Olympic Ski Complex. . . . In February 2013, the group issued an open statement to the IOC asserting that deforestation and the release of toxic effluents had degraded the natural landscape in the Sochi region.[25]

Notwithstanding the IOC's rhetorical embrace of sustainability, Sochi construction has left a problematic environmental footprint. A Reuters reporter observed, "Locals in Sochi say that chemicals used in Olympic construction have polluted the water and damaged the prospect of the city turning into a major Russian tourist destination anytime soon." A tourist from Moscow told the reporter, "You don't want to swim in the water here. Even the locals have stopped swimming here." The Human Rights Watch report echoed these concerns, citing innumerable complaints from residents and suggesting that much of the construction work for the games was performed without following the environmental review procedures mandated in Russian law.

An article in the *Moscow Times* reported: "Prominent among the critics are ecologists, who say that the massive construction projects are destroying local wildlife. In 2010, the United Nations Environment Program said in a report that the government had ignored the cumulative effects of the various projects on the regional ecosystem."[26]

Steven Meyers, writing for the *New York Times Magazine,* commented on the "rapacious development under way in the region's protected parks, including a supposed research center above Sochi that is widely believed to be a personal mountain resort, replete with helipads and several Swiss-style chalets, for Putin."[27]

The locals and the environmentalists who protested these ecological transgressions were subject to scorn and repression. According to an Associated Press 2013 report, the protesters "have been detained, put on trial and even barred from going on the beach."[28]

There was perhaps an even larger environmental fallout from the Sochi games—the relaxation of legislation for environmental protection around the country. Martin Müller, professor of urban geography at the University of Zurich, observed: "It is even more cause for concern that some of this environmental damage was facilitated through the targeted relaxation of environmental jurisdiction. This applies to the law on protected areas, which was modified to allow for sports mega-events to be held there, and the forest code, which was modified to allow for the cutting of rare species of trees."[29]

Terrorism

As became painfully apparent following the two bombings of the railway station in Volgograd in December 2013, killing thirty-four, and the shootout in Dagestan, which killed another seven, the Sochi area is politically unstable and dangerous. Terrorist groups seeking independence are very active in Dagestan, Chechnya, and Abkhazia, among other nearby regions. A Chechen terrorist leader threatened to disrupt the Winter Games. While the Sochi area may have been thought of as a peaceful, subtropical retreat on the Black Sea prior to its exposure to the world press around the 2014 Olympics, now there are few who regard the region as safe.

Weather

As many had feared, the weather did not cooperate for the Winter Games. For nearly a week, thermometers broke 60 degrees Fahrenheit at the ski resort in the mountains outside Sochi. The organizing committee had to use the tons of artificial snow they had stored under thermal blankets to spread over the competition areas. Even then, events were delayed, and competitors complained copiously.

Subtropical Sochi has served for decades as a summer retreat, mostly for Russian politicians and, more recently, wealthy business leaders.[30] The expressed hope was to convert Sochi into a year-round resort. The warm weather during the Winter Games, broadcast to the world on television, the Internet, and social media, could not have promoted the image of Sochi as a winter resort very successfully.

Hospitality

As has often been the case with mega-sporting events, the scale of construction was so grand that it was inevitable that certain projects were not completed on time. For the hotel construction projects in Sochi, this problem was experienced in spades. The media outlets were swarming with jokes about hotels that did not open for the games despite having booked tourists or athletes, hotel rooms without water or with water pooling on the bathroom floor, rooms without phones or television sets, bathrooms without toilets or ceilings, and so on. There were abundant complaints about the lack of evening entertainment, the paucity of restaurant choices, and the level of service.

Alexander Maklyarovsky, the head of the internal tourism department at the major Russian tour operator company KMP, commented, "The city has no experience with foreigners and locals struggle to communicate in English." Sochi's mayoral adviser, Olga Nedelko, added that "hospitality is also an issue . . . locals are used to seeing tourists as a nuisance."[31]

Impact on Tourism

The 2013 official report of the Sochi organizing committee noted that tourism in the Sochi area declined in 2010 and 2011, sending it back down to its 2006 level. The report speculated that the decline may have been due to excessive construction work in the region. With all the negative publicity from the games, there was little optimism that tourism would pick up. The facts that Sochi is far away from most population centers in Russia and Europe, difficult to get to, and encumbered by Russian visa requirements did not augur well. There were widespread concerns that the overbuilding of hotel rooms for the games (22,000 new rooms) would lead to occupancy rates as low as 30 percent and put downward pressure on room prices, which in turn would lead to extensive bankruptcies.

A comprehensive study on the prospects for Sochi tourism by the Czech Center for Security Analysis and Prevention was not sanguine. The study concluded:

> The developers who build new hotel complexes are losing their interest in these projects in Sochi. . . . The returns . . . after the Olympic Games are over remain the main investment risk. The emergence of competitive tourism seems to be the biggest problem with the investment. . . . Instead of staying in Sochi for three days, the Russians prefer to fly to Egypt or Turkey for one week, all inclusive and with services at a higher level. Some of the private investors realized the impossibility of achieving a return on realized buildings and they demand a percentage subsidy on loans from the state bank and want the state to buy a share in their companies.[32]

In fact, the massive Olympic construction was just that: construction for the seventeen days of the Olympics. Although there were visions of a new international, year-round luxury resort in Sochi, no careful feasibility studies were done and there was no serious planning. After the games were over, David Segal, writing in the *New York Times,* made the following observations:

> It also seems that few people in the upper echelons of the Russian government have given the future of Sochi much thought.
>
> "I don't think anyone is sure what to do with it," said Sufian Zhemukhov, co-author of a coming book on the Sochi Games. "I say that because President Putin and Prime Minister Medvedev have changed the concept many times. First, it was going to become a kind of capital of southern Russia. Then they talked about dismantling the arenas and taking them north. A few months ago, Medvedev said they were going to open casinos there. Virtually everything about the Sochi Games has been improvised, it seems, and their aftermath will not be any different."[33]

Brian Gleeson, the general manager of the Radisson Blue Beach Resort and Spa in Sochi, is not sure where the additional tourists will come from. He has written off U.S. and European tourists, who have better options closer to home for which they need not put up with the expense and hassles of procuring a Russian visa.[34] The annexation of Crimea is making things even worse: the beaches in Crimea are the one immediate competitor for Sochi in summer tourism. Once the Russian government annexed Crimea, it began pouring money into subsidizing flights and getting the tourism industry up and running again to hasten the integration of Crimea into Russia.

Complicating any constructive legacy still further is that the combination of corruption and the myopic vision of the overall project led to most of the building being done on the cheap. Martin Müller, who has spent five years studying the area, commented that he spoke with engineers in charge of quality assurance on the various construction projects and was told, "There is no quality to assure. Quality wasn't an issue. It wasn't demanded by investors, and nobody asked for it. Builders would sometimes even try to bribe their way through the quality assessment phase."[35]

As of the time of writing, July 2014, the Olympic venues and hotels appeared to be in financial trouble. The Russian government issued a rule in May 2014 that exempted Olympic-related businesses from regional property taxes. This move would reportedly cost the regional government $114 million in tax revenue during 2014. One official commented that the businesses did not have the money to pay the tax, so there was really no choice.[36]

Meanwhile, hotel vacancy rates soared, and officials scrambled to develop plans to entice tourism. Several ideas were floated, including the creation of an extreme sports park and a Russian Disneyland, but as of July 2014 nothing had been decided. Some previous plans were scrapped, such as the conversion of the Iceberg Skating Palace into a velodrome.

Ironically, in June 2014 the government announced that the Sochi games had produced a record Olympic surplus of $261 million.[37] This figure refers to the *operating* revenues and *operating* costs directly connected to the staging of the games and has little economic meaning. The central government could write the Sochi Olympic Organizing Committee a check to boost its revenues or to reduce its costs for any amount to generate such a surplus. And the designation of *operating* surplus means that all capital costs are excluded.

Thus, in the end, Putin had an inordinately expensive mess on his hands, with the potential for political pushback. Although not so proficient at planning economic development, Putin is masterful at political and military strategy. So, either by serendipity or by design, Putin was able to divert the eyes of the Russian people away from Sochi just days after the Winter Olympics ended and toward a much weightier nationalist matter—the annexation of Crimea to Russia.

Russia is currently committed to hosting yet another "most expensive ever event" with the World Cup in 2018. That extravaganza is estimated to cost a minimum of $21 billion already three years before the event (with further cost increases likely to occur down the line, as seems to be the rule).[38]

The contrast between Barcelona and Sochi couldn't be starker.

For Barcelona, the Olympics were put at the service of the preexisting city plan; for Sochi, the city plan was put at the service of the Olympics. Barcelona had deep, unrealized potential as a tourist destination, whereas Sochi's potential arguably had already been approached. In Barcelona, the financing scheme took full advantage of existing infrastructure and maximized the use of outside funds; in Sochi, virtually everything was built from scratch, and financing was overwhelmingly public. For Barcelona, management was intelligent and efficient; for Sochi, management was often feckless and corrupt. The different economic outcomes of the 1992 and 2014 Olympic Games reflected these underlying realities.

6

Rio-Brazil and London

Brazil and London represent the two most recent experiences with hosting the World Cup and the Summer Olympics, and Rio, of course, will become the newest host of the Summer Games in 2016. The contrasts between the Rio-Brazil and London experiences are manifested along several dimensions: degree of economic development, planning model and goals, administrative style and efficiency, and the extent of buy-in from the local population.

Rio and Brazil

Two for one. Not a bad idea. Brazil hosted the 2014 World Cup and Rio de Janeiro will host the 2016 Summer Olympics. In theory, there should be some savings, or what economists call economies of scale, from such a double engagement.[1] The final match of the World Cup was played at the refurbished Maracanã Stadium in Rio, and the same venue is slated to serve as the Olympic Stadium in 2016.[2] The Brazilian Ministry of Sport is overseeing both events, and many of the same executives are supposed to be involved. If all goes according to plan, a pacification of the favelas, a more efficient political and administrative apparatus, and various infrastructure improvements will result from the doubleheader, helping to carry Brazil's fame and fortune forward in the coming decades.

When Rio was awarded the host status for the 2016 Games, it became the first city in South America slated to host the Olympics. Rio's Organizing Committee for the Olympic Games (OCOG) took some interesting initial steps. It hired several outside consulting firms (AECOM from Los Angeles, Wilkinson Eyre Architects from the United Kingdom, Pujol Barcelona Architects from Spain, and IMG and McKinsey from New York) to design an urban strategy and style for the games. The final master plan for the 2016 Games was meant to emulate that of the successful 1992 Games in Barcelona—four urban clusters rather than one focal area, with new transportation routes and technologies connecting them. Superficially, the plan resembled Barcelona's. In substance and outcome, however, the two plans had little in common.

The 2014 World Cup

But first things first. Although the 2014 World Cup was pulled off with relatively minor hitches evident to the international television audience, on the streets of the host cities the situation was far from normal. A *New York Times* reporter described the scene in Rio on July 13, the day of the final match between Argentina and Germany, this way: "The authorities had assembled what ranked as one of the largest security operations ever in Brazil, with 25,000 soldiers and police officers giving Rio a martial feel throughout the day with sirens blaring and motorcades halting traffic."[3]

Also not visible to the international television audience was that preparations on the ground lagged woefully. The transportation infrastructure was far from completed. Buildings around the stadiums were left half-finished. The building that was supposed to serve as the media center in the southern city of Curitiba, the capital of Paraná, for example, was left as a "six-story metal skeleton jutting out from the World Cup soccer stadium."[4] Other projects abandoned in midstream included the monorail to São Paulo's domestic airport, a passenger terminal at the Fortaleza International Airport, and WiFi networks at six of the twelve stadiums, among many others. Some construction was so rushed that quality was uncertain, such as the overpass on the way to the stadium in Belo Horizonte, which collapsed on July 3, leaving at least two people dead and nineteen injured.[5]

According to a Reuters report, "In Salvador de Bahia, construction of a planned subway system was handed over to a private company halfway through, and work will not be completed until after the tournament is over. A new runway was proposed for the World Cup at Rio de Janeiro's Galeão International Airport, but now it is unclear if it will be finished even in time for the 2016 Games."[6] Five of the twelve host cities admitted that they didn't complete the promised transportation infrastructure (bus lanes, metro, or monorail) on time for the Cup. Sinaenco, a trade group of architects and engineers, stated that nationwide, "only 36 of 93 major projects are complete" in time for the World Cup.[7]

FIFA requires that each host country have eight modern stadiums of at least 40,000 capacity, one of which must have 60,000 seats, for the opening match, and another with 80,000 capacity, for the final contest. That threshold alone would have been difficult enough to meet, but Brazil decided to go one better. In the hopes of exposing twelve of its cities to the world and resolving some internal political squabbles, Brazil committed to having twelve venues, each with a minimum 40,000 capacity.[8] In 2009 the Brazilian Football Confederation initially estimated that refitting or building the twelve stadiums required for the World Cup would cost about $1.1 billion. The total stadium budget eventually rose to over $4.7 billion.[9] Nine of the stadiums were new, and of these, seven were built on the site of existing stadiums that were demolished.[10] With the exception of the new stadiums in Manaus and Cuiabá, all the facilities were publicly financed yet are now under private management. In these so-called public-private partnerships, the taxpayers fund the construction and the private sector gains the usufruct rights. Manaus and Cuiabá, whose new stadiums were also built with public funds, are actively looking for private companies to manage their stadiums, which have little prospect of profitable use.

Estimates for the total cost (including all infrastructure, security, and operations) of the World Cup for Brazil run from $15 billion to $20 billion. (Of course, these estimates, like others concerning the cost of hosting mega-events, are affected by what auxiliary, infrastructural investments are deemed to be directly related to the event. The more tangentially related investments are included, the higher the cost estimates go.)

White elephants seem inevitable. Four stadiums were built in cities with no football team in the first division of Brazil's soccer leagues. In Manaus, there is a second-division team that draws an average attendance of around 1,500. Manaus now has a new stadium with a capacity of 42,374, built at a cost of $325 million.[11] It was used for a grand total of four games during the World Cup. Meanwhile, a sewerage system and monorail that were part of the Manaus Cup plans were never built. A year later, no professional soccer team was playing in the stadium because it was too expensive and only eleven events had been held in the facility.[12]

New stadiums were also built in Cuiabá, Brasília, and Natal, all with lower-division teams and low attendance. In Natal, another perfectly good playing field was bulldozed so that a new stadium could be erected that met FIFA standards. Dave Zirin quotes Jan-Marten Hoitsma, a project manager brought in to make sure that Natal's new facility was completed on time: "There are no big football teams here—the biggest team gets gates of around 5,000 and we're building a 42,000-seater World Cup stadium."[13]

The Natal stadium cost $450 million, not including the cost of the new highway that leads to it. That highway cost Maria Ivanilde Oliveira her livelihood. She used to sell ice to locals on their way to the beach. The locals no longer travel on her street. She can no longer afford electricity for her house.[14] Marília Sueli Ferreira works at a stationery store next to the new stadium in Natal. During the competition, she raised the question, "What are we going to use this stadium for after the World Cup? The World Cup is made for tourists, not for residents, and the tourists are going to disappear very soon."[15] In May 2015 the Natal stadium was being used for weddings and childrens' parties.

The Mané Garrincha Stadium in Brasília cost a reported $900 million to build and has a capacity of over 70,000.[16] The stadium was initially budgeted at $300 million. An official audit of the stadium completed in May 2014 found that the tripling of the costs owed in large measure to construction company payoffs and price gouging. For example, the 140-page auditor's report states that the transportation of prefabricated grandstands was supposed to cost just $14,700, but the construction company billed the government $1.5 million. The auditors found $2.3 million in overcharges for materials that were listed multiple times on invoices. All told, the report estimates that one-third of the $900 million cost was due to fraudulent billing.

Brasília's professional football team, Brasiliense, is in Brazil's fourth division. They have chosen not to play in the Mané Garrincha Stadium. The team's coach, Marcos Soares, explains why: "You have to pay [to rent the stadium], you have the employees, cleaning, security staff, the clubs have to pay for this. It's a gigantic stadium, for 70,000 people; Brasiliense will not fill a stadium like that. To make a profit, you need, I imagine, 25,000 people and you're not going to get that in a fourth division match in the Brazilian championship."[17] In May 2015 the Brasilia stadium was being used as a bus parking lot.[18] In Fortaleza, Recife, and Salvador they do have football teams in the first division, but the teams average around 15,000 attendance per game, with an average ticket price of $10. Recife already had three large, multipurpose stadiums. The populations in these cities do not come close to having the purchasing power to pay ticket prices high enough to maintain those stadiums, let alone to service the construction debt. In Curitiba, in early October 2013, with construction 78 percent complete, the new stadium construction was suspended because of numerous safety violations and out of fear that the structure would collapse. It was eventually completed in time for the competition.

Meanwhile, an Associated Press report found "skyrocketing campaign contributions by the very companies involved in the most Cup projects." And Renato Rainha, an arbiter at Brasília's Audit Court, stated, "These donations are making corruption in this country even worse and making it increasingly difficult to fight. These politicians are working for those who financed campaigns."[19]

Rainha speaks with good authority. Two mega-construction companies, Andrade Gutierrez and the Odebrecht consortium (which includes IMX and the Los Angeles–based AEG), received the bulk of World Cup construction projects. Political contributions from Andrade Gutierrez jumped 500-fold, from $73,180 in 2008 to $37.1 million in 2012, and those from Odebrecht went from $90,909 in 2008 to $11.6 million in 2012.[20] Fully 40 percent of federal members of congress had criminal cases pending against them in the nation's highest court.[21]

In São Paulo, the venerable Morumbi Stadium was excluded from the World Cup by FIFA because it failed to meet technical requirements.[22] The local organizing committee for the World Cup decided to build a new stadium that would meet FIFA's requirements. After its overview visit to Brazil in May 2011, FIFA required enhancements to the new facility's design. The enhanced design carried an estimated price tag of $650 million, a 30 percent increase in the total cost. The construction was disrupted in early 2014 when a crane collapse destroyed a good section of the stadium and killed two workers; a work stoppage followed. The construction company in charge of the venue admitted on May 19, 2014, that the glass covers for the roof would not be installed in time for the World Cup, meaning that the fans who were supposed to be protected from the elements would not be.[23] The final cost of the facility was expected to exceed $650 million by a substantial margin. The renowned Brazilian journalist and television commentator Juca Kfouri mused, "A stadium is built in São Paulo, with public money, to deliver to a private club [the Corinthian football team], when São Paulo has a stadium that for more than 50 years has served world football . . . and could perfectly host an event that lasts one month and would host a maximum of six games."[24]

At the famous Maracanã Stadium in Rio, which was originally built for the 1950 World Cup, there was a $200 million renovation for the Pan American Games in 2007.[25] That renovation was not suitable, in FIFA's judgment, so after the Pan American Games, Maracanã Stadium was partly demolished and then rebuilt for over $500 million. The initial plan for the rebuild included the demolition of the Indigenous Cultural Center (the first indigenous museum in Latin America), as well as of a school and a gymnasium, to make room for a parking garage.[26] Fierce local resistance and social movements, however, have preserved the venues for the time being.

There was also the leveling of a nearby favela (Favela de Metro) and the relocation of its residents. The journalist Dave Zirin described the scene at this former favela in mid-June 2014:

> Two middle-aged men, former residents of Favela de Metro, sat around a plastic table between the sidewalk and a demolished home. We asked them why the city would hastily evict this community only to leave wreckage behind: "They didn't give us a reason why we had to leave. They just came, pushed us out, and knocked the building down."[27]

The land was slated to become a parking lot, but, as the World Cup matches began on June 12, 2014, there was no lot there. Seven hundred families had been displaced. The first 100 were removed at gunpoint and resettled two hours away in a western suburb of Rio. The remaining families protested and sued, and eventually received better treatment.

The plan was to have Brazil's most popular soccer team, Flamengo, continue to play at Maracanã after the games. The proximate problem was that the Consórcio Maracanã, a group led by Brazil's largest construction company, with the now fallen Brazilian billionaire

Eike Batista's company IMX and the U.S-based AEG, was awarded a thirty-five-year contract to manage the stadium.[28] The consortium initially proposed to Flamengo that it pay the team a fixed sum per game and that it keep all the revenue generated by signage, concessions, and luxury seating. Flamengo demurred, but a settlement was eventually reached.[29]

The white elephants not only cost hundreds of millions of dollars each to build, they cost millions of dollars annually to operate and maintain. Anyone who has ever owned a car or a house knows that such maintenance costs are not trivial. They also present an aesthetic issue, for they are ultramodern facilities surrounded by a sea of parking lots anomalously situated in open areas or in communities with older, more modest construction.

These massive sports facility and infrastructure expenditures are taking place against a backdrop of sharp income inequality, a relatively low level of economic development, poor social services, increasing prices, and rising expectations. At $11,300, Brazil's per capita income is approximately one-fifth that of the United States. Measured by the Gini coefficient, Brazil's income distribution is roughly 40 percent more unequal than in the United States.[30] Approximately 20 percent of Brazil's 200 million-plus people live in poverty. The Brazilian GDP, which grew at close to 6 percent per year during 2000–10, slowed to a 2 percent rate during 2011–13. Meanwhile, inflation accelerated from the 3–4 percent range during 2000–10 to around 6 percent during 2011–13, and as the World Cup approached in 2014, prices rose at a still faster clip.

Housing prices spiked even faster. While gentrification is appealing to some, it means unaffordable housing to others. It is a pattern familiar to mega-events, as land becomes scarcer and demand often rises. According to the Knight Frank Global House Price Index, the rate of increase in home prices in Brazil during 2012 was the third highest in the world. The rate of increase in Rio was even higher, jumping 58.3 percent (in real terms) between August 2010 and June 2013.[31]

Rio has a housing deficit estimated at 500,000 units. The shortage was aggravated by the widespread evictions of slum (favela) dwellers to improve the visual appearances for the World Cup and Olympics and to allow developers to benefit from the rising real estate value of propitiously situated favelas.[32]

The provision of health services, public transportation, and education for most Brazilians is woeful. So, in hindsight it was not surprising when the announcement of a nine-cent increase in bus and metro fares in the summer of 2013 pushed hundreds of thousands of Brazilians over the edge.

During FIFA's 2013 Confederations Cup warmup for the World Cup, over a million Brazilians spontaneously poured into the streets, carrying placards declaring "Death to the World Cup" and "We Want a FIFA Level Education System." (At the time, Brazil's entire national education budget was $37 billion.) Many of the 2013 protests turned violent. A CNN reporter interviewed a teacher taking part in a demonstration in Belo Horizonte, who asserted that the World Cup was lining the pockets of the rich and corrupt while the poor continued to suffer. The teacher added, "Tonight this is about all of Brazil, we are moving against corruption. We have been suffering too long. And this year we rise. We have woken up."[33]

The protests continued well after the Confederations Cup and into 2014. During the last week of February 2014, a demonstration in São Paulo of more than a thousand people protesting the "waste" of $15–$20 billion[34] on hosting the World Cup turned violent as the protesters "went on a rampage, smashing bank windows and setting up roadblocks with garbage set on fire." Military police put down the protest and arrested more than 230 people.[35]

Toward the end of March 2014, less than eighty days before the start of the World Cup, the head of Rio's police pacification (of the favelas) program was shot during a wave of violence directed against the police. The popular movement seemed to confirm former FIFA secretary general Jerome Valcke's observation: "Less democracy is sometimes better for organizing a World Cup."[36]

In the final weeks before the opening match, worker strikes broke out across the country, affecting police, teachers, and transit workers in São Paulo. Political groups threatened disruptive demonstrations, and the government sat down to reach a compromise with all of these groups.[37] According to an article in the *New York Times,* in the six months leading up to the first match on June 12, 2014, in São Paulo, ten banks were vandalized (the front glass was shattered) and two car dealerships were damaged. In the same period, 505 people were arrested in São Paulo and 89 were injured (according to GAPP, a group of first-aid volunteers).[38] A poll conducted by the Pew Research Center in June 2014 found that only 34 percent of Brazilians felt the World Cup would have a positive impact on the country, and 72 percent were dissatisfied with the nation's direction.[39]

After the Confederations Cup, it was increasingly clear that the Brazilian government needed to take drastic security measures. The government announced the formation of a 10,000-member federal-level shock security force in addition to the normal public and private security personnel, complete with surveillance drones, to deal with expected protests during the World Cup.[40] The final security bill for the World Cup surpassed $1 billion.[41] (The original contract for London's security force in 2012 was 10,000 as well. In the end, the London games required more than 20,000 military and security personnel.)[42] Protests during the first several Cup matches were decisively squashed by security personnel using tear gas, clubs, and reportedly bullets. At a joint meeting between the Brazilian security chief and FIFA after one week of the competition, it was decided to further beef up security procedures and personnel around the stadiums.

Fueling the resistance movement were concerns regarding FIFA's demands for special tax treatment. Romário de Souza Faria, the former Brazilian soccer star turned politician, claimed that FIFA would make a profit of $1.8 billion from the 2014 World Cup, which would normally yield $450 million in tax revenues. While Romário's assertion may lack accuracy (Brazil's Internal Revenue Service estimated the loss at $248.7 million),[43] it was enough to elicit anger. (It is true that FIFA does generate surpluses from the World Cup cycle approaching a billion dollars. However, since FIFA is a nonprofit organization, whether these surpluses are taxed is a function of the peculiarities of the tax code in each host country. FIFA did qualify as a tax-exempt nonprofit organization during the 1994 World Cup in the United States. There are other, smaller exemptions that FIFA insists on, such as the importation of materials and television equipment and some sales taxes. FIFA's tax privileges are similar to those received by other sports mega-event sponsors and organizations.)

Nor has Brazil's international embarrassment—the ever-present uncompleted projects, the deaths of at least nine construction workers, the crane collapse at the stadium construction site in São Paulo, the decertification of Rio's drug laboratory by the World Anti-Doping Association (necessitating the shipment of samples to Lausanne, Switzerland), and FIFA executives' statements that the preparations in Brazil were the worst they had ever seen—helped dampen the people's protests. Meanwhile, activists in Cuiabá and Manaus were motivated by the fact that their new stadiums cost 50 percent more than their cities' educational budgets.[44]

Further exacerbating local tensions was the shabby treatment of migrant construction workers at World Cup sites. A 2013 report released by the Brazilian Labor Attorney General's office stated that 111 workers on the renovation of São Paulo's airport were living in poor conditions next to the building site. They were lured from the northeast sector of Brazil on promises of monthly wages of $625. Many were not employed and had to stay in one of eleven makeshift camps in "slave-like conditions" next to the airport. Some had to pay more than $220 to secure the job.[45]

Protest passions were also stoked by the forced relocation of entire favelas. Estimates are that 250,000 people living near construction sites were displaced.[46] According to Clean Games, a transparency organization created to monitor the World Cup and Olympics, no government body communicated with the displaced.[47] The razing of favelas is for many reminiscent of a policy of Brazil's military dictatorships in the 1960s and 1970s. Most of the recent evictions took place without consultation with the residents, many of whom had lived in their favela communities for decades and had worked and schooled their children there. If they could prove title to their homes, they received compensation ranging from $1,500 to $5,000.[48] Many were relocated 10 or more kilometers away. Christopher Gaffney, a professor at Rio's Fluminense Federal University, commented, "These events were supposed to celebrate Brazil's accomplishments, but the opposite is happening. We're seeing an insidious pattern of trampling on the rights of the poor and cost overruns that are a nightmare."[49]

Many favelas not slated for destruction instead experienced siege-like conditions. The *Financial Times* reported that several favelas "now resemble no-man's land as military police clutch assault rifles to their bullet-proofed chests" and quoted Carlos Melo, a leading Brazilian political scientist, as saying that the World Cup had put Brazil in the spotlight and was encouraging gangs and other favela residents "to exploit a moment of visibility and the vulnerability of the government."[50]

While there was little question that Brazil needed massive infrastructure investment,[51] the popular sentiment questioned whether the best interests of the country's development were really being served by spending some $5 billion on soccer stadiums, the specialized nature of much of the infrastructure spending, and the ubiquitous waste and corruption.

Part of Brazil's World Cup dilemma seemed to emanate from a peculiarity in FIFA politics. FIFA president Sepp Blatter had promised that South Africa would get to host the World Cup. When South Africa narrowly lost out to host the 2006 World Cup, Blatter persuaded FIFA to change its selection system by introducing a continental rotation. The African continent would go first, in 2010, thereby assuring South Africa as the host. The 2014 Cup would return to its continent of origin, South America. When 2007 rolled around and it was time to pick the South American host for 2014, there was only one bidder, Brazil.

The existence of only one bidder set up an interesting dynamic. Without competition from other countries, Brazil was not compelled to get its organizational act together. So, for instance, Brazil's initial bid did not designate which cities in the country would host the matches. Nor did Brazil take advantage of the absence of competition to lowball its bid; rather, the goal was to impress the world with Brazil's level of development and readiness to become a major economic player in world trade and tourism. So Brazil boldly declared that it would build or refurbish not the requisite eight but twelve stadiums, along with undertaking a variety of very ambitious infrastructural projects.

Aggravating Brazil's problem of finding domestic political compromise in the selection of the twelve locations, the final determination was not made until 2009—two years after the designation of Brazil as the host of the 2014 Cup.[52] This delay increased the construction costs and left less money available for important transportation and energy projects. Based on its unsatisfactory experience in Brazil, FIFA ended its experiment with continental rotation.

A key part of the initial Brazilian World Cup plan was former Brazilian president Lula's promise that the stadiums would be financed with private funds. But with the state on the hook for delivering the games to FIFA and the IOC, there was no incentive for the private sector to commit financing. Nearly all the stadium financing was paid for with public funds—another sore point for Brazil's World Cup detractors.[53]

Romário denounced the preparations: "The stadiums are constantly late, the rise in costs is way over the top, and public money is being used to build them before they are handed over to private firms who reap the benefits." A 2014 poll in Curitiba found that 58 percent of respondents were against Brazil hosting the World Cup and 87 percent were against using public money to fund the completion of the new stadium (over 70 percent of the funding for which came from the public treasury).[54]

There was more than a little irony, then, when Brazilian sports minister Orlando Silva declared there would be another special legacy of the World Cup: "The World Cup will leave us among other things more attractive stadiums. Clubs will be able to demand higher ticket prices, and our football will be able to finance itself better."[55]

2016 Olympic Games

Even though the Olympic Games last only seventeen days, compared to thirty-four days for the World Cup, the Olympic Games are immensely more complicated to pull off than the World Cup. The World Cup involves 736 athletes; the Summer Olympics involve 10,500. The World Cup has one championship; the Olympics have dozens. Host-generated broadcasting for the World Cup amounts to a few hundred hours; the Olympics in Rio are expected to generate almost 5,000 hours. The crowds and the traffic are concentrated in one city for the Olympics, rather than being dispersed among twelve.

Whatever deficiencies cropped up in hosting the 2014 World Cup, they appear to be magnified severalfold for the 2016 Summer Games. At Olympic Park, 2,500 construction workers went on strike during April 2014 for several weeks, just as various IOC officials were visiting Rio and declaring that the city was the most behind schedule they had ever seen. The IOC took the extraordinary step of sending a supervisory team to set up shop in Brazil and oversee the progress on the various construction projects over the final two years of preparation. Among other problems, facing environmental challenges, the planned Olympic golf course in Barra da Tijuca still hadn't planted grass as of June 2014, and at least two years is needed for course preparation to be done properly.[56]

At Guanabara Bay, the prospective site for sailing and water sports, pollution levels remain far above even the lax Brazilian standards, and, according to Rio's state environment secretary, Carlos Francisco Portinho, there is no longer any possibility that Rio can meet the pollution reduction metrics promised to the IOC. A May 2014 letter that Portinho sent to Brazilian sports minister Aldo Rebelo stated that it will take at least another decade to significantly reduce pollution levels in the bay, even if the requested $70 million for abatement facilities were immediately allocated. Meanwhile, several Olympic sports federations expressed fears that Rio's polluted waters could prove harmful to athletes' health, potentially exposing them to fecal matter that can cause hepatitis A, cholera, and dysentery.[57] Frustrated by the slow progress being made on Rio's new basketball arena, the head of the International Basketball Federation began looking into the possibility of holding the hoops tournament at an arena in São Paulo, 275 miles away.

In an interview with Brazil's *Colectiva* magazine, leading Brazilian journalist, television personality, and soccer commentator Juca Kfouri opined:

I think that [hosting the Olympic Games] does not make any sense for a country that does not even have a sports policy, as it has been admitted by the Minister of Sports. It is putting the cart before the horse. Sport should be handled as a factor of public health, disease prevention, following the dictates of the World Health Organization, which reveals that every dollar that you invest in democratization and mass sport, you save three in public health. . . . What worries me is that the Olympics are in the hands of those who committed the debacle that was the Pan American Games in Rio de Janeiro. I have no reason to believe it will be different. And we should remember that we spent almost 10 times more public money than it was anticipated. From 400 million to nearly 4 billion, while leaving strictly no legacy for the city of Rio de Janeiro. The Bay of Guanabara was not depolluted, as had been promised. The Rodrigo de Freitas lagoon was not depolluted. The metro linking the Pan American Village to the Galeao Airport was not built. . . . The Maria Lenk Aquatic Park is not good. The Velodrome is not good. Engenhão, which in theory is the most modern stadium of Brazil, is not planned to be used in the World Cup. At Maracanã . . . a stadium was imploded and another is being built instead. I fear the lack of transparency of our spending and by the legacy promised to the city of Rio de Janeiro. We're seeing the displacement of people from their homes against the law, the *manu militari,* to take them much further from [where] they reside, from their jobs, their children's schools and everything else.[58]

Similar to Brazil's experience with the World Cup, the implementation of Rio's grand plans is proceeding at a slow pace. The IOC has expressed its concern over and over. After a three-day site visit in March 2014, the IOC delegation was as diplomatic as it could be in its assessment: "The delivery timelines of some of the venues for test events and the games have faced delays, and now leave no margin for any further slippages." The next month, John Coates, IOC vice president, stated, "We've become very concerned, to be quite frank. They really are not ready in many, many ways."[59]

The plans include extensive construction in four separate clusters of Rio (following one defining feature of Barcelona's Olympic plan),[60] encompassing sports facilities, bus rapid transit (BRT) lanes, metro connections, cleaning up of the port, a new golf course, an Olympic Village in Barra da Tijuca, new sewer systems, new parks, airport upgrades, and a museum, among other things. The Olympic village is scheduled to include 3,600 apartments, and all are slated to become luxury housing. Much of the new transportation network is intended to connect the airport to the hotel districts, the hotel districts to the Olympic sites (such as the BRT from Ipanema Beach to Barra da Tijuca), or the Olympic sites to each other. They appear either tangential or irrelevant to public needs or the city's economic development.

Equally significant, the TransOlímpica freeway that is slated to connect the four Olympic clusters to each other poses both human and environmental challenges. The $634 million freeway is expected to be 23 kilometers long, and its construction will require the relocation of at least 875 families. It will also have a major ecological impact because it will destroy 200,000 square meters of Atlantic shrub, an endangered form of vegetation in one of the largest conservation areas and the biggest urban park in Brazil. The affected residents will be moved some 2 kilometers away, and many are complaining that their new apartments are far inferior to their current homes. One sixty-two-year-old woman told a Rio newspaper, "I have a house with three bedrooms, three baths, a kitchen, a living room and space for my business. The apartments they are offering are very small. . . . I respect that they want us to leave, but I do not want to."[61]

Meanwhile, costs are exploding on the Rio Olympics. While the original bid for the 2016 games was estimated at $14.4 billion, as of July 2015, the tab had already run to $20 billion, with a year's left of overruns still to happen.[62] We return to discuss the 2016 Olympics and Brazil's trouble economic and political situation in the postscript.

Assessment

It is too early to do a statistical assessment of the economic impact of hosting the World Cup and the Olympics on Brazil and Rio. It is not too early, however, to consider some of the factors that make economic success seem improbable.

Initially, it was projected that Brazil would have 600,000 foreign visitors during the World Cup. The Brazilian government has claimed that the actual number was 1 million. The large number owes to the participation of teams from four neighboring South American countries plus Mexico in the final sixteen.[63] The largest groups of foreign tourists came from Argentina, Chile, and Colombia. According to anecdotal reports, they were not big spenders. As has been noted, large numbers of them slept on the beach or in trailers and used public restrooms.

Meanwhile, President Dilma Rousseff declared that the national workday for public employees would end at 12:30 p.m. every day on which a World Cup match was played. This meant shorter work days, so that the Brazilian people would all have the opportunity to watch and enjoy the World Cup. Though this measure might have lowered the intensity of popular protest, it might also have reduced worker productivity directly through shorter work hours and, perhaps, indirectly through the effect of extra celebration. One study estimated a drop in productivity of 30 percent.[64]

Brazil's political system is nothing short of a labyrinth. Years of trying to undo the authoritarian style of the country's long-standing dictatorship has produced a complexly encumbered decisionmaking process. Even once spending projects are approved, moving the funds from the national treasury to the institution that is supposed to spend them requires multiple departments and people to sign off. Not only can these steps take months, but inevitably many individuals may require payoffs to expedite the process. Sometimes state agencies even hire private consulting firms to make it all happen. At other times parallel government bodies or temporary authorities with no accountability are created.

It is hard enough for a relatively well-functioning democracy to pull off the gargantuan commitments for a sport mega-event. For a crippled system, it is next to impossible. Long delays are unavoidable, which leads to higher costs, which lead to less urgent projects being postponed or canceled.

Of course, autocratic political systems do not get a pass on mega-event construction delays and incompletions. Putin proved that in spades in Sochi. The sheer magnitude of the financial and physical commitments needed to host either the World Cup or the Olympic Games should serve as a code red warning to all developing countries. Olympic PR spin to the contrary, legacies can be negative, especially when they entail billions of dollars of debt.

Writing for the Atlantic Council, where he is a nonresident senior Brazil fellow, Ricardo Sennes casts a critical but ultimately hopeful light on the impact of mega-events. On the one hand, Sennes states that the coming-out party vision has backfired: "The image of Brazil as a global leader has given way to the image of a country experiencing an active democratic debate about its future." On the other hand, Sennes sees a possible, though unintended, silver lining:

Governments will have to address the new social demands on the quality of life, reflected in the quality of public services and a path of inclusion for the new middle class, not only as consumers, but as citizens as well. This new process implies important changes in Brazil's political democratic system considering its representative model, the pattern of public resource allocation, and social participation in public policy decision-making processes.

Change may be slow, but change will come. If the World Cup has had some role in clarifying and synthesizing these desired changes, that shall be the best legacy to expect from the 2014 championship in Brazil.[65]

These are hopeful words, though perhaps unrealistic. The political dynamic could instead turn toward more repression. If Sennes is right, then it is a rather twisted path toward social inclusion and deepened democracy. Mega-events, in his view, succeed because they first create crisis, and out of the ashes arises a more responsive, egalitarian society.

A more pessimistic and critical view is articulated by Christopher Gaffney:

Since the announcement of the 2016 host city in October 2009, the Rio de Janeiro city government has pushed through a revised master plan that was adopted to include the multiple Olympic projects. . . . The improvised revision of the city's master plan has been accompanied by an extensive list of executive decrees that have "flexibilized" urban space in order for Olympic related projects to occur. These measures have undermined Rio's fledgling democratic institutions and reduced public participation in urban planning processes.[66]

More growth or less? More equity or less? More democracy or less? Time will tell.

London

The 2012 London Olympic Games distinguished themselves in several ways. Most significant, the legacy planning was more detailed and more ambitious than in any previous Olympics. The central legacy goal was to rejuvenate five depressed boroughs in East London—Newham, Hackney, Tower Hamlets, Waltham Forest, and Greenwich. Although they each have their distinct traits, as a group they are characterized by rising population numbers, a relatively young and minority demographic, and comparatively high levels of social deprivation (measured by levels of employment, income, health, skills, education, housing, and crime, and certain attributes of the living environment).

In the nineteenth century and much of the twentieth, East London was a center for manufacturing and the city's docklands. Accordingly, it was a working-class neighborhood and poor relative to western districts in London. During the 1970s and 1980s, however, in the wake of labor troubles and technological change, the docks closed, and East London suffered extensive job loss in traditional manufacturing and processing industries. By the late 1980s a regeneration process had begun, first with the new docklands project, which was followed in 1990 by the launching of the more dispersed Thames Gateway scheme,[67] and then by a movement of cultural and artistic businesses as well as nonprofit organizations into the area, seeking lower rents and prices. Small pockets of relative affluence began to appear in an area that was still economically depressed and crime-ridden. One outstanding problem was the paucity of public transportation connecting East London to the city center.

A major focus of London's Olympic Plan was to redevelop these five boroughs. It is important to emphasize, however, that a regenerative dynamic in favor of East London development had already begun in the 1990s. The London Docklands Development Corporation was established in 1985. The original scheme was to develop 8.8 million square feet of offices, hotels, shops, and restaurants and 8,000 parking spaces. The docklands light railway was the only form of public transportation connecting part of the area to the central city.

By the late 1990s, Canary Wharf, part of the docklands project, had begun to attract financial firms, and subsequently expanded to include other businesses and upscale housing. One study on the docklands project commented that "criticism has focused upon the removal of local democratic controls and the replacement of the existing population by a new, more prosperous group of young professionals. . . . Tower Hamlets, the borough in which Canary Wharf is located, experienced a significant change in population. . . . In 1981 the authority had 85 percent council (public) housing and 15 percent private housing and by 2008 nearly 60 percent was private housing."[68]

The new Stratford rapid train station and nearby housing are part of a project of the London and Continental Railways that was initiated in 1997.[69] Hence, by 2003, when the government decided to pursue its Olympic bid, an extensive transportation plan and related development plan were already in place.

Short-Run Effects

In May 2011, the London Organizing Committee for the Olympic Games (LOCOG) put out a request for proposals (RFP) seeking to identify a group to produce an economic impact study. The RFP stipulated that LOCOG was anticipating significant public pushback with respect to the games because of the massive allocation of taxpayer monies to finance the necessary infrastructure and operations and that the LOCOG was therefore seeking a study that would be sufficiently robust to silence the critics. In the end, the consulting firm Grant Thornton got the contract and obliged with a study (for which it was paid a reported $2 million) that estimated a substantial economic boost. Stefan Szymanski, one of the economists working on the study but who was not involved in the final write-up, expressed alarm to Ari Shapiro of National Public Radio, calling the study "a political document . . . tantamount to a whitewash," and went on to say, "I'm very uncomfortable about the triumphalist tone of this which does not reflect what the data is saying."[70]

Let's take a look at the available evidence. Anne Power, professor and head of the London School of Economics program on Housing and Communities, has studied the impact of the Olympic construction on East London. The borough of Newham was the actual site and main host of the games. Because of the paucity of skilled local labor, only a small minority of the thousands of construction jobs created in preparation for the games went to Newham residents. Together with a growing population, this meant that the unemployment rate in Newham increased 42 percent between 2005 and 2012. Crime in the borough was 50 percent above the London average. The supply of subsidized housing declined during 2005–12, as the Olympic regeneration scheme removed thousands of homes, and the 1,300 homes in the Olympic Village that were slated to be affordable were still well beyond the financial reach of most Newham households.[71]

Dan Brown and Stefan Szymanski studied employment change in the five host boroughs in the run-up to the games and compared them with changes in the rest of London. They found that changes were more positive where Olympic construction was either nonexistent or minor and concluded that "the direct employment effects of the Olympics are small."[72]

What about the direct financial effect of hosting? The bottom line was certainly not helped by the special treatment in the IOC demands for the "Olympic family." The IOC required that LOCOG set aside 250 miles of VIP lanes for exclusive use by members of the Olympic family, to secure nearly 2,000 rooms for IOC bigwigs and associates in the finest five-star hotels, and to control commercial space in support of Olympic sponsors. In particular, the IOC's *Technical Manual on Brand Protection* stipulates that "candidate cities are required to obtain control of all billboard advertising, city transport advertising, airport advertising, etc., for the duration of the games and the month preceding the games to support the marketing program."[73]

As is the case for other host cities since 2010, corporate partners

and foreign nationals participating in the Olympics (including athletes, media workers, and referees) were exempt from earnings taxation in England during the games. Since the status of some nonprofit
organizations, such as LOCOG and the IOC, is likely to be tax-
exempt even without the special tax treatment required by the IOC,
it is not a simple matter to estimate what the cost of these privileges is
to the London and English treasuries. One study put the costs of the
tax exemptions at more than $130 million.[74]

As we have seen, a principal claim for sports mega-events is that
they boost tourism both during the games and in the long run. The
evidence for London tourism during 2012 is not encouraging. The
number of London tourists during the summer of 2012 was 8 percent below the level in 2011. Thanks to higher hotel prices and the
purchase of tickets to Olympic events, reported total tourist spending
increased slightly. However, much of the increase had to be shared
with the IOC and with the home offices of the hotel chains, many
of which were outside London. Businesses in central London, from
taxis, to restaurants, to museums and theaters, reported a reduction
in demand of 20 to 40 percent. Not only were traditional tourists
scared away by Olympic congestion and higher prices but Londoners
by the hundreds fled or avoided the city.[75]

Despite an initial security snafu, the staging of the games went
well.[76] LOCOG *operating* costs totaled $4.1 billion (infrastructure
and facility costs are not included in this number), including $185
million to put on the opening and closing ceremonies.[77] LOCOG
itself broke even, but only after a significant infusion of $1.67 billion
in public funds.[78]

At least up through the games, it does not appear there was a
net gain in revenue to the national treasury or the London economy.
On the other side of the ledger, the costs were high. As with other
mega-events, there is always a good deal of subjectivity about what
investments should be included in the budget of the games. Some infrastructural investments are peripheral to the games, others would
have been undertaken without the games, and so on.

This is what we do know. When London won the bid in 2005, the initial total cost estimate was approximately $5 billion.[79] The National Audit Report asserted that total costs up through the end of the games included £8.92 billion of public monies and £2.41 billion of LOCOG funds, totaling £11.33 billion or roughly $18 billion.[80] Some estimates go considerably higher, up to £24 billion (approximately $40 billion).[81] Indeed, the December 2012 report of the National Audit Office refers to "the lack of realism in the original estimates."[82] Even if one uses the lowest of the final cost figures, the cost overrun was at least three times the initial estimate.

Thus, as in practically all other cases, the London games cannot be justified as a sound economic investment in the short run. If the investment can be justified economically, it must be on the basis of any long-run or legacy effect.

It should, however, be noted that the London organizers corrected the underbudgeting early on. By 2007 the budget was adjusted upward to £9.3 billion of public funds, excluding LOCOG's operating budget, but including £2.75 billion of contingency funds.[83] Significantly, the contingency funds were 41.7 percent of the base budget, and practically all of the funds were eventually used. Nonetheless, more recent bidders have used appreciably lower contingency budgets. The initial Los Angeles bid budget for the 2024 games, for instance, includes only 10 percent for contingency.

Legacy Effects

London's legacy plan was ambitious, but many question whether it was realistic. In 2005, Jack Straw, England's secretary of state, commented in Parliament on the IOC's selection of London to host the 2012 Games:

> London's bid was built on a special Olympic vision. That vision of an Olympic Games that would not only be a celebration of sport but a force for regeneration. The Games will transform one of the poorest and most deprived areas of London. They

will create thousands of jobs and homes. They will offer new opportunities for business in the immediate area and throughout London . . . it reaches out to young people in two important respects: it will encourage many more to get fit and to be involved in sport and, whatever their physical prowess, to offer their services as volunteers for the Olympic cause.[84]

The various legacy goals included:

—Making the UK a world-leading sporting nation
—Transforming the heart of East London
—Inspiring a new generation of young people to take part in volunteering and cultural and physical activity
—Making the Olympic Park a blueprint for sustainable living[85]
—Demonstrating that the UK is a creative, inclusive, and welcoming place to live, visit, and do business
—Increasing foreign investment

The National Audit Report of December 2012 estimated that the costs of implementing the legacy programs would be approximately $1.4 billion.[86] The $1.4 billion would be on top of the $18 billion-plus that had already been spent through the end of the games.

One of the key legacy projects was the conversion of the Olympic Stadium into the home field for the West Ham United soccer team. The stadium renovation was more complicated and expensive than it might have been. One reason for this was that the design of the Olympic Stadium did not anticipate the conversion needs of a soccer team, namely, the need to remove the running track so that the pitch (field) could be close to the stands. Had this been anticipated, then the last row of seats would have been higher and field seating could have been added on top of the track. The second reason is that the Olympic Stadium was far too big for the West Ham soccer team. The upper deck, with its 55,000 seats, had to be removed. In the end, the renovation carried an initial projected cost of $323 million, to be paid by taxpayers.[87] In early September 2014, according to a report by Sky News, the projected renovation cost rose by another $25 million, with further increases possible.[88] Final cost estimates for the stadium and its renovation were cited at $1.1 billion in August 2015. Of this, the West Ham club paid $23.1 million, or approximately 2 percent of the total cost. West Ham also benefits because the London Legacy Development Corporation (a taxpayer-funded entity) will contribute an estimated $3.8 million to the stadium's operating expenses (including "the cost of stadium utilities, security, maintaining the pitch, and even the goalposts and corner flags"). Partially offsetting these operating subsidies, West Ham will pay yearly rent of $3.1 million, leaving a net subvention from the government to the club of $700,000 yearly.[89]

Hackney is one of the five boroughs in East London where the games took place. It lies just west of the Olympic Park and about five miles east of the city center. In February 2014, *Sports Illustrated* ran a feature story about a community center in Hackney Wick, which lies a couple of blocks from the $735 million Olympic Stadium.[90] The area used to be home to a peanut factory, which closed in the 1970s. Other manufacturing firms closed as well, leaving behind vacant industrial buildings. Over time, many of these were converted into lofts for artists and a new, still low-income, community of artists and artisans developed.

When the Olympic planners arrived in the neighborhood after 2005, they promised a strong economic rebound. The community center invested in opening a café to cater to the expected Olympic visitors and growing workforce. But apart from higher rents, as of February 2014, little had changed in the local economy. The main metro stop, Stratford, was on the east side of the park, in the borough of Newham. There was next to no additional foot traffic in Hackney. Moreover, many of the planned investments were never made because public money ran out and private money was uninterested.

Lance Forman, owner of the H. Forman & Son salmon-smoking plant, commented, "People were not allowed to look out and see what

East London had to offer. The Olympic Park could frankly have been in a big bubble on the moon. It was an opportunity missed. They said it would create great business opportunities. My experience is they failed spectacularly."[91]

Part of the transformation of East London entailed a plan to build 12,000 new homes and create 10,000 jobs. [92] The new-homes plan was scaled back to 8,000 in mid-2013. In spring of 2014, the Olympic Village conversion into housing had not been completed.[93]

The Olympic Village was supposed to cost £1 billion (approximately $1.7 billion) and to be financed privately by the Australian developer Lend Lease. (The head of London's Olympic Delivery Authority had been the CEO of Lend Lease until February 2011.) When the 2008 financial crisis hit, Lend Lease dropped out, and the Olympic Village was paid for out of public funds. In August 2011 the Village was sold to the Qatari ruling family's real estate company for £275 million (approximately $460 million), for a taxpayer loss in excess of $1 billion.[94]

More generally, there has been a decreasing commitment to affordable housing (which carries a 30 percent discount to market rents). It is worth quoting Gavin Poynter, economics professor at the University of East London and a student of the London games, at length on the process:

As part of the Mayor of London's *First Steps* programme, for example, tenants in social housing in London boroughs could apply to move into the Olympic Village. Those seeking to rent could secure a discount of up to 30 percent on the market rent for their property though they had to be in employment and meet other criteria. . . . But, as the Park's conversion gathered pace, such aspirations were much diluted. The first major mixed community development, Chobham Manor, provided about 25 percent affordable housing, 10 percent [age points] below the widely published target, and subsequent developments, to be completed by the early 2020s, are unlikely to achieve even this level. As the social or public gain dimension of the Games' urban legacy has waned, so the commercial has flourished.[95]

The Olympic, now East, Village has become part of a high rise, high density and high price area of development around the transport hub that is Stratford. The vision for the creation of affordable housing has receded. As developers have privileged scheme viability, the proportion of the value captured for investment in social housing and public spaces has diminished particularly on the south side of the former Olympic Park and within the developments on its borders. In the absence of significant levels of public investment post-2012 (far more than that earmarked in the LDDC's business plan), the social transformation focused on the needs of the local community has amounted to a wish list. Its achievement was undermined by a combination of insufficient public resources to deliver an ambitious city building programme, the impact of government social policies that capped housing benefit support for the lower waged and unemployed—putting the purchase or rent of new housing units out of the reach of many local people—and the operations of a London property market in which the activities of international investors pushed up rent and property prices in iconic locations such as the Olympic Park and its borders.[96]

Another problem, common to mega-event hosting, is that funds to finance an Olympic bid or hosting often come at the expense of allocations to nonprofit companies. According to the British charity Directory of Social Change (DSC), the government diverted $665 million from monies designated for nonprofits via the lottery in order to finance the 2012 games. The government says it will replenish the funds by 2030, but the DSC asserts the money is needed now.[97]

What about the other legacy goals?

One goal was to advance the greening of London. The reduction of the carbon footprint from the games' facilities beyond the regulatory standards was accomplished, but the set targets were not met.

For instance, one pledge was to supply 20 percent of the power for Olympic Park from renewable energy sources; according to the *New York Times,* the actual amount during the games was closer to 9 percent.[98]

Another goal was to transform the United Kingdom into a leading sports state and to inspire its citizens to engage in more physical activity. Here the early evidence is not as positive. Sports participation figures published in June 2013 by Sport England showed that nearly a year on from the 2012 Games, twenty out of twenty-nine sports recorded a fall in the number of adults taking part between April 2012 and April 2013. Overall, the numbers of people exercising for thirty minutes once a week fell by 100,000 to 15.3 million over the same period, or by an even greater margin of 200,000 since October. The number of those exercising three times a week also fell.[99] In its June 2014 report, the nationwide participation numbers for April 2013 to April 2014 were up slightly, but they were down again for London, where, one presumes, any positive Olympic effect would be more visible.[100] The negative trend continued during the six months between October 2014 and March 2015 when around 222,000 stopped undertaking regular physical activity in England.[101] It appears that London and England are not alone in not reaching this goal. According to a 2007 study performed for the Culture, Media and Sport Committee of the British Parliament's House of Commons, "No host country has yet been able to demonstrate a direct benefit from the Olympic Games in the form of a lasting increase in participation."[102]

The goal to regenerate development in East London, to create thousands of new jobs, and to reduce poverty also has encountered difficulties. It is always possible to change the character of some micro-neighborhoods by displacing lower-income with higher-income groups. Such gentrification has necessarily occurred to a degree with the billions of dollars of new investments in pockets of East London. Such a process, however, is simply relocating, rather than producing, wealth.

In assessing the changes brought to East London from the games,

Gavin Poynter comments that East London got a stadium it didn't need, more four- and five-star hotels it didn't need, and additional high-rise, high-priced developments it didn't need. Poynter adds that there was not much in it for lower-income people.

The London 2012 organizers also claimed that the games brought a significant uptick in foreign investment. In particular, they boasted that at a meeting a few weeks prior to the games sixteen foreign companies made commitments for new investments in the United Kingdom. Were this true, it would suggest that the level of foreign investment in the U.K. would have risen in 2013. In fact, it fell by £900 million. More significantly, during the three pre-financial crisis years (2005–07), there was a yearly average of £91.6 billion of foreign direct investment (FDI) in the United Kingdom. But during 2012–13, the annual average was £44.15 billion, or less than half the previous level.

It is undoubtedly too early to make any definitive judgments, but a couple of take-aways seem appropriate. First, London gave careful thought to the legacy of the 2012 Games and made a bold attempt to redevelop a low-income, socially underserved, crime-ridden area of the city. London planners also provided for administrative continuity to allow ongoing attention to the legacy process after the games ended. These are certainly commendable aspects of the London games. The problem, however, appears to reside in the weakness in the plan's conception and the inadequate financial commitment to carry forward the ideals set out.

Second, from the time a plan is made to bid for the games to the time of the games themselves, eleven or more years pass. When there is an expectation of enticing private money to help finance construction, it is important to anticipate that financial markets may hit snags along the way. It is also important to understand that the dynamics of urban development can shift over the course of the decade-plus of gestation. In the case of East London, the low rents and low prices, together with some earlier government initiatives, were already beginning to transform the socioeconomic environment of the area. A rational plan for development would have understood and incorporated these changes.

A plethora of issues notwithstanding, London 2012 did a marvelous job planning and implementing its public relations. Sebastian Coe and his collaborators have spoken eloquently and repeatedly about the purported success of the London games, and the media have largely portrayed the games in a positive light. Impact reports from Grant Thornton, no matter how compromised they are in fact, help to further promote the triumphalist tone. One can only hope that the low-income residents of East London will one day come to experience the gains that the official line trumpets.

7 | Bread or Circuses?

The perennial claims that hosting the Olympics or the World Cup is an engine of economic development find little corroboration in independent studies. In the short run, the increasingly massive costs of hosting cannot come close to being matched by the modest revenues that are brought in by the games. The payoff, if there is one, must be realized in the long run. But even the legacy return is at best dubious. Much of the alleged legacy comes in the form of qualitative gains, and the rest comes over very long periods of time, difficult to trace back to the several-week period of the games or the prior construction. But more often than not, the main legacy consists of white elephants that cost billions to build and millions annually to maintain, along with mountains of debt that must be paid back over ten to thirty years.

The Difficult Calculus of Economic Gain

Even where specific areas of benefits can be identified, they must be evaluated against not only the size of the financial investment in hosting but also the opportunity costs of land used and of the human talent committed to planning and implementing the games. Cities must ask themselves what the best long-term use of scarce land and other resources is. Areas that today are blighted or underutilized may face bleak prospects for the coming years, but filling these areas with stadiums for the next three decades or more may preclude a more productive use that may not become apparent for another five or ten years.

One of the more important rebuttals to the calculus that shows more expense than revenue in hosting is that much of the expense is connected to infrastructure that will support the city's or country's long-term development needs. This certainly may be true in theory, and may even be so in practice, but it requires very careful and clever planning, which is more noticeable for its absence.

That careful planning was certainly present in Barcelona for the 1992 Summer Games. But in Barcelona the city planners had begun reconceptualizing their city soon after the Franco regime ended in 1975. The Catalan region had been largely neglected under Franco, and Barcelona itself had suffered under decades of unregulated industrial development. As a result, people in this seaport city were cut off from the Mediterranean by blocks of manufacturing, warehousing, and railways. Together with poor traffic circulation and underdeveloped infrastructure, this situation made a city that could be a shining jewel of tourism, with its magnificent architecture, cultural history, climate, and location, mostly a tourist afterthought.

The new government began to hatch a master plan for Barcelona to change the entire picture in the late 1970s and elaborated the plan in the early 1980s. The plan preexisted the thought of hosting the Olympics, but hosting was seen as a vehicle to put the plan into action. Barcelona used the Olympics; the Olympics didn't use Barcelona.

If other cities were able to emulate Barcelona—and many have tried but failed—then the problems that have been discussed in this book may be attenuated, or even in some cases avoided. The difficulty is that the conditions that contributed to Barcelona's success are not present elsewhere, and the political systems in other countries have shown themselves increasingly unwilling or unable to engage in effective long-term planning.

Los Angeles in 1984 is another case that lends some hope. But Los Angeles mostly worked for a different reason. Hosting the Olympic Games produced more negative than positive imagery during the period from Mexico City in 1968 through Montreal in 1976. When it came time to select a host for the Summer Games in 1984, there were no suitors. The IOC had no leverage, and Los Angeles and Peter Ueberroth (the head of the local organizing committee) took full advantage. Los Angeles passed an ordinance stipulating that it would not spend public money on the games and got the USOC/IOC to guarantee the city against any operating losses. With major venues still in place from the 1932 games, the IOC further agreed to a minimal construction budget for minor venues only, and Ueberroth arranged for corporate financing of these. Ueberroth also profitably redesigned Olympic sponsorships. Moreover, in the 1980s it was acceptable to use university dormitories for housing the athletes and trainers. Los Angeles used the dorms at the University of Southern California and the University of California at Los Angeles and, consequently, avoided the multibillion-dollar expense of building an Olympic Village. The end result was a surplus of $215 million and a new, positive image for hosting the games. Even so, according to an econometric study by Rob Baade and Victor Matheson, the Los Angeles games did not bring any long-term employment gains to the city.[1]

Bidding to host the Olympics since 1984, until recently, has been more competitive. Costs have skyrocketed and planning has been incomplete. Because the direct fiscal and economic impact has been neutral or negative, it is important to consider the opportunity costs of hosting.

One of the most significant costs is land use. The modern Olympic Games are huge affairs. At the 1896 Games in Athens, there were 295 athletes, 43 medal events, and 7 venues; at the 1936 Games in Berlin, there were 3,963 athletes, 129 medal events, and 25 venues; at the Tokyo Games in 1964, there were 5,151 athletes, 172 medal events, and 33 venues; and, most recently, at the 2012 London Games, there were 10,500 athletes, 302 medal events, and 31 venues. The IOC's guidelines for the *minimum* surface area for the footprint of the venues alone is 1,660 acres. For a smaller city like Barcelona, this represents almost 7 percent of the city's surface area. When ceremonial green space, large-scale public space, parking, transportation, and communication facilities are included, the amount of needed acreage can quadruple. Beijing used an estimated 8,400 acres of real estate to stage the 2008 Games.[2] The magnitude of these numbers suggests a substantial opportunity cost (opportunities forgone for alternative uses) from hosting the Summer Olympic Games.

If instead of spending some $5 billion tearing down old stadiums, then building new ones or renovating existing facilities, Brazil had spent $5 billion on public transportation networks in its major cities or on an intercity train system, what might have been the impact on the Brazilian economy? If instead of building an Olympic park in East London, London had provided rental subsidies or tax credits to artisanal industry and retail businesses or additional funding for, say, technical education, what enduring effect on employment in the surrounding boroughs might that have wrought? The questions about trade-offs are practically endless.

It is frequently argued that it is not possible to secure funding for more effective development projects. Political gridlock and partisan politics stand in the way of such appropriations in democratic countries, but somehow hosting the Olympics or World Cup breaks political stalemate. The irony is that in countries where political decisionmaking is so encumbered, the same obstacles that prevent more productive development projects without hosting the Olympics or World Cup are likely to thwart efficient implementation of mega-event plans. In authoritarian countries, gridlock is unlikely to be an issue, but skewed decisionmaking is common nonetheless.

In either democratic or authoritarian countries, the tendency is for event planning to hew closely to the interests of the local business elite. Construction companies, their unions (if there are any), insurance companies, architectural firms, media companies, investment bankers (who float the bonds), lawyers, and perhaps some hotel or restaurant interests get behind the Olympic or World Cup project. All stand to gain handsomely from the massive public funding. Typically, these interests hijack the local organizing committee, hire an obliging consulting firm to conduct an ersatz economic impact study, understate the costs, overstate the revenues, and go on to procure political consent. According to one study, in the buildup to hosting the 2010 World Cup, the average profits of five big construction companies in South Africa rose from R158 million in 2004 to R1.67 billion in 2009—a 10.5-fold increase.[3]

Inevitably, there are some short-term employment gains from the extensive construction required for the Olympics or World Cup. The problem is twofold: first, the government has to pay back the money it borrowed over the ensuing decades, which reduces funding for other government projects and reduces public employment; and second, the typical pattern has been to import thousands of workers from other areas, often from out of the country, and pay them a pauper's wage. Further, when used after the games, the stadiums, ski slopes, golf courses, and road networks are more likely to serve the consumption habits of upper-income groups. Hosting sports mega-events, then, tends to reinforce the existing power structure and patterns of inequality.

The Bidding Process Erodes Possible Gains

The fact that the existing power structure imposes itself on the bidding process has another unfavorable implication. Consider the following stylized model of the bidding process. In each of the three cases, there is a monopoly seller of hosting rights (either FIFA or the IOC).

Case One

—*Perfect information and no principal-agent problem*
—*Outcome: Expected net gains are bid away*
In this case, it is assumed that the IOC or FIFA each has complete information about the bidders and each of the bidders has complete

information about its own bid and those of its competitors. It is further assumed that there is no principal-agent problem. This means that the body representing the city or country (the local organizing committee) fairly represents the interests of the entire resident population. The local organizing committee is the agent of the entire resident population (the principal). With the assumption of perfect information, each bidder will know what its potential gain from hosting is and will continue to bid until just before its gain is fully eroded. (In theory, if each bidder also knows the gains of other bidders, it will stop bidding at just above the gain to the second highest bidder, leaving a small potential gain.) Note that if the overall return to hosting approaches zero, and if there are feel-good benefits from hosting, this implies that there will be a negative financial result. That is, the host will have to pay to achieve the feel-good effects, bringing the overall net return to zero.[4] This case is the most favorable for the bidding cities or countries. It is also the least realistic of the three cases.

Case Two

—*Imperfect information and no principal-agent problem*
—*Outcome: winner's curse and net loss*

The sole difference between this case and the prior one is that the assumption of perfect information is dropped, making case two a better approximation of reality. In this case, each bidder does not know what its potential benefits and costs might turn out to be when it participates in the bidding competition. The winning bid in such a case usually goes to the most exuberant bidder, who not only outbids all the other bidders but also generally bids higher than the possible gain, an outcome known in game theory as the winner's curse. The result is a net financial loss and a net overall loss, even though the organizing committee (agent) in this case is still assumed to fairly represent the interests of the local population (the principal).

Case Three

   —Imperfect information and a principal-agent problem
   —Outcome: outlandish overbid

This case moves yet closer to reality by acknowledging a principal-agent problem. That is, the local organizing committee, the agent, is controlled by the private interests that stand to gain the most from hosting, and these interests are not coincident with those of the host country's or city's population (the principal). The condition of imperfect information again facilitates extravagant bids from each of the prospective hosts. The expected outcome is substantial financial and overall losses, which will only be exacerbated by cost overruns.

Cycles of Leverage

The foregoing discussion makes an implicit assumption, namely, that the good being auctioned—the right to host the Olympics or World Cup—is highly desired. We have seen that this has not always been the case in the past, such as with the bidding for the 1984 Summer Games. Indeed, monopolists (single sellers of a good or service) can exploit their situation only when they produce a good in demand. If I open up a fast food chain that sells hamburgers made of rubber, even though I may be the only producer of rubber hamburgers, it is improbable in the extreme that I will have any market power or leverage.

Alternatively, if I make edible hamburgers from beef, and if Burger King, McDonald's, Wendy's, and their ilk all go out of business, I will be able to raise my prices, and my chain will become very profitable. I will not, however, be able to raise my prices as high as I might want. The price will still be constrained by demand, even though I have a monopoly. The reason is that at some high price (say, $7 a burger), my customers will decide to patronize other fast food options, such as Taco Bell, Kentucky Fried Chicken, or prewrapped sandwiches at a convenience store.

Similarly, the IOC and FIFA have a lot of market power or leverage that enables them, within bounds, to extract excessive bids from prospective hosts. Yet if either body overplays its hand and if consecutive hosts have bad experiences, then the demand for hosting diminishes and the IOC and FIFA lose leverage. In the extreme case, no prospective hosts bid, as in the case of the Los Angeles Games in 1984, when the IOC lost all leverage.[5]

At least since Beijing in 2008, as the BRICS began to dominate World Cup and Olympic hosting, the youthful exuberance of the developing countries has led to outlandishly expensive games. What may have been more subtle miscalculations and losses in Atlanta, Sydney, Salt Lake City, and Athens became glaring missteps in the cases of Beijing, South Africa, Sochi, and Brazil.[6] The negative news from the recent Olympics and World Cups has meant that the demand for hosting has fallen. FIFA thickened the imbroglio with revelations of corruption in its selection of Qatar to host the 2022 World Cup, as well as Germany (2006), South Africa (2010), and Russia (2018), and of syndicate-rigged match fixing in previous Cups.[7]

From their behavior, it seems that both the IOC and FIFA see the writing on the wall. Table 2-3 listed the evidence: a diminishing number of bidders for the Summer and Winter Olympics since 2001. Over the last five bidding cycles, the number of applicant cities for the Summer Games has declined steadily from twelve (for the 2004 Games) to ten to nine to seven to five (for the 2020 Games), while the number applying for the Winter Games has gone from nine (for the 2002 Games) to two (for the 2022 Games).

Bidding for the 2022 Winter Olympics practically ground to a halt in 2014. Failing to receive popular support, early bids from Krakow, Stockholm, Munich, Davos, and Lviv were withdrawn in 2013 and 2014. The Norwegian government, citing excessive costs, then refused to backstop Oslo's bid. The IOC was left with the embarrassing choice between two host cities from authoritarian countries: Almaty, Kazakhstan, and Beijing, China: the former with no experience hosting sport mega-events, a shortage of financial resources, and a poor human rights record, the latter with an environmental/water crisis, ski slopes 120 miles north of Beijing, and an abysmal human rights history. Notably, a report commissioned by the Dutch government in 2012 predicted that in the future, it was likely that only nondemocratic countries would host the Olympics because only they would "have the centralized power and money to organize them."[8]

The IOC's selection of Oslo as a candidate city, before the Norwegian government withdrawal, is also noteworthy. One of the explicit selection criteria in the IOC's rule book is broad support from the local population. Norway and Oslo hardly meet this standard. In a March 2014 poll, 59.2 percent of Norwegians and 55.8 percent of Oslo residents opposed the bid. The tables may be turning on the IOC.[9]

The IOC is well aware of this problem. In a June 2014 study prepared by the National Olympic Committees (NOCs) of Austria, Germany, Sweden, and Switzerland and titled "Olympic Agenda 2020: The Bid Experience," the internal report had this to say:

> In Switzerland and Germany, citizens rejected potential bids in public referenda with 53%, in Sweden national politics decided not to support a bid and in Austria public opposition even received 72% in a referendum . . . in Krakow 70% opted against hosting the Games.
>
> What is the problem of established European nations to bid for the Olympics? The grounds cited sound very similar in all four countries: public and politics seemingly fear the high costs of bidding for and hosting the Games, especially in the aftermath of the increase of costs that was witnessed in Sochi as well as concerns relating to human rights and sustainability.[10]

The mayor of Paris, Anne Hidalgo, reflected an increasingly common perspective when asked whether her city would bid for the 2024 Summer Games: "I love sports. I love competitions. I know what it can bring to a society and a city. . . . But today we are all under financial and budgetary restraints that do not make it possible for me to say that I support such a candidacy. Parisians expect me to provide housing, public services, justice, economic ease."[11] (Under political pressure and with the assurance that Paris would not have to build the most costly Olympic venues, Mayor Hidalgo was eventually to change course and back the city's bid for the 2024 games.)

As the worker strikes and popular protests in South Africa and Brazil have underscored, it is not just the Parisians who have this expectation. A new protest movement in Japan emerged in 2014 in opposition to Tokyo's extravagant plans to host the 2020 Summer Games. Street demonstrations in Tokyo in July 2014 denounced the projected $2.1 billion Olympic Stadium (already reduced in scale by almost 50 percent from the original bid) as ecologically damaging and financially wasteful. The protesters called for the renovation of Tokyo's existing Olympic Stadium from the 1964 Games, rather than the construction of another facility. John Coates, IOC vice president, responded that further changes in the venue plan could occur only if the IOC approved.[12]

When Thomas Bach replaced Jacques Rogge as head of the IOC in September 2013, one of his first projects was to tour prospective host cities around the globe to drum up interest in bidding for future games. His message in each instance was similar: the IOC would look very favorably on a bid from your city. Subsequently, Bach has discussed other reforms to put the bidding process back on track from the IOC's perspective. I discuss these reforms later in the chapter and in the postscript, along with other proposals.

Sepp Blatter and FIFA have also been tinkering. FIFA's basic pattern had been to alternate host nations between Europe and the Americas. This pattern was disrupted in 2002 with the World Cup's first Asian finals and again in May 2004, when the rights to host the 2010 finals were awarded to South Africa. The new policy was to rotate the hosting rights among the six continents. It was South America's turn for 2014. But when the World Cup was awarded in October 2007, there was only one bidder from the continent, Brazil.

Without competition among potential hosts, FIFA lost its leverage, so FIFA aborted its policy of continental rotation. The new policy is that countries of the same continent as either of the last two World Cup hosts are ineligible. This way, rather than identifying a single continent that could bid to host the tournament, countries from four continental confederations would be eligible to bid for each World Cup.

What Is to Be Done?

Reform from Above

On June 10, 2014, the United States Olympic Committee (USOC) gathered for a quarterly meeting on the MIT campus in Cambridge, Massachusetts. The expectation was that the USOC would announce a handful of finalist cities it had chosen to bid to host the 2024 Summer Games. Back in February 2013, the USOC had sent out letters to fifty cities inviting them to apply to be the host. It is not uncommon for U.S. cities that compete to represent the United States in the worldwide hosting contest to spend up to $10 million on the domestic selection process.

But Larry Probst, the head of the USOC, made no announcement of finalists. Rather, reminding the press that the U.S. entries for the 2012 Summer Games (New York) and the 2016 Games (Chicago) had been rejected by the IOC, Probst said that he wanted to see how the IOC would reform its selection process before announcing a final U.S. entry. It sounded a bit like a threat: guarantee that the United States will win the games bid or we won't play.

The IOC should have a natural inclination to have a U.S. city host, which it hasn't had for the Summer Games since Atlanta in 1996, because the largest TV contract comes from the United States. The IOC currently has a contract with NBC for nearly $8 billion for U.S. broadcast rights through 2032. NBC will get higher ratings if the games are held in U.S. time zones and the domestic population can watch the competition live during prime time. Higher ratings will keep their NBC partner happy and lead to a higher rights fee next time around. Further, most leading U.S. cities have large, wealthy populations who can fill the Olympic venues, buying high-priced tickets and catering services, while U.S. companies purchase signage in and around the facility.

Probst and the USOC believe that if a U.S. city gets the right to host in 2024, it will mark the end of a twenty-eight-year hiatus, and that is longer than it should be. So Probst said that the USOC would not show its hand until the IOC Working Group on reforming the selection process, created by Thomas Bach in 2013, made its report in December 2014. Strangely, two weeks later Probst announced the four U.S. finalists—San Francisco, Los Angeles, Washington, D.C., and Boston—anyway.

When Bach entered office in September 2013, he immediately recognized that there was a declining number of bidding cities and that the situation was untenable. He told *Inside the Rings,* a newsletter that covers the business of the Olympics, that the IOC's bidding process was too onerous and that he wanted to make it simpler and more flexible:

> We are asking too much too early. We approach potential candidate cities like you would in business with a tender for a franchise. We are putting out our conditions. "You have to do this, you have to do that, here are our conditions, here are the guarantees." This leads to a situation that all the bid books are written by the same people [consulting firms] around the world. You get the same answers in all the bids and when you have the Q&A in the Session or in the briefing I could give you the answers beforehand. I would like to change the mentality. . . . I want to invite potential candidates to study how the Olympic Games would fit into their long-term city and regional and country development.[13]

These are all reasonable thoughts, and Bach went on to set up his working group to study how the process could be reformed. The previous IOC head, Jacques Rogge, also called for a reformed, more supple process in the early 2000s. Nothing substantial came of it; in fact, the process only became more involved and more expensive.

Early indications from the working group were not encouraging about more substantial change. At the IOC meeting prior to the Sochi Olympics in February 2014, two reform ideas were discussed. The first was to allow countries as well as cities to bid to host. Such a change might lower the burden on the city but raise it on the country, and would entail higher transportation costs (and carbon footprint) and security spending. As a reform, it is hardly a game-changer. The second was to reinstate the pre–Salt Lake City policy of having IOC members visit the bidding cities.[14] The idea here is that first-hand visits provide more information than videos, so the plausibility of each city's plan could be better assessed. Perhaps, but such visits would raise costs and reopen avenues for payoffs and bribes, which of course is why they were scrapped in the first place.

Any fundamental change would have to affect the monopoly power that the IOC and FIFA wield. One way this could be accomplished, at least in theory, would be to introduce competition to the Olympics and the World Cup. This has been tried before, and failed. Witness the Goodwill Games, spawned by U.S. media mogul Ted Turner back in 1986 and shown on his own network. Turner lost $26 million on the Goodwill Games in that year and another $40 million in 1990, after which the games died a slow death, taking their last breath in Brisbane, Australia, in 2001.[15] If Turner with his media empire and deep pockets couldn't compete, it is not likely others could. The Olympics and the World Cup have deep branding and appear to be natural monopolies. Worldwide fans don't seem to want two Olympics or two World Cups.

Another way to reduce the leverage of the IOC and FIFA would be to control the number of bidders. A sensible way to do this would be to reintroduce the continental rotation system that FIFA briefly tried in the early 2000s but quickly abandoned when it saw its leverage decline. Yet such a system, which would involve the six continents, would not only delimit the geographic span of the competition in each cycle, it would also save the bidding cities from continents not in play the energy and expense of bidding—an expense that can rise to $100 million per city or more. (Tokyo reportedly spent $150 million on its failed bid to host the 2016 Summer Games.)[16] The question is not whether such a reform would be desirable, engendering at least incremental improvements, but whether Bach's working group or a parallel effort in FIFA would accept such a change.

Of course, it would also help if (1) FIFA and the IOC accepted the use of older, more modest stadiums or if they paid for all venue construction, (2) they encouraged repeat hosting, and (3) they made a more serious and professional effort to identify which bids made the most sense for a city's development. While the IOC and FIFA give lip service to a concern over development, sustainability, and other desiderata, the IOC and FIFA voters are ill equipped to make judgments about a city's or country's development needs.[17]

The IOC's selection in September 2013 of Tokyo over Madrid (and Istanbul) to host the 2020 Summer Games raises questions about the constituency for real reform. Madrid's bid anticipated extensive use of existing sports facilities and only minor infrastructure work. Its total budget, shared by three levels of government over seven years, was only $1.9 billion, one of the lowest in modern Olympic history. Tokyo's bid budget was approximately $6 billion, including a very elaborate and lavish Olympic stadium and village (initially projected to cost $4 billion). If the IOC was interested in sending a message that it wanted to avoid fiscal excess and financial imprudence, it certainly did not manifest that desire in its selection of Tokyo.[18]

There are also calls for Athens to be designated the permanent home of the Summer Games. It's not an awful idea, but too many nations would object to not having the opportunity to host the games, and the internationalist image of the Olympics might suffer.

The World Cup has a simpler solution because there are so many countries around the globe with mature professional soccer leagues that have at least eight suitable stadiums. If FIFA moderated its demands for stadium capacity and luxury seating, the investment demands on the host country would be more modest and manageable.

Both FIFA and the IOC could also opt to share more of the generated revenue from the games with the host city or country. The Summer Games currently generate around $6 billion from television and media rights, ticket sales, corporate sponsorships, and memorabilia sales. The Winter Games earn between $3 and $4 billion, and the World Cup earns nearly $4.5 billion.

As of December 2013, FIFA had over $1.4 billion in its reserve investment portfolio. These reserves grew further following the 2014 World Cup. Why can't some of those riches be shared with host countries, especially those less-developed countries with the largest infrastructure investment requirements? Such a policy would allow a more even distribution of hosting between the richer and poorer nations.

In short, there are a variety of options for FIFA and the IOC to lessen the burden on their hosts. It is questionable, however, whether as monopolies, with little competitive challenge in the mega-event marketplace, they will yield much of their market power. Of course, to the extent that cities and countries lose interest in bidding or corporate sponsors insist on improved public relations, FIFA and the IOC will find themselves obligated to introduce some reform. It is a good bet that the reform will be calibrated to be just enough to spark the necessary interest among prospective hosts and the necessary legitimacy in the eyes of the media and corporate sponsors.

The June 2014 report, mentioned above, by the NOCs of Austria, Germany, Sweden, and Switzerland, "Olympic Agenda 2020," outlined some possible tinkering reforms. The report's authors studied the bid process for the 2010, 2014, and 2018 Winter Olympics and discovered that the cost of bidding alone had quadrupled over this period while the size of the bid book had doubled. The proposal is to simplify the bidding process. The report lamented the increasing public opposition to hosting and suggested stronger propaganda campaigns to convince the public of the value of hosting, and even that "the IOC might also think about financial support to co-fund communication campaigns in interested countries."[19] The authors hinted that it might be possible to lower IOC-mandated venue seating capacities and to modify other requirements so that host countries could more often use existing facilities rather than build new ones. They also suggested that it might be acceptable to reduce the size of the Olympic family (which now requires 42,000 rooms for the Summer Games) so that hosts do not have to overbuild hotel capacity. Finally, the report noted that for all the IOC's talk of promoting sustainability since the 1990s, the IOC has lacked specific environmental standards, any monitoring protocol, and any system of penalties. The report stated that it might be desirable to establish a sustainability monitoring body, and that to be effective, such a body would need enforcement powers. These thoughts, of course, were nothing more than suggestions for the IOC to deliberate and, presumably, decide on at its December 2014 meeting. Ultimately, at that meeting the IOC adopted the so-called Agenda 2020, which proclaimed the IOC's renewed interest in sustainability, affordability, and flexibility—all desiderata that the IOC had previously embraced.

The 2014 bribery scandal surrounding the awarding of the 2022 World Cup to Qatar, along with the earlier payoffs to bring the 2010 Cup to South Africa and the 2018 competition to Russia, commend another type of reform from above—transparency. The voters who award the World Cup and Olympic hosting rights are protected by anonymity rules.[20] (Unfortunately, FIFA seems to be moving in the wrong direction, announcing in July 2014 that the report it commissioned on the possible corruption in the selection of Qatar will not be made public.)[21] If the choices of each voter were made public, then the process would be more accountable and less prone to corruption.

Following the bribery scandal connected to the awarding of the 2002 Winter Olympics to Salt Lake City, the IOC reduced the number of voters and ended the practice of having its voting members visit the candidate cities. The IOC procedures are still far from democratic and cry out for further reform.

The current process for selecting the candidate cities and then the winning city involves 115 people, called IOC members. These members include fifteen active athletes who are elected by their peers at the Olympic Games; fifteen individuals chosen from NOCs and fifteen from the International Federations; and seventy individual members, who are self-perpetuating. Thus, a solid majority (60.9 percent) of the IOC members belongs to a self-generating elite and is accountable to no one, other than to the Olympic Movement and the IOC president. Members on the selection committee serve terms of eight years and can be reelected indefinitely, with an age limit of seventy years (except for those members who joined the IOC before 2000, whose age limit is eighty). Why not have all the IOC members be elected by a constituent part of the Olympic Movement every four or eight years, with limits of two terms?

Reform from Below

Absent substantial change emanating from the international monopolies, cities and countries will have to be smarter and more responsible. Gigantism needs to be eschewed. Bids need to be more cautious and to take greater advantage of already installed infrastructure. If their bids don't meet the standards of FIFA and the IOC, then cities and countries must be willing to stand their ground.[22]

Tokyo's governor Yoichi Masuzoe may have adumbrated a new, more entitled approach to hosting in late July 2014 when he informed the IOC that Tokyo was reconsidering its approved plan for the 2020 Olympics. The Tokyo Organizing Committee has been under popular pressure not to build a new Olympic stadium but rather to use the existing one built for the 1964 Games. The governor noted that Tokyo had promised a compact games geographically but that it was also necessary for the games to be compact financially. Accordingly, Tokyo is considering moving some of the events as far away as 60 miles to save on venue construction costs. As Masuzoe explained, "Expenses can be 30, 40, 50 times more than the original plan. How can I persuade the taxpayers to pay this kind of money?"[23]

Cities would also be well advised to follow the examples of Los Angeles and Barcelona. To do so would require that the contexts and preconditions for the success of those cities be fully understood. Rio's plan for the 2016 Olympics attempted to emulate Barcelona by designing four urban clusters of Olympic activity—a strategy in distinct contrast to the more common single central complex model followed by Atlanta in 1996, Sydney in 2000, Athens in 2004, Beijing in 2008, and London in 2012. Unfortunately, Rio followed Barcelona in form but not in substance. The two cities and their circumstances were entirely different.

The most important aspect of Barcelona's plan for other prospective hosts is not the four clusters but the fact that the urban redevelopment plan preceded any thought about hosting the Olympics. The Olympics were made to work for the plan. The plan was not created posthaste to work for the Olympics.

Many other factors worked in Barcelona's favor as well. Among them, 60 percent of the financing for the games came from the private sector, and of the 40 percent of financing that came from public money, only 5 percent came from the city of Barcelona. Of the thirty-seven venues used during the games, twenty-seven preexisted and five more were already under construction. Fully 83 percent of the total cost was connected to nonsports facilities. Barcelona's location, climate, architecture, and culture, as well as its entry into the European Common Market, regional airline deregulation, and intelligent marketing, were also key elements.

However, just as monopolists won't surrender power voluntarily and will be inclined toward minimalist, cosmetic reform, city and country politicians will be concerned with not alienating their donors and the most powerful elements in their constituencies. They will be inclined, absent political reform, to shill for the interests of the construction, insurance, finance, and hotel industries.

In most cases, the electorate has been willing to settle for circuses and the promise of bread. When the electorate demands bread itself, as it has in Brazil, then politicians will be forced to take notice.

Postscript

The year 2015 was action-packed in the world of FIFA and the IOC. While worthy of a full tome, I will focus on some highlights that pertain most poignantly to the economic gamble behind hosting the World Cup and the Olympics. Sepp Blatter and FIFA cry out for top billing.

FIFA

After the corrupt regime of Joao Havelange ended in 1998, Sepp Blatter, with the aid of hefty bankrolling by Qatari billionaire Bin Hammam and envelope stuffing to buy the support of FIFA's 203 voting delegates, squirmed his way to the top of the FIFA leadership.[1] Courtesy of some promises from Blatter to favor Qatar in a future hosting bid and to support Bin Hammam personally in the 2006 FIFA presidential election, the two teamed up again to enable Blatter's re-election in 2002. But, promises to the contrary, Blatter held the key to indefinite reelection: he controlled FIFA's massive budget and he spread it liberally around the globe to the heads of FIFA's 200-plus member associations. The trick is that in a FIFA election each associated country, whether the United States with its population of 320 million or Montserrat with its 4,900 people, gets one vote. A

$100,000 check for a soccer field and some personal enrichment can go a long way in garnering the votes of scores of member associations around the globe. And this, together with some strategically placed, substantially larger payoffs, is what enabled the 79-year-old Blatter to be elected president once again in May 2015, leading him famously to boast: "I am the president of everyone."

Blatter's reelection in 2015 may have been as uneventful as previous ones had it not been for a spectacular intervention by the U.S. Department of Justice. On May 26, the eve of the FIFA vote for president, Swiss police, acting on behalf of the U.S. DOJ, swept into the Baur au Lac Hotel in Zurich to arrest fourteen FIFA officials and business partners. Each was charged with corruption in connection to receiving kickbacks for awarding media rights or payoffs for supporting certain hosting candidates.

The U.S. DOJ had been looking into FIFA malfeasance ever since December 2010 when FIFA chose Qatar over the United States, Australia, and South Korea to host the 2022 World Cup. The selection of Qatar utterly defied common sense on several grounds. With a permanent population of fewer than 278,000 nationals and a land area less than half the size of Massachusetts, Qatar will be the smallest host ever of the tournament. Qatar has no meaningful soccer history and only a fledgling national league. Amid poor transport, hospitality, and venue infrastructure, Qatar is expected to spend in excess of $220 billion to host the event. Finally, with its dubious human rights record, Qatar will bring embarrassment not only to itself but to FIFA as well.

Yet, on December 2, 2010, Blatter announced not only that Qatar would host the 2022 Cup, but also that Russia would host the 2018 World Cup. England, for one, seemed a more logical choice than Russia. The sport's birthplace had not hosted the World Cup since 1966. England, of course, enjoys a superb infrastructure with modern stadiums, and its bid committee had spent more than $30 million in preparing a plan. The decision to hold two host selections at the same time fit Blatter's scheme perfectly, allowing delegates to trade votes for each other's first choices.

If FIFA's selection of Russia over England displayed an insensitivity to cost and to human rights in Russia, its selection of Qatar over America for 2022 betrayed an utter blindness to these concerns. Not only was the 1994 U.S.-hosted World Cup the most heavily attended in the tournament's history, but America had the best infrastructure and was in the process of developing football as a leading professional sport. Further development of U.S. soccer would have been a great boost to the game, internationally and to FIFA.

So what is the explanation for FIFA's quixotic choice? In the case of Qatar, a cache of millions of emails and other documents uncovered in June 2014 suggested that Bin Hammam had used secret slush funds to make dozens of payments totaling more than $5 million to senior soccer officials. One of those officials was Jack Warner, former FIFA vice president and erstwhile president of CONCACAF (FIFA's organization in North American, Central America, and the Caribbean), who reportedly received $2 million for his support of Qatar as the 2022 host.[2] It also seems that several European votes were procured by Qatar's promise of a large order of jets from Airbus.

The massive construction works for the 2022 World Cup is being undertaken almost entirely by an estimated 1.5 million migrant workers from Nepal, India, Sri Lanka, Bangladesh, and the Philippines. Their labor is governed by Qatar's infamous kafala system, which requires workers to turn over their passports to the company sponsoring them. In effect, they become prisoners, unable to switch jobs or leave the country without the company's permission.

As of May 2014, more than 1,000 worker deaths had already been reported in connection with construction for the tournament. The International Trade Union Confederation projected that at the existing rate there will be 4,000 deaths by 2022.

Making matters still worse, the 2022 World Cup cannot be played in Qatar during the summer months when daytime temperatures frequently exceed 120 degrees Fahrenheit. Even if the stadiums themselves were air-conditioned, at great financial and carbon-footprint expense, there would be practice fields and tourists to worry about. After much sturm and drang, it was finally agreed to hold the 2022 World Cup in November and December, disrupting the middle of the European soccer seasons. One unhappy camper was FOX television, which had purchased the broadcast rights for the 2022 Cup, thinking that the games would be televised during the summer. The network's strongest ratings come in November and December when the National Football League season enters its dramatic final weeks. Now, the World Cup would be competing for eyeballs with the NFL. Sepp Blatter mollified FOX's protests by offering the network the right to televise the 2026 World Cup before any competitive bidding took place with the other networks. Thus, the back room deals that Blatter had worked to award Qatar the 2022 tournament engendered another cost to FIFA in the form of lower television rights fees.

Confounding the picture even more, FIFA suppressed a report, released in 2014, that it had commissioned from former U.S. federal prosecutor Michael J. Garcia. The report found certain FIFA officials were paid $1.5 million each to vote to award Qatar the tournament. FIFA suppressed the publication of Garcia's report. On August 7, 2015, FIFA announced that it had hired L.A.-based law firm Quinn Emanuel Urquhart & Sullivan to do a new internal investigation into FIFA's corruption. It remains to be seen if FIFA will suppress this report as it did Garcia's.

So, the U.S. DOJ had good cause to investigate Mr. Blatter and his lieutenants. In the course of doing so, it uncovered many unexpected transgressions. One of them was a $10 million payoff that lay behind the selection of South Africa to host the 2010 World Cup. A few days after Blatter's reelection, FIFA's second in command, Secretary General Jerome Valcke, was linked to this payoff. Meanwhile, some of the fourteen who were arrested a few days earlier agreed to talk to the DOJ about their knowledge of FIFA's corruption. The circles around Blatter were beginning to close.

Several members of UEFA's (the European soccer organization) executive committee began to talk about the possibility of not participating in the 2018 World Cup in Russia and instead holding their own tournament in Europe. If UEFA did this, it was likely that the United States, Canada, Japan, South Korea, and much of Latin America would follow. The Russian Cup would be upstaged and FIFA's very existence would be threatened. Moreover, increasing numbers of FIFA's corporate sponsors began to express dismay and to call for deep reform.

This was too much for Blatter to contemplate. On June 2, he called a press conference to say that he was resigning as FIFA's president. There was a catch however. He was not going to resign until elections were held to choose his successor, and these elections would not be held until February 26, 2016. This would give Blatter ample time to align forces so that one of his acolytes could be chosen allowing Blatter to serve as éminence gris. This might also enable him to receive an obscene salary and perquisites as president emeritus, just as Blatter had arranged for his predecessor, Joao Havelange.

But Blatter also had to attend to possible legal challenges that would be brought against him. He and Valcke hired a team of high-priced lawyers, and Blatter began to proclaim his innocence, asserting "I cannot monitor everyone all the time."[3]

Yet, if Blatter and Valcke were innocent, why did neither of them show up for a single match of the 2015 women's World Cup in Canada? They were both in Brazil for every game of the 2014 month-long men's World Cup. After all, Blatter considered himself to be the "grandfather" of women's soccer, responsible for the sport's growth over the last few decades.

The truth is that FIFA has held back progress of the women's game on several fronts. Consider the following. First, FIFA refused to compel Canada to provide grass fields for the women's competition—the kind that the men's World Cup is played on. Not only does the ball move differently on artificial turf, but the surface is made of chemicals and rubber pellets that fly off into the players' faces, uniforms, and hair.

Second, FIFA's prize money distribution is acutely imbalanced. According to the BBC, the total prize money offered to the men's teams in the 2014 World Cup was $576 million; the total offered to the women's teams in 2015 was $15 million. Do the math: the men's prize money is 38.4 times larger than the women's![4]

Third, FIFA's policy accepts having opposing women's teams frequently stay in the same hotel. Again, an awkward practice not experienced at the men's World Cup.

All the more remarkable, given the lack of attention from FIFA, the women's championship game between the United States and Japan in 2015 set the all-time record for television viewership of any soccer match, men's or women's, in the United States. The overnight TV ratings for the championship match hit 15.2. This broke the previous ratings record, also set by U.S. women in the 1999 World Cup final between the United States and China, at 13.3. In a distant third was the men's 2014 World Cup match between the United States and Belgium at 9.8.

Not only did the U.S.-Japan game break records for soccer viewership, but it also crushed the ratings for the NHL Stanley Cup championship game in 2015 that drew only a 5.6 rating (just over one-third of the women's rating). The women also came within a hair of matching the NBA championship game in June 2015 between the Cleveland Cavaliers and the Golden State Warriors, which garnered a 15.9 rating.

The DOJ says that the fourteen arrests at the Baur au Lac Hotel in May were only the beginning. It appears now to be hot on the trail of Blatter himself, as does a team of Swiss investigators. If Blatter is indicted, then it is likely that the path to reforming FIFA will be more straightforward. At one level, it is clear what must be done: presidential term limits; voting transparency; voting weighted by the number of registered soccer players in a country; an independent board to oversee FIFA's actions and to vet members of the executive committee; compensation disclosure for FIFA executives; more women on the executive committee; and a commitment to equal prize money for men and women as is practiced in the grand slam tournaments of tennis.

At another level, FIFA stands to remain a worldwide monopoly without government oversight, with the ability to extract extravagant investments from prospective host countries, bloated rights fees from broadcasters, handsome sponsorship deals from corporations, and inflated ticket prices from its well-healed clientele. A Blatterless FIFA will remain a dominant force, and one deserving of constant vigilance.

IOC

When Thomas Bach took over as IOC's president in September 2013, he knew that something was amiss. The long-term trend of disappearing bidders was given an exclamation point as prospective host cities for the 2022 Winter Games dropped out of the competition one by one. Eventually, the IOC was left with only two possible hosts Almaty, Kazakhstan, and Beijing, China—each fraught with problems.

Bach's strategy to redress the issue was twofold. First, he began globetrotting to tell dozens of municipalities that the IOC would look very favorably upon a strong bid from their city. Second, he began to promote the idea of reform to make bidding more attractive. The latter ultimately resulted in Agenda 2020 being passed at the IOC Congress in December 2014.

Agenda 2020 contained dozens of elements, with a few of them heralding a commitment to making the hosting experience more affordable and sustainable. In fact, these were not newly professed values for the IOC. Sustainability became an IOC mantra back in the 1990s. Affordability was introduced as a valued criterion in 2002. Nonetheless, the publicity around these reforms led several cities to view hosting as a more viable option and the number of early bidders for the 2024 Summer Olympics ticked up. Let's turn to consider some of the news from 2015 on the upcoming games and current bids.

Rio de Janeiro, Brazil 2016

An Associated Press report on May 8, 2015, about Rio's preparations for the 2016 Summer Olympics noted the following potential problems:[5]

—Possibility of heavy street violence
—Government refusal to fund water polo venue
—Serious ongoing pollution in Guanabara Bay
—Construction of one-fourth of venues not yet under way
—Only 10 percent of Olympic construction, overlay, and energy projects funded
—No contract yet to supply power to Olympic venues

Then, on July 10, 2015, the Olympic organizing committee revealed that the cost of the Olympic Village had grown fivefold since the initial bid. Cariocas, as residents of Rio are called, had grown accustomed to such news, and worse. A few weeks earlier, the remaining residents of the disappearing favela, Vila Autodromo, had taken to the streets to protest the leveling of their community adjacent to the Olympic Park. Meanwhile, nearby on the edge of the new Olympic golf course, a new housing community had begun selling units that cost between $2.3 million and $23 million.[6] Unfortunately, Rio has fallen victim to the Olympic overbuild disease that afflicted Sydney, Lillehammer, Sochi, and other hosts. As of early November 2015, only 230 of the 3,604 (a mere 6.4 percent) of the planned luxury apartments bordering the golf course had been sold. The widespread overbuild here and elsewhere is causing property values to plummet, portending a possible financial crisis triggered by the real estate market.[7]

Vila Autodromo is but one of scores of favelas that are being eliminated (or partially torn down) as part of Rio's hosting effort. Originally, the official plan (*morar carioca*) was to modernize services in the favelas and integrate them into the mainstream life of the city. Many favelas, however, are located both at the margins of the four

Olympic clusters and also in the proximate hillsides of Rio with enviable views of the sea. Developers saw an opportunity to invest and build new, high-income housing. That spelled the razing, not the integration, of these communities, as the *favelados* were relocated hours away in the western suburbs of the city, separated from their friends, their children's schools, and their jobs. This radical facelift will be one of the enduring legacies of Rio 2016.[8]

The largest operational issue faced by the 2016 games is the boating and swimming events, particularly sailing in Guanabara Bay, but also open swimming at Copacabana Beach and canoeing and rowing on the Rodrigo de Freitas Lake. These waters are the depository of waste and untreated sewage from Rio homes and factories. A July 2015 analysis of the bacteria and virus levels in these bodies of water

> revealed dangerously high levels of viruses and bacteria from human sewage in Olympic and Paralympic venues—results that alarmed international experts and dismayed competitors training in Rio, some of whom have already fallen ill with fevers, vomiting and diarrhea. . . . Olympic athletes are almost certain to come into contact with disease-causing viruses that in some tests measured up to 1.7 million times the level of what would be considered hazardous on a Southern California beach. . . . As part of its Olympic project, Brazil promised to build eight treatment facilities to filter out much of the sewage and prevent tons of household trash from flowing into the Guanabara Bay. Only one has been built.[9]

Compounding the problem, a massive corruption scandal at Petrobras, the state oil company, was engulfing many members of President Dilma Rousseff's government and threatening to implicate the president herself. Meanwhile, the economy continued in an extended recession with rising unemployment and inflation, an exploding national budget deficit that has reached 9 percent of GDP, output falling at a 2.3 percent annual clip in 2015, and its currency having lost practically half its value over the last three years.[10] One joke making the rounds in Rio in July 2015 was that the rate of inflation (approximately 8 percent) was now higher than the president's plummeting popularity rating.[11]

Yet, whatever transpires in the real Rio economy, there's a strong likelihood that, abetted by an extensive military and police presence, the 2016 summer games will be delivered with few blemishes to the worldwide television audience.[12] The IOC will be on hand to declare the games a resounding success, as the Cariocas struggle to find sustenance and stability in their daily lives.

Pyeongchang, South Korea 2018

While the infrastructure and venue construction appear to be more or less on schedule at this early juncture, Pyeongchang has faced a common obstacle in preparing for the 2018 Winter Olympics: money. The organizing committee's budget called for $158 million in corporate sponsorship revenues in 2013 and $611 million in 2014. But in 2013 sponsorship revenues were zero, and in 2014 they were only $31.6 million. The committee has had to borrow the shortfall from the government.[13] Pyeongchang has also witnessed its share of political protest. A coalition of fifty civic groups has filed complaints against the game organizers for malfeasance. Among the complaints is the destruction at Mount Gariwang, where a ski slope is being built for the games.[14] More than 50,000 trees, many older than 500 years, have been cut down. Future bidders would be prudent to take note.

Tokyo, Japan 2020

In 2013 the IOC selected Tokyo over Istanbul and Madrid to host the 2020 Summer Games. If the IOC believed in the affordability mantra that it has been peddling since 2002, it seems that Madrid, whose budget was less than one-third of Tokyo's, would have been the better choice. Indeed, the extravagance of Tokyo's bid came home to haunt the organizing committee and the city.

Tokyo's initial bid boasted venue compactness—twenty-eight of the thirty-three venues were planned to be within five miles of the $4 billion Olympic Village. Early on, however, it was recognized hundreds of millions of dollars could be saved by locating some of the venues outside of Tokyo because of the high cost of land, labor, and materials in the city. The IOC, seeking to vaunt Agenda 2020, accepted the dispersion of Tokyo's 2020 venues.

Next, a larger and knottier issue surfaced in the plans for the Olympic Stadium. The original plan entailed razing the 54,000-capacity stadium from the 1964 Olympics and erecting a modern facility, initially budgeted at $1 billion. This plan provoked popular protests among taxpayers seeking to know why the 1964 stadium was inadequate. The protests magnified as the projected costs of the new facility ballooned. By early July 2015, the projected costs had risen to $2.5 billion (with a retractable roof) or $2.1 billion (sans roof).[15] According to the stadium architects, the building contractors were chosen before they presented cost estimates for the project.[16] A poll published by NHK, the Japanese national broadcaster, found that 81 percent of those surveyed were against the new stadium.[17] Finally, the political pressure grew too strong, and on July 17 the government put the kibosh on the stadium, announcing a competition for a new design and issuing an apology to the IOC. Among other things, this meant that the stadium would not be ready for World Rugby Championship in 2019, as intended.

Beijing, China 2022

Commenting on the bidding process for the 2022 Winter Games, Olympics historian Jules Boykoff observed: "Voters in Munich, Stockholm, Krakow, and Graubunden, Switzerland, said thanks but no thanks to the Olympics, citing high costs, low public support, and security demands. Lviv was forced to pull out due to unrest in Ukraine. Oslo was a clear frontrunner, but its bid was derailed when conservatives and progressives joined forces to say no. This left a dubious duo: Almaty and Beijing."[18]

The IOC was confronted with a Hobson's Choice. Its response was to enact a program of apparent reforms intended to lessen the hosting burden, dubbed Agenda 2020, and to have Thomas Bach repeatedly aver that Almaty and Beijing each had strong bids. The IOC wants it both ways: credit for its rhetoric, on the one hand, and to do whatever it wants, on the other. The Olympic Movement professes certain values and respect for human rights is prominent among them. Indeed, the IOC reasserted its supposed commitment to human rights in its Agenda 2020. Yet the human rights record in both Kazakhstan and China is abysmal. Despite claims that shining a bright light on China and bringing the country into the community of nations with hosting the 2008 Olympics would lessen political repression, China's human rights ranking actually deteriorated between 2008 and 2014, according to Human Rights Watch and the Reporters without Borders Press Freedom Index.[19] Rather than a salutary effect on human rights, the typical pattern when China hosts international events is a clampdown on political expression, a roundup of activists, and tighter censorship.

Kazakhstan is hardly any better. It has had the same president since 1989, and Human Rights Watch has criticized the country's repression of dissent and religious freedom as well as its use of torture on detained persons.[20] Ever the soothsayer and spin artist, Bach declared: "We have two excellent candidates."[21]

Agenda 2020 also professes a concern for affordability, and the Beijing organizing committee has cooperated by noting that it will use some of the venues from the 2008 Olympics. Bemusingly, China also has cooperated by not including the cost of the high-speed railroad that will link Beijing to the Alpine and Nordic ski areas (54 miles and 118 miles from the capital, respectively) in the Olympic budget. Chinese state media has estimated the cost of the high-speed rail at $5 billion.[22]

Also excluded from the budget will be the substantial expense of new water diversion and desalination programs that will be necessary for drinking, ice making, and artificial snow making in the water-starved northern cities. China's northern climate is arid and only 25 percent of the country's exiguous water resources lie in the north, although nearly 50 percent of the population resides in the north.[23] Accordingly, China launched an $80 billion water diversion program from the south prior to the 2008 summer Olympics, but the north's per capita water availability still remains below what the United Nations deems to be the critical level. Zhangjiakou, the site of the Nordic skiing competition, only gets eight inches of snow per year and Yanqing, the site of the Alpine skiing events, gets under fifteen inches of precipitation annually. With the warming climate in recent years, little of the snowfall remains on the ground. Both venues will require copious water supplies for artificial snow making.[24] Beijing, Zhangjiakou, and Yanquing are part of the North China Plain, encompassing the four provinces of Shandong, Henan, Jiangsu, and Hebei, all part of China's most important agricultural region, producing sorghum, winter wheat, corn and other vegetables, and cotton. The demand for water from the ski areas will divert water from vital agricultural uses.[25]

Even without considering the lost agricultural output, it is evident that the published budget for Beijing 2022 will be understated by billions of dollars, enabling the IOC to trumpet the success of its Agenda 2020 affordability campaign. Further, China's purported legacy of ski resorts in the mountains bordering Inner Mongolia and the Gobi desert only threatens to worsen an acute and unsustainable water shortage. If the ski resorts survive, only China's rich will be able to afford them, while food supplies will be adversely impacted and food prices will rise.

Another strike against Beijing 2022 is that the winter is one of the worst times for air pollution in the city. Studies have shown this pollution to be responsible for a significant increase of cardiovascular and respiratory diseases.[26] Deforestation of the northern mountains will only compound the problem. Before the 2008 games, Beijing succeeded in temporarily reducing airborne particulates by placing strict controls on traffic, closing nearby factories, discouraging residents from engaging in outdoor activities, and using cloud seeding to induce rain. Similar strategies are bound to be employed again in 2022. Still, it is hard to imagine that athletes' health will not be put at some risk.

Boston and Bidding for the Summer 2024 Games

Thomas Bach's globetrotting and Agenda 2020 appear to have found some early resonance. The decline in suitors has been arrested, at least for the time being. Paris, Rome, Budapest, Hamburg, and Los Angeles have entered the IOC's competition to host the Summer Olympics in 2024.[27] (As this edition goes to press in December 2015, news has come from Hamburg that in a referendum the citizens of that city rejected Hamburg's bid by a 51.6 to 48.4 percent margin. Toronto and Baku previously decided against bidding. The Los Angeles City Council has until the summer of 2016 to decide whether to sign on to the mandatory financial guarantee to the IOC. Agenda 2020 may be losing its luster.)

The United States Olympic Committee (USOC) selected Boston to be the U.S. representative for 2024 over Los Angeles, San Francisco, and Washington, D.C., on January 8, 2015.[28] Then, seven-and-a-half months later, on July 27, 2015, the USOC decided to withdraw its support for Boston. The short version of the story is that both the mayor of Boston, Marty Walsh, and the governor of Massachusetts, Charlie Baker, refused to offer the IOC the mandatory financial backstop in the event of cost overruns or revenue shortfalls.

The longer version is that practically nothing went right for Boston 2024, the organizing committee for the games, after the USOC's January selection. Boston 2024 was a private group, made up largely of corporate executives, many connected to the construction industry. It appropriated the name of Boston and submitted bid documents to the USOC in the city's name in December 2014. Neither the Boston city council nor the state legislature voted to endorse the bid. After the USOC anointed Boston on January 8, there were numerous public calls for Boston 2024 to release the bid documents. Taxpayers wanted to know: what venues would be built and where would they be, what infrastructural investments would be made, and how was it all going to be financed? After two weeks of pressure, Boston 2024 released several bid documents, but withheld others.

The bid documents revealed an initial plan that called for $4.7 billion to be spent on the games' operations, $3.4 billion on permanent venues, $5.2 billion on infrastructure improvements, and $1 billion on security (hopefully to be fully picked up by the federal government). The released documents also declared that no new public money would be needed: the operations budget would be covered by Olympic revenues, the permanent venues would be built by private sector developers, and the infrastructure investments would be made anyway and were already funded in the state's plans. Further, the documents asserted that Boston 2024 had entered into constructive conversations with the private landowners in Widett Circle (planned home of the Olympic Stadium), Columbia Point (planned for the Olympic Village), and other sites.

But, there were problems. The Olympic revenues were optimistically projected. There were no private sector companies or universities expressing an interest in building the sporting venues. Much of the infrastructure, in fact, was not funded, and representative Bill Straus, chair of the House transportation committee, estimated the actual infrastructure costs of Boston 2024's plans would approach $13 billion. Moreover, contrary to Boston 2024 claims, the private landowners in Widett Circle and Columbia Point said that the first they heard of the plans was when they read the partially released documents, and a $1 billon plan to expand the convention center had never even been mentioned to Governor Charlie Baker. Boston 2024 had gotten off to a bad start and the trust factor became a salient issue.[29]

Matters got more difficult still for the Boston bidders when it was revealed in March that they had hired, at $7,500 a day, former governor Deval Patrick (who helped launch the Olympic effort by appointing a biased committee to study the feasibility of hosting) to be an international goodwill ambassador. Then in May, pursuant to a Freedom of Information Act request, it was discovered in previously suppressed bid documents that Boston 2024's financing plan did, in fact, involve the use of public funds. The list of gaffes and embarrassments continued to grow and public support continued to wane. Polls indicated that 51 percent of voters supported Boston's bid in early January, but by July this percent had diminished to around 40 percent.

Although Boston 2024's handling of public relations left much to be desired, the fundamental problem was that neither its first plan (dubbed 1.0) from December, nor its second plan (2.0) released at the end of June made economic sense. Plan 2.0 was born when Governor Baker insisted that Boston 2024 produce a more detailed plan that convincingly demonstrated public monies would not be necessary.

Plan 2.0 was, in fact, very different from 1.0. It no longer called for private corporations to build the Olympic venues. In 2.0 all the venues would be temporary.

Having all temporary venues raised new issues. While it sidestepped the problem of white elephants, why spend hundreds of millions of dollars for venues that would be used for only three weeks? How could there be a sporting legacy if facilities were taken down? How would the IOC feel about a 69,000-capacity stadium (up from 60,000 in 1.0) in Boston without premium seating, when the Paris bid's Olympic Stadium was the 80,000-seat Stade de France with all the modern revenue-generating accoutrements? If Boston 2024 wanted to compete successfully against Paris, Hamburg, Rome, and Budapest between September 2015 and September 2017 (when the IOC would crown a winner), wouldn't it have to substantially upgrade many of its thirty-three temporary venues, engendering hefty cost overruns?

But Boston's bidders were not worried about winning in September 2017 quite yet. They were worried about winning over Massachusetts taxpayers by persuading them that no public money would be spent. Besides all temporary venues, Boston 2024 had a few other tricks up its sleeve.

First, via deus ex machina, Boston 2024 proposed to slash the cost of certain venues. The velodrome, for which the group never identified a location, would cost only $64 million (London 2012 initially budgeted $32 million for its velodrome but ended up spending $169 million). The aquatics center, also locationless, would cost only $70 million (London 2012 budgeted $121 million, but ultimately paid $431 million).[30] The media and broadcasting center, which was projected to cost $500 million in version 1.0, in 2.0 would require only $51 million.

Second, with unrealistically cheap venues, the bulk of the development costs were slated to be picked up by private companies. At Widett Circle, where the Olympic stadium would be housed, the private developer was expected to build an approximately twenty-acre deck over the rail yards and wholesale food markets, to add an MBTA stop, to cover all utility and remediation costs, and eventually to build out the mixed-use facilities. In order to make such a project attractive to a developer, Boston 2024 had to load it up with record tax subsidies and pay no air rights fees to the MBTA (the state-owned mass transit system in greater Boston).

Consider these figures. The Boston 2024 plan called for the Widett Circle developer to pay only 15 percent of its normal property tax obligation through 2039. The average annual loss in the city's property tax collection would be over $41.3 million.[31] During the 2040s, the developer would pay 30 percent of the normal tax.[32]

All told, the Widett Circle developer would be receiving a tax subsidy of an estimated $269 per square foot. The tax abatement for the developer at Columbia Point (where the Olympic Village would have been situated) was estimated at $199 per square foot. Compare this to more typical development tax subsidies in Boston: the current mixed-use project under way called Fenway Center is receiving $4 per square foot and the Vertex Pharmaceutical development at the seaport received $11 per square foot.

Boston 2024 claimed that the planning for the Olympics revealed exciting development opportunities for the city. While it may be that developing Columbia Point and even Widett Circle without the constraints of IOC requirements would make sense for Boston at some point in the future, it is implausible to suggest that projects requiring such massive and unprecedented subsidies are the best developments for Boston in the coming decade. Increasing Boston's density—a city already short on open space—must be planned extremely carefully and with a macro-vision of the city's needs. Boston 2024's plans for Widett Circle included 4,000 housing units, yet it did not include space or financing for preschools, primary, middle, or high schools, nor for police or fire services, among other things. Further, based on the air rights paid at Fenway Center to the MBTA, which entails building a deck over the Massachusetts Turnpike, the air rights at Widett Circle should exceed $350 million. Yet the Boston 2024 plan only included a $10 million air rights payment to Amtrak, with nothing paid to the MBTA. The roughly twenty-acre deck at Widett Circle would have cost more than $1.4 billion (yet was budgeted in plan 2.0 at $314 million).[33] Clearly, this proposal did not represent careful planning and was not in the city's best interests.

Third, Boston 2024 claimed to have developed several layers of insurance that would protect taxpayers against cost overruns or revenue shortfalls. Most of this insurance involved the use of standard policies, such as surety and performance bonds or capital replacement insurance. Boston 2024 also claimed to have envisioned an umbrella policy, but it never identified a willing carrier, nor the details of what and how much would be covered. It was clear, however, that changes in the scope of the thirty-three venues (such as adding luxury boxes or catering facilities to the temporary Olympic Stadium), which may have been necessary to effectively compete with Paris, Hamburg, Rome, or Budapest, would not have been covered by any of the touted policies. In the end, if Boston 2024 had had effective insurance that truly protected the taxpayers, then it should have sold the IOC on the idea and thereby obviated the IOC's required financial guarantee from the city.[34]

Fourth, many of Boston 2024's projected revenues were optimistic. For instance, it projected $1.52 billion (in 2016 prices) in domestic corporate sponsorships, which would have been an Olympic record. It also projected average ticket prices of $137 for preliminary games in the basketball, baseball, and soccer competitions. While such a high price point is hard to imagine even for those games when the United States is involved, it seems utterly fanciful for a soccer match, say, between Chile and Turkey. It is also implausible that Major League Baseball (MLB) would allow its players to participate, interrupting the season and risking injury for its stars. After all, the IOC booted baseball out of the Olympics at the beginning of the century and MLB has since invested hundreds of millions of dollars to develop the World Baseball Classic.

In the end, what started as one of Boston 2024's principal selling points—a highly educated population in a city of world-class universities—turned out to be its downfall. The citizens were too intelligent to be duped, or, at least, too weary from spending over $20 billion on the budgeted $2 billion Big Dig project and from an increasingly dysfunctional mass transit system, to buy the no-public-money sales pitch. It didn't help statewide support that Boston 2024 did not contemplate spending a penny on infrastructure improvements outside the greater metropolitan area; nor that Boston 2024 was intending to bypass key state locations—Springfield (the birthplace of basketball) and Holyoke (the birthplace of volleyball)—in favor of larger, fancier venues in New York and other northeastern cities to play the early rounds of competition in these sports.[35]

After the USOC pulled the plug on Boston, Thomas Bach couldn't contain his criticism. Bach scolded:

> What we could see in a nutshell, what happened is that Boston did not deliver on its promises to the USOC when they were selected. . . . I gave up following it. It was pretty confusing. Every day, there was a new project coming from Boston or new people or new ideas. I really gave up following it in detail.[36]

Boston mayor Marty Walsh, who had been one of Boston 2024's biggest boosters, testily responded:

In Boston and I'm pretty sure probably in the rest of America, we don't get forced into putting taxpayers' money at risk. And if that's confusing to the IOC president, than it shows exactly why the IOC is in the position they are, in not having multiple countries bid for the Olympics. And I think that's what they have to realize. I saw his comment today, and the USOC will never admit this but, it's that guarantee that ultimately helps with poor polling numbers, concerned the senate president, the speaker, the governor. Concerned the taxpayer. So if you think about how this thing has gone down over the last several months, it really comes down to the guarantee that the IOC demands the United States Olympic Committee's host city sign. That's really what it . . . , but I think it's just unfortunate that the President of the IOC involved himself in this conversation.[37]

Mayor Walsh seemed to have finally learned the lesson: it is prudent to be vigilant when dealing with unregulated, international monopolies. And sometimes it is even a good idea to fight back.

Notes

Preface

1. See, for instance, Roger G. Noll and Andrew Zimbalist, eds., *Sports, Jobs and Taxes: The Economic Impact of Sports Teams and Stadiums* (Brookings Institution Press, 1997).

2. Stefan Szymanski and I follow the same practice in our book, *National Pastime: How Americans Play Baseball and the Rest of the World Plays Soccer* (Brookings Institution Press, 2006).

3. For a humorous discussion of this etymological issue, see Sarah Lydall, "Up in Arms over 'Soccer' vs. 'Football,'" *New York Times*, June 19, 2014.

Chapter 1

1. Only Los Angeles and Moscow had bid to host the 1980 Summer Games. Los Angeles has bid to host the Olympics more than any other U.S. city.

2. See http://leastthing.blogspot.com/2013/06/further-thoughts-on-sepp-blatters-fifa.html.

3. According to Dominico Scala, a member of the three-man Compensation Sub-Committee, the pay levels chosen are meant to emulate the compensation paid to executives in similarly sized companies in the private sector. See www.fifa.com/aboutfifa/organisation/footballgovernance/news/newsid=2384045/index.html.

4. Jonathan Calvert and Heidi Blake, "Fifa's Chiefs Pocket Secret 100% Pay Rise," *Sunday Times*, June 22, 2014.

5. Jonathan Calvert and Heidi Blake, "Calling Time on Fifa's Watch Scandal," *Sunday Times* (London), September 14, 2014 (www.thesundaytimes.co.uk/sto/news/article1459174.ece).

6. "Fifa ExCo Members Ordered to Return Watches," *The Guardian,* September 18, 2014 (www.theguardian.com/football/2014/sep/18/fifa-exco-return-watches-gift-brazil-world-cup).

7. See, for example, Heidi Blake and Jonathan Calvert, *The Ugly Game* (New York: Simon and Schuster, 2014); Tariq Panja, A. Martin, and V. Silver, "How Sepp Blatter Controls Soccer," at www.bloomber.com/graphics/2015-sepp-blatter-fifa, viewed May 15, 2015; and ESPN E60 report by Jeremy Schaap, "Sepp Blatter and FIFA," at espn.go.com/video/clip?id=12880456.

8. In 2014 President Bach had an expense account of $243,000 on top of the IOC covering his rented apartment in Lausanne, and members of the executive committee are reimbursed up to $450 a day for IOC travel, along with $7,000 a year for administrative support. See Nick Butler, "Bach Receives $243,000 a Year for Being IOC President," Insidethegames.com, April 2, 2015.

9. Prince Nawaf Faisal Fahd Abdulaziz resigned from the IOC on July 11, 2014.

10. See www.businessinsider.com/finances-of-the-ioc-2012-8?op=1. There is also a potential upside to having such elite members on the committee. As Wolfgang Maennig pointed out to me, at least these persons cannot be corrupted.

11. It is common for bid committees to add a former Olympic athlete as a figurehead.

12. Rick Burton and Norm O'Reilly, "Bach's History a Signal That His Leadership Will Be Proactive," *Sports Business Journal,* February 10–16, 2014. Stockholm's potential bid had special significance because Stockholm would have become the first city to host both the Summer and the Winter Games. Munich's bid had Thomas Bach's interest because he hails from Wurzburg, just north of Munich.

Chapter 2

1. Coubertin's commitment to a modern Olympics was inspired by his contact with the English physician William Penny Brookes. See Robert Barney, Stephen R. Wenn, and Scott G. Martyn, *Selling the Five Rings: The International Olympic Committee and the Rise of Olympic Commercialism* (University of Utah Press, 2004), chap. 1.

2. Coubertin changed his mind on the importance of amateurism over time. See *Olympism: Selected Writings of Pierre de Coubertin,* ed. Norbert Muller (Lausanne: IOC, 1970).

3. International Olympic Committee (IOC), "Olympic Charter" (Lausanne, 2013) (www.olympic.org/documents/olympic_charter_en.pdf).

4. Brundage finished sixth in the pentathlon and didn't finish in the decathlon. See, for example, Bruce Lowitt, "Thorpe Becomes 1st Olympic Star," *St. Petersburg Times,* October 31, 1999 (www.sptimes.com/News/103199/news_pf/Sports/Thorpe_becomes_1st_Ol.shtml).

5. Allen Guttmann, *The Olympics: A History of the Modern Games* (University of Illinois Press, 2002), chap. 3.

6. Roland Renson and Marijke den Hollander, "Sport and Business in the City: The Antwerp Olympic Games of 1920 and the Urban Elite," *Olympika: The International Journal of Olympic Studies* 6 (1997): 73–84.

7. Guttmann, *The Olympics,* p. 44.

8. Five countries sought to host the first World Cup: Italy, Holland, Spain, Sweden, and Uruguay. In the competitive bidding spirit, Uruguay, a country of but 2 million and about to celebrate the centenary of its independence, offered to pay the full travel and lodging expenses of visiting teams and to build a new stadium. Yet two months before the 1930 competition was to begin, no European countries were willing to make the three-week boat trip to Uruguay. The Latin American soccer federations threatened to withdraw from FIFA, and political arm twisting began in Europe. In the end, France, Yugoslavia, Romania, and Belgium—hardly the powerhouses of European soccer at the time—agreed to participate. See Brian Glanville, *The Story of the World Cup* (London: Faber and Faber, 1993), chap. 1.

9. Tensions between FIFA and the IOC have asserted themselves on several occasions over the years. Notably, FIFA refused to accept the stadiums designated for soccer in Southern California matches by the Los Angeles Organizing Committee of the 1984 Games. As a consequence, the 1984 Olympic soccer competition was played at four sites: Harvard University, the U.S. Naval Academy in Maryland, Stanford University, and the Rose Bowl. See Peter Ueberroth, *Made in America* (New York: William Morrow and Co., 1985), p. 104. In 2015 IOC president Bach became outspoken after the FIFA corruption scandal, calling for deep, structural reform of FIFA.

10. See Guttmann, *The Olympics,* chap. 4, for a fuller discussion of this and other issues confronting the 1936 Games.

11. There were, however, two "alibi" Jews, Rudi Ball (ice hockey) and Helene Meyer (world-class fencer). They had Jewish fathers but non-Jewish mothers. By Jewish custom, only someone with a Jewish mother is considered Jewish. For a more detailed discussion, see Arnd Kruger, "Germany: The Propaganda Machine," in *The Nazi Olympics: Sport, Politics and Appeasement in the 1930s,* ed. A. Kruger and W. Murray (University of Illinois Press, 2003).

12. Marty Glickman and Sam Stoller were the two replaced athletes. See, for example, Donald Harrison, "Jewish Athlete Still Bitter about Ruined Shot at Gold Medal," *San Diego Jewish Press-Heritage,* July 2, 1999 (www.jewish sightseeing.com/germany/berlin/olympic_stadium/19990702-glickman.htm). See also Marty Glickman and Stan Isaacs, *The Fastest Kid on the Block: The Marty Glickman Story* (Syracuse University Press, 1999).

13. Germany did, however, take home the most gold medals from the 1936 Games, with the United States coming in second and Hungary third.

14. The Melbourne games were boycotted by Egypt, Iraq, and Lebanon to

protest Israel's takeover of the Suez Canal in 1956. They were also the site of a vicious and bloody water polo contest between the Hungarian and the Soviet teams following the Soviet invasion of Hungary in that year.

15. IOC, *Olympic Marketing File*, 2014 (www.olympic.org/Documents/IOC_Marketing/OLYMPIC_MARKETING_FACT_%20FILE_2014.pdf), p. 22.

16. Barney and others, *Selling the Five Rings,* chap. 4. Mexico City's games in 1968 were the first to be broadcast in color (ibid., p. 84).

17. See ibid., pp. 80–98, for an extended discussion of these tensions and their compromises.

18. Guttmann, *The Olympics,* p. 113. There is one International Federation for each sport.

19. In his memoir of the Los Angeles games, Peter Ueberroth, the president of the Local Organizing Committee, states that the IOC received one-third of the U.S. television rights fee of $225 million (*Made in America,* pp. 66–68). As pointed out in the text, this is inaccurate. The IOC received one-third of the cash payment of $100 million only.

20. The technical services deduction allowed to Calgary for the 1988 Winter Games was set at 20 percent of the gross value of the rights fee. Barney and others, *Selling the Five Rings,* p. 207.

21. Ibid., chap. 8.

22. The Partido Revolucionario Institucional has held power for more than seventy years since its founding in 1929.

23. The Mexico City games witnessed another first. Some of the athletes were paid by Adidas and Puma to wear their running shoes. Apparently, endorsements by Olympic athletes continued quietly for the next decade, and most in the IOC looked the other way.

24. Neither scaling the fence nor entering the balcony posed major physical challenges. The Israeli team had asked to be transferred to a more secure location at the beginning of the games, but its request was denied.

25. John Gold and Margaret Gold, "Olympic Cities: Regeneration, City Rebranding and Changing Urban Agendas," *Geography Compass* 2, no. 1 (2008): 305.

26. See Guttmann, *The Olympics,* pp. 143–44, for a discussion of the causes of the massive cost overrun in Montreal. See also Barney and others, *Selling the Five Rings,* pp. 123–25.

27. The first recorded use of performance-enhancing drugs in the Olympics was during the 1904 marathon when the winner, Thomas Hicks, was found to be using strychnine. The use of steroids, erythropoietin, and other substances has been widespread beyond the East Germans; such well-known figures as Marion Jones, Ben Johnson, and many others have admitted to drug use or have tested positive.

28. See Ueberroth, *Made in America,* p. 83.

29. Most commentaries in the West state that the true finances of the Moscow games are unknown, held as state secrets by Alexei Kosygin and

Leonid Brezhnev. Ueberroth, however, suggests that the 1980 Games cost the USSR more than $5 billion (*Made in America*, p. 60). Barney and others (*Selling the Five Rings*, p. 148) report that Moscow's official figure put the cost at $1.3 billion, while other estimates rose as high as $9 billion.

30. On the verge of its Islamic revolution, Teheran, Iran, was also an applicant to host the 1984 Olympics, but withdrew before the final bidding stage.

31. Ueberroth adds that "donations [to finance the games] were out of the question. . . . It would have been insensitive and ill advised to compete against churches, synagogues, hospitals, YMCAs, Girl Scouts and all the other worthy organizations that rely on charity for their survival. Also, the USOC relies almost entirely on donations and we didn't want to compete for the same dollars" (*Made in America*, p. 60).

32. Ueberroth, *Made in America*, p. 121.

33. The extent to which it does one or the other depends on what economists call the price elasticity of demand. The more sensitive consumers are to price changes (the higher the elasticity), the more the tax on hotels or car rentals will lower demand for travel to the city.

34. An exclusive product category refers to a type of product, for example beer, and a single company being the only one allowed to advertise in that category during the competition or in association with the Olympics. The company would also be allowed to promote itself as an official sponsor of the Olympics. Ueberroth states in his book that the idea of fewer, larger, and exclusive sponsorship contracts came from his aide, Joel Rubenstein (*Made in America*, p. 61). The IOC adopted this strategy in its TOP program immediately after the L.A. games.

35. Although different surplus amounts have been cited in the literature, $215 million is the figure that Ueberroth cites several times in his book (for example, *Made in America*, p. 369.) Ueberroth states that the figure was revised upward from the September 1984 report of a $150 million surplus. The surplus was given 60 percent to the USOC and 40 percent to Southern California, in both cases to benefit the development of youth sports. The official IOC report on the Los Angeles games also states that the surplus was $215 million, although it notes the possibility that the figure could increase with some additional revenue trickling in by the time the LAOCOG dissolved. See http://library.la84. org/6oic/OfficialReports/1984/1984v1pt2.pdf, 11.01.10, p. 309.

36. IOC official report, ibid., p. 370. Ueberroth contrasts Los Angeles' good luck with what happened in Lake Placid, New York, where an expected operating surplus of $1 million turned into a $6 million operating deficit when the organizing committee had to throw money at a series of last-minute problems.

37. ABC paid the IOC $225 million for U.S. rights, and managed to turn a nifty profit of more than $400 million. The U.S. ratings soared, and ABC was able to charge $250,000 for a thirty-second advertising spot. Meanwhile, Peter Ueberroth thanked the thousands of volunteers and paid himself a modest bonus of $475,000.

38. There was actually a crack in the armor of amateurism under Lord Killanin. In 1978, Rule 26 of the Olympic Charter was modified so that athletes were allowed openly to earn money from endorsements if the money went to their national sports federation or their country's Olympic Committee. The receiving organization was then permitted to pay the athlete's expenses in connection with the games, including "pocket money." "Broken-time" payments for time away from the athlete's regular job were also authorized if the athlete had a regular job. But the rule continued to declare that professional athletes were ineligible.

39. The IOC at the time consisted of 109 men and seven women. Members elected prior to 1966 had life membership, and those elected subsequently until the age of eighty. Today, the age limit for new members is seventy years.

40. Because of the growing size of both the Winter and the Summer Games, alternating the events also made administrative sense.

41. Elmer Sterken, "Economic Impact of Organizing Large Sporting Events," in *International Handbook on the Economics of Mega Sporting Events,* ed. Wolfgang Maennig and Andrew S. Zimbalist (Cheltenham, U.K.: Edward Elgar, 2012), p. 340.

42. See, for example, Stephen Wenn, Robert Barney, and Scott Martyn, *Tarnished Rings: The International Olympic Committee Bid Scandal* (Syracuse University Press, 2011), chap. 6, and A. Jennings and V. Simson, *The Lords of the Rings: Power, Money and Drugs in the Modern Olympics* (Transparency Books, 2012).

43. See, for example, the story provided by Ueberroth about payoffs to IOC members from South Korea in its successful pursuit of the 1988 Games (*Made in America,* p. 106).

44. See, for example, Helen Lenskyj, *Inside the Olympic Industry* (SUNY Press, 2000), chap. 1.

45. "Nagano Olympics Records Destroyed," CNNSI.com, January 15, 1999 (www.sportsillustrated.cnn.com/features/1999/year_in_review/flashbacks/olympics1/).

46. Even after the Salt Lake City scandal and the appointment of Mitt Romney to head the local organizing committee, the Salt Lake City OCOG was not above chicanery. While Romney had pledged "complete transparency," the committee's actions did not live up to its rhetoric. According to a *Boston Globe* report, "Most key records about the Games' internal workings were destroyed under the supervision of a staff member" shortly after the Olympics ended. Kenneth Bullock, a committee member who represented the Utah League of Cities and Towns stated: "Their [the Salt Lake OCOG] transparency became a black hole. It was nonexistent." Christopher Rowland and Callum Borchers, "Mitt Romney's '02 Olympics Short on Transparency," *Boston Globe,* July 24, 2012.

47. Michael Payne, *Olympic Turnaround* (London Business Press, 2005), p. 234.

48. A similar imbroglio unfurled earlier with regard to the split of corporate sponsorship revenues. After the IOC introduced its TOP program of exclusive sponsorships in 1985, the USOC argued that since most of the large sponsors were based in the United States (and, if they didn't sign with the IOC, they would do a national sponsorship deal), it was entitled to a disproportionate share of TOP revenues. The other NOCs, of course, strenuously disagreed. The IOC sponsorship negotiator was ISL, and ISL offered the USOC 20 percent of all TOP revenues. The USOC successfully held out for 30 percent, but not until after a significant amount of ill will had accumulated. See Barney and others, *Selling the Five Rings,* pp. 174–80.

49. This and other financial data on the Olympic Games are available in the *Olympic Marketing File* from various years and also the official IOC reports on each Olympics.

50. "IOC, USOC Finalize Revenue Deal," ESPN.com, May 24, 2012 (http://espn.go.com/olympics/story/_/id/7967000/ioc-usoc-resolve-differences-revenues). See also Barney and others, *Selling the Five Rings,* chap. 11.

51. Some estimates for Sochi expenditures go as high as $70 billion. Putin has not released a careful accounting of the investments, so even though the figure of $51 billion is frequently cited, there is no authoritative estimate. The matter is further complicated because the ruble-to-dollar exchange rate has fluctuated significantly during and subsequent to the games.

52. This estimate does not include an additional $600 million that Brazil is planning to spend on athlete training, with the goal of earning enough medals in 2016 to be in the top ten medal-winning countries at the Olympics. The country's announced goal is to win thirty medals, thirteen more than were won in 2012. Tariq Panja, "Brazil to Spend Record $600 Million to Boost Olympic Medal Hopes," Bloomberg.com, July 23, 2014 (http://brazil portal.wordpress.com/2014/07/24/brazil-to-spend-record-600-million-to-boost-olympic-medal-hopes/).

53. To be sure, the London Organizing Committee for the Olympic Games reported that it received only $700 million from the IOC, substantially less than the IOC numbers suggest. See, for example, "London Olympics 2012: Where Does the Money Come From—And Where's It Being Spent?," *The Guardian,* July 26, 2012 (www.theguardian.com/sport/datablog/2012/jul/26/london-2012-olympics-money).

54. IOC, *Olympic Marketing File,* 2014, pp. 7, 26.

55. Zjan Shirinian, "Rio 2016 'Top Priority' after World Cup, Pledges Brazilian President," *Inside the Games,* July 11, 2014 (www.insidethegames.biz/olympics/summer-olympics/2016/1021254-rio-2016-top-priority-after-world-cup-pledges-brazilian-president).

56. Argentina and Uruguay boycotted the 1938 World Cup in France because of an internal dispute over FIFA procedures. They each believed that FIFA's policy was to rotate the hosts between Europe and the Americas. Since

the 1934 competition was held in Italy, the choice of France for 1938 violated the presumed policy. Between 1958 and 2010, FIFA scrupulously followed the continental rotation policy, as discussed later in the text. Although it was not a boycott of the World Cup finals, in 1974 the Soviet team refused to travel to Chile for an intercontinental playoff match in protest over Pinochet's overthrow of Allende and the new regime's brutality.

57. For further discussion of soccer and violence, see Stefan Szymanski and Andrew Zimbalist, *National Pastime: How Americans Play Baseball and the Rest of the World Plays Soccer* (Brookings Institution Press, 2006); Franklin Foer, *How Soccer Explains the World* (New York: Harper Perennial, 2010); and David Goldblatt, *The Ball Is Round: A Global History of Soccer* (New York: Riverhead Books, 2008).

58. See, for example, Paul Darby, "Africa, the FIFA Presidency, and the Governance of World Football: 1974, 1998 and 2002," *Africa Today,* 2003.

59. "Qatar's 2022 World Cup Bid Hit with Fresh Corruption Claims, FIFA Refuses to Comment," *Sports Business Daily Global,* June 2, 2014. For an earlier report, see Claire Newell, Holly Watt, Claire Duffin, and Ben Bryant, "Qatar World Cup 2022 Investigation: Former Fifa Vice-President Jack Warner and Family Paid Millions," *The Telegraph,* March 21, 2014. Andrew Zimbalist, "Shameful Qatar Has Sold FIFA a Dummy," *Sunday Times,* March 8, 2015. Heidi Blake and Jonathan Calvert, *The Ugly Game: The Qatari Plot to Buy the World Cup* (London: Simon and Schuster, 2015). On the match-fixing scandal, see "FIFA Report on Match-Fixing Casts Shadow over This Month's World Cup in Brazil," *Sports Business Daily Global,* June 2, 2014.

60. It is interesting to note that FIFA's expenses during the previous four-year cycle were only $3.57 billion. That is, they increased by almost $2 billion while revenues grew by $1.5 billion. The increased expenditures reflect Blatter's doling out of higher compensation to members of the Executive Committee and larger subsidies to certain member countries apparently in order to solidify his control and re-election chances.

61. Following substantial pushback over the twelve new or fully renovated stadiums in Brazil, FIFA chiefs seem to be getting religion. A few days after the 2014 World Cup competition ended, Sepp Blatter announced that FIFA may ask Russia to build only ten instead of twelve new stadiums for the 2018 competition.

62. Dennis Coates, "World Cup Economics: What Americans Need to Know about a US World Cup," University of Maryland Baltimore County, Department of Economics Working Paper 10-121, pp. 18–20. For the 1994 World Cup in the United States, the only appreciable facility investments were $2.5 million to replace the artificial turf at the Silverdome outside Detroit, Michigan, and $2.8 million to slightly widen the field at the Cotton Bowl in Dallas, Texas. While most studies report that Germany spent under $1 billion on facilities to host the 2006 Cup, one article cites a figure of $1.9 billion. See Victor Matheson, "Were the billions the Brazilians Spent on World Cup Stadiums Worth

It?," Five-Thirty-Eight.com, 2014 (http://fivethirtyeight.com/features/were-the-billions-brazil-spent-on-world-cup-stadiums-worth-it/). This article seems to be confounding original stadium construction costs and facility preparation expenses for the 2006 World Cup.

Chapter 3

1. Ex ante methodology means that the estimated impact is forecast before the event takes place. To create such an estimate, one must make assumptions about the number of foreign visitors, number of days spent in the city or country, amount of spending per day, and so on. It is a simple matter to inflate the estimates by making unrealistic assumptions. As discussed in the text, there are numerous other issues with this methodology.

2. To be sure, there is also a literature of ex ante event analysis that looks at how financial markets respond to the announcement of a city being selected as a mega-event host. The findings in this literature are mixed. In both Beijing and Sydney, the national stock markets did not experience a lasting boost from the awarding of the games to their cities, although the share prices of construction companies in New South Wales did rise. See, for example, R. Brooks and S. Davidson, "The Sydney Olympic Games Announcement and the Australian Stock Market Reaction," *Applied Economics Letters* 7, no. 12 (2000); M. Leeds, J. Mirikitani, and D. Tang, "Rational Exuberance? An Event Analysis of the 2008 Olympic Announcement," *International Journal of Sport Finance* 4, no. 1 (2009); and N. Veraros, E. Kasimati, and P. Dawson, "The 2004 Olympic Games Announcement and Its Effect on the Athens and Milan Stock Exchanges," *Applied Economics Letters* 11, no. 12 (2004).

3. These problems are potentially ameliorated by the use of Computer General Equilibrium (CGE) models, which incorporate the effect of price changes on production coefficients and also recognize resource constraints. See, for one, James Giesecke and John Madden, "Evidence-Based Regional Economic Policy Analysis: The Role of CGE Modelling," *Cambridge Journal of Regions, Economy and Society* 6 (2013), pp. 285–301.

4. Most input-output models contain highly aggregated data on imports and exports.

5. John J. Siegfried and Andrew Zimbalist, "The Economics of Sports Facilities and Their Communities," *Journal of Economic Perspectives* 14, no. 3 (2000): 95–114.

6. See www.travelingguide.com/tourism/2008statistics.

7. This computation is based on the standard finance formula, Payment = Principal * $[r(1 + r)^n/((1 + r)^n - 1)]$, wherein part of the principal, as well as the interest, is paid off each year, such that the payments are spread out equally over the thirty-year period of the loan. The interest rate is denoted by r and the number of years by n.

8. Sources for table 3-1 follow: A. Feddersen, A. Grotzinger, and W. Maennig (2009), "Investment in Stadia and Regional Economic Development: Evidence from FIFA World Cup 2006 Stadia," *International Journal of Sport Finance* 4 (4), pp. 221–39; R. Baade and V. Matheson (2004), "The Quest for the Cup: Assessing the Economic Impact of the World Cup," *Regional Studies* 38, pp. 343–54; S. Du Plessis and W. Maennig (2011), "The 2010 World Cup High Frequency Data Economics: Effects on International Tourism and Awareness for South Africa," *Development Southern Africa* 28 (3), pp. 349–65; F. Hagn and W. Maennig (2008), "Employment Effects of the Football World Cup 1974 in Germany," *Labour Economics* 15 (5), pp. 1062–75; F. Hagn and W. Maennig (2009), "Large Sport Events and Unemployment: The Case of the 2006 Soccer World Cup in Germany," *Applied Economics* 41 (25), pp. 3295–302; S. Allmers and W. Maennig (2009), "Economic Impacts of the FIFA Soccer World Cups in France 1998, Germany 2006, and Outlook for South Africa 2010," *Eastern Economic Journal* 35 (4), pp. 500–19; S. Szymanski (2002), "The Economic Impact of the World Cup," *World Economics* 3 (1), pp. 169–77; S. du Plessis and C. Venter, "The Home Team Scores! A First Assessment of the Economic Impact of World Cup 2010," Stellenbosch Working Paper Series WP21/2010 (Stellenbosch University, Department of Economics); S. Jasmand and W. Maennig (2008), "Regional Income and Employment Effects of the 1972 Munich Summer Olympic Games," *Regional Studies* 42 (7), pp. 991–1002; P. K. Porter and D. Fletcher (2008), "The Economic Impact of the Olympic Games: Ex Ante Predictions and Ex Post Reality," *Journal of Sport Management* 22 (4), pp. 470–86; A. Feddersen and W. Maennig (2013), "Employment Effects of the Olympic Games in Atlanta 1996 Reconsidered," *International Journal of Sport Finance* 8 (2), pp. 95–111; A. Feddersen and W. Maennig (2012), "Sectoral Labour Market Effects of the 2006 FIFA World Cup," *Labour Economics* 19(6), pp. 860–69; J. Giesecke and J. Madden (2011), "Modelling the Economic Impacts of the Sydney Olympics in Retrospect: Game Over for the Bonanza Story?," *Economic Papers* 30 (2), pp. 218–32; S. B. Billings and J. S. Holladay (2012), "Should Cities Go for the Gold? The Long-Term Impacts of Hosting the Olympics," *Economic Inquiry* 50 (3), pp. 642–47; R. von Rekowsky (2013), "Are the Olympics a Golden Opportunity for Investors?," *Leadership Series—Investment Insights* (Boston: Fidelity Investments, August); R. Baumann, Bryon Engelhardt, and Victor A. Matheson (2012), "Employment Effects of the 2002 Winter Olympics in Salt Lake City, Utah," *Journal of Economics and Statistics* 232 (3), pp. 308–17; Robert Baumann and Bryon Eldon Engelhardt (2012), "Labor Market Effects of the World Cup: A Sectoral Analysis," in *International Handbook on the Economics of Mega Sporting Events,* ed. Wolfgang Maennig and Andrew S. Zimbalist (Cheltenham, U.K.: Edward Elgar), pp. 385–400; R. A. Baade and V. Matheson, "Bidding for the Olympics: Fool's Gold?," in *Transatlantic Sport,* ed. Carlos Pestana Barros, Muradali Ibrahímo, and Stefan Szymanski (London: Edward Elgar, 2002), pp. 127–51; J. L. Hotchkiss, R. E. Moore, and S. M.

Zobay (2003), "Impact of the 1996 Summer Olympic Games on Employment and Wages in Georgia," *Southern Economic Journal* 69(3), pp. 691–704.

9. J. L. Hotchkiss and others, "Impact of the 1996 Summer Olympic Games on Employment and Wages in Georgia," *Southern Economic Journal* 69, no. 3 (2003): 691–704. The Hotchkiss and colleagues' study may be interpreted to be picking up medium-term employment gains, as it goes four years past the 1996 Games. The authors claim that the main employment effect of the games begins to occur two years before the games, so they compare performance between two periods, 1985–93 and 1994–2000. They arrived at this division by testing dummy variables for different period breakdowns beginning with 1990, the year the IOC awarded the games to Atlanta, and then picking the breakdown that best fit the data. This technique arguably involves data mining and is further questionable because a good deal of Olympic construction takes place more than two years in advance of the games. It is also noteworthy that they do not conduct separate tests for counties with venues and counties nearby counties with venues. Also, without explanation, in two cases the counties included are not contiguous with counties with venues. These are included without explanation. Further, there are problems with serial correlation in their regressions. See also Arne Feddersen and Wolfgang Maennig, "Employment Effects of the Olympic Games in Atlanta 1996 Reconsidered," *International Journal of Sport Finance* 8, no. 2 (2013): 95–111.

10. Stan Du Plessis and Wolfgang Maennig, "The 2010 World Cup High-Frequency Data Economics: Effects on International Tourism and Awareness for South Africa," *Development Southern Africa* 28, no. 3 (2011): 349–65; Thomas Peeters, Victor Matheson, and Stefan Szymanski, "Tourism and the 2010 World Cup: Lessons for Developing Countries," *Journal of African Economies*, January 2014, pp. 1–31.

11. Estimates for the 2010 South African World Cup have the average foreign tourist spending a total of $1,650 in the country, while estimates for the German World Cup in 2006 put total spending per visitor at $1,286. Our estimate in the example is in the upper part of this range, at $1,500. See Peeters and others, "Tourism and the 2010 World Cup."

12. As discussed later in the text, Brazil reported that the number of visitors during the period of the 2014 World Cup, including a few weeks before the beginning of the matches, was 1 million, denoting a gain of around half a million above normal levels. The majority of these visitors came from neighboring South American countries with teams in the final sixteen. Anecdotal reports suggest that these visitors in large numbers stayed on the beaches and trailers, used public bathrooms, and spent little money.

13. Michel de Nooij, "Mega Sport Events: A Probabilistic Social Cost-Benefit Analysis of Bidding for the Games," *Journal of Sports Economics* 15, no. 4 (2014): 412. Indirect costs are estimated at an additional $142 million.

14. The consulting studies were undertaken by the engineering firm, DHV,

and an economic advising firm, Rebel. Together their studies produced a base case cost/benefit analysis that projected a negative net present value from hosting of between –1.1 billion and –1.8 billion euros. Communication from Enno Gerdes of the Rebel consulting firm.

15. Michael Feblowitz, "The Legacy Games: Social and Economic Impacts for Olympic Cities," *Social Impact Research Experience Journal,* January 1, 2012, p. 20.

16. European Tour Operators Association (ETOA), "Olympic Hotel Demand," ETOA Report 2010 (www.etoa.org).

17. Bent Flyvbjerg and Allison Stewart, "Olympic Proportions: Cost and Cost Overrun at the Olympics 1960–2012," Said Business School Working Papers, University of Oxford, 2012.

18. See www.latimes.com/business/la-fi-rio-high-prices-20140314,0,543820 .story#axzz2w95MLCBY.

19. For more on the human costs of poor design associated with mega-events, see, for example, Christopher Gaffney's June 30, 2014, discussion of the lack of design integration of Brazil's World Cup stadiums, surrounded by parking lots, in their communities, at geostadia.com. An extensive treatment of the human costs associated with mega-events can be found in Dave Zirin, *Brazil's Dance with the Devil* (Chicago: Haymarket Books, 2014), chaps. 6 and 7.

20. The reported balanced *operating* budget or small *operating* surplus in Atlanta 1996, Salt Lake City 2002, Vancouver 2010, London 2012, and Sochi 2014, among others, all depended on government subsidies. See, for one, The Brattle Group, *Analysis of the Boston 2024 Proposed Summer Olympic Plans.* Prepared for the Commonweath of Massachusetts Office of the Governor, President of the Senate, and Speaker of the House, August 17, 2015.

21. Kavetsos and Szymanski, using survey evidence, considered three mega-events in Europe and found that there is a short-term increase in self-defined happiness in two of the three host countries, but that the effect is not lasting. They also found that having the home team win does not produce a significant increase in self-defined happiness. Georgios Kavetsos and Stefan Szymanski, "National Well-Being and International Sports Events," *Journal of Economic Psychology* 31, no. 2 (April 2010): 158–71.

22. Andrew Zimbalist, "Shameful Qatar Has Sold FIFA a Dummy," *Sunday Times* [London], March 8, 2015.

23. *Guardian* report cited in "Pay Slips Show Qatar World Cup Stadium Workers Earn as Little as $0.76 an Hour," *Sports Business Daily Global,* July 31, 2014.

24. Arrivals at the Atlanta International Airport did increase in the four years following 1996, but they increased at a slower rate than in the previous four years. The Atlanta airport is a Delta Airlines hub and serves as an entry point into the United States for fifty-one countries, so there are many factors that affect Atlanta's airport arrivals besides the Olympic Games. P. K.

Porter and D. Fletcher (2008), "The Economic Impact of the Olympic Games: Ex Ante Predictions and Ex Post Reality," *Journal of Sport Management* 22, no. 4 (2008): 470–86.

25. ETOA, "Olympic Hotel Demand," ETOA Report 2010 (www.etoa.org).

26. In 1996 in Georgia, home state of the host city Atlanta, hotel occupancy rates fell from 73 percent in the previous year to 68 percent. Sydney in 2000 saw hotel occupancy rates fall steadily as the games approached, from 83 percent in March to 68 percent in July and August, before a modest recovery to 80 percent during the games themselves. Cited in Mark Perryman, "Do the Olympics Boost the Economy? Studies Show the Impact Is Likely Negative," *Daily Beast,* July 7, 2012 (www.thedailybeast.com/articles/2012/07/30/do-the-olympics-boost-the-economy-studies-show-the-impact-is-likely--negative.html), p. 7.

27. Ibid.

28. M. Saayman and R. Rossouw, "The Economic Value of the 2010 Soccer World Cup" (www.actacommercil.co.za/index.php/acta/article/viewfile/55/55).

29. ETOA, "Olympics and Tourism," ETOA Report 2006 (www.etoa.org).

30. Vancouver bed nights followed a similar pattern, reaching 8.415 million in 2010, below the 8.91 million level set in 2007.

31. *Statistics Canada*, various years (www.statcan.gc.ca/start-debut-eng.html).

32. Talia Marcopoto, "Brazil Claims 'Victory' in World Cup," CNN.com, July 16, 2014.

33. See, for example, Eduardo Campos, "Gasto de Turista Estrangeiro Pode Chegar a R$2,4 Bi," *De Brasilia,* July 16, 2014 (www.valor.com.br/financas/3616670/gasto-de-turista-estrangeiro-pode-chegar-r-24-bi#ixzz37jqFNkjL).

34. Author conversations with Luiz Martins de Melo, Christopher Gaffney, and various journalists covering the World Cup.

35. Foreign tourism in Brazil had been growing at 5.7 percent annually from 2009 through 2012.

Chapter 4

1. Christopher Gaffney, "Between Discourse and Reality: The Un--Sustainability of Mega-Event Planning," *Sustainability* 5 (2013): 3926–40.

2. IOC publications enumerate the perceived legacy benefits after each Olympic Games. See, for instance, IOC, *Fact Sheet: Legacies of the Games.* Update December 2013. See also Grant Thornton, "Report 5: Post-Games Evaluation: Meta-Evaluation of the Impacts and Legacy of the London 2012 Olympic Games and Paralympic Games," July 2013.

3. Points 15 and 16 were added in a June 2014 public relations brochure titled "What You Need to Know about the 2014 FIFA World Cup Brazil," put out by the Secretariat for Social Communication, Presidency of the Federative Republic of Brazil. The brochure was prepared by a New York City public relations firm, Fleishman-Hillard.

4. European Tour Operators Association (ETOA), *Olympic Report,* ETOA Report 2006 (www.etoa.org), p. 6.

5. Ibid.

6. J. R. Brent Ritchie and Brian H. Smith, "The Impact of a Mega-Event on Host Region Awareness: A Longitudinal Study," *Journal of Travel Research* 30, no. 1 (1991): 3–10.

7. ETOA, "Olympics and Tourism," ETOA Report 2010 (www.etoa.org), p. 1. It is perhaps reasonable to question the objectivity of the ETOA. On the one hand, as a tourist trade association, one would suspect that the ETOA would be a proponent of any event that lifted tourism and hence would be inclined to be supportive of the Olympics if the games indeed lift tourism. On the other hand, since the Olympics tend to concentrate any effects within one city of one country, it may be that the majority of ETOA members oppose them. I am not in a position to evaluate the internal politics of the ETOA, and it seems reasonable, a priori, to assume that it is in the best interests of the ETOA to understand the true economic impact from hosting the games.

8. The report, *The Sydney Olympics and Foreign Attitudes to Australia,* was written by authors that included Nancy Rivenburgh, a former professor at Barcelona's Centre for Olympic Studies. It is cited by Perryman in "Do the Olympics Boost the Economy?," p. 7.

9. Cited by Perryman, ibid.

10. ETOA, "Olympics and Tourism," ETOA Report 2006 (www.etoa.org), p. 15.

11. Cited in ibid.

12. Tourism New South Wales, "Facts and Figures" (corporate.tourism.nsw.gov.au/Facts_And_Figures_p10.aspx).

13. ETOA, "Olympics and Tourism," ETOA Report 2010 (www.etoa.org), p. 3.

14. Jon Teigland, "Impacts on Tourism from Mega-Events: The Case of Winter Olympic Games," *Western Norway Research Institute,* October 1996, p. 45.

15. ETOA, "Olympics and Tourism," ETOA Report 2010 (www.etoa.org), p. 3.

16. A. Rose and M. Spiegel, "The Olympic Effect," *Economic Journal* 121 (2011): 652–77. Interestingly, another 2011 study by Billings and Holladay found that Olympic host cities between 1950 and 2005 did not experience any increase in trade openness (or real GDP) as a result of hosting. S. Billings and J. Holladay, "Should Cities Go for the Gold? The Long-Term Impacts of Hosting the Olympics," *Economic Inquiry* 50, no. 3 (2012): 754–72.

17. Wonho Song, using the Rose and Spiegel data set, found increases to exports and to tourism. However, these findings suffer from the same selection bias found in Rose and Spiegel. W. Song, "Impacts of Olympics on Exports and Tourism," *Journal of Economic Development* 35, no. 4 (2010).

18. W. Maennig and F. Richter, "Exports and Olympic Games: Is There a Signal Effect?," *Journal of Sports Economics* 13, no. 6 (2012): 636.

19. Robert Baumann, T. Ciavarra, and B. Engelhardt, "An Examination of

Spectator Sports and Crime Rates," *Economics and Labour Relations Review* 23, no. 2 (2012): 83–97.

20. For instance, during the World Cup in Germany (2006) and in South Africa (2010), sex trafficking is reported to have increased between 30 and 40 percent. See "Nuns, Backed by the Pope, Warn of Human Trafficking at World Cup," Reuters, May 20, 2014. (www.reuters.com/article/2014/05/20/us-soccer-world-trafficking-idUSBREA4JDIS20140520), and Chen Jiang, "Forced Prostitution and Modern Slavery: Brazil's Response," Council on Hemispheric Relations, April 6, 2015 (www.coha.org/forced-prostitution-and-modern-slavery-Brazils-Response).

21. In São Paulo there was also a metro line built that goes out to the new stadium and adjacent real estate development.

22. Of the total spending on the World Cup in excess of $15 billion, approximately $4 billion was spent on road, bus, and rail transportation, $3.8 billion on airport upgrades, $315 million on port improvement and $180 million on telecommunications. Deputy Sport Minister Luis Fernandes emphasizes the importance of the investment to extend the nation's broadband network to Manaus for the Cup. This was a minor investment and certainly could and would have been undertaken without hosting the World Cup. "Seeking a Silver Lining," *Sports Pro*, July 2014, pp. 56–65.

23. Gaffney, "Between Discourse and Reality," p. 3933.

24. Associated Press, "Rio's Olympic Golf Course in Turmoil," September 4, 2014 (http://espn.go.com/espn/print?id=11463567&type=story).

25. Gaffney, "Between Discourse and Reality," 3928.

26. Christopher Gaffney, "Hunting White Elephants/Caçando Elefantes Brancos," blog entry, June 6, 2014 (www.geostadia.com/).

27. The idiom "white elephant" derives from an ancient tradition of Southeast Asian monarchies. White elephants were very rare and were regarded as sacred. If the king gave one as a gift, it was an honor. However, the gift was a terrible burden to the person who received it. He had to feed and care for that elephant throughout its long life.

28. *CBS News*, "Olympic Challenge: How Do Host Cities Fare after the Games?," February 24, 2014 (www.cbsnews.com/news/olympic-challenge-host-do-host-cities-fare-after-the-games).

29. Ibid.

30. Doug Saunders, "Is the World Cup a Giant Waste of Money?," *Globe and Mail*, May 31, 2014 (www.realclearworld.com/2014/06/12/brazil_needs_more_than_a_world_cup_win_159149.html).

31. Perryman, "Do the Olympics Boost the Economy?"

32. In 2014, however, Barcelona turned its Olympic Stadium at Montjuic into an upscale sports theme park.

33. Gaffney, "Between Discourse and Reality," p. 3929.

34. *CBS News*, "Olympic Challenge: How Do Host Cities Fare after the Games?"

35. Juliet Macur, "When Dazzle of Stadiums Gives Way to Desolation," *New York Times,* June 29, 2014.

36. E. Cottle, ed., *South Africa's World Cup: A Legacy for Whom?* (University of KwaZulu-Natal Press, 2011).

37. Ian Austen, "Vancouver Journal: A $1 billion Hangover from an Olympic Party," *New York Times,* February 24, 2010 (www.nytimes.com/2010/02/25/ sports/olympics/25vancouver.html?_r=0). Although all the records have not yet been released, the author may have been too ebullient in his estimate of the public debt incurred. The provincial assembly did have to pass special legislation to provide almost a half billion dollars for the completion of the village after the financier Fortress Investor Group pulled out. "Vancouver Assumes Financial Control of Olympic Village," Associated Press, February 18, 2009.

Chapter 5

1. Anna Sanchez and others, "Barcelona 1992: International Events and Housing Rights: A Focus on the Olympic Games" (Geneva: Center on Housing Rights and Evictions [COHRE], 2007), p. 20. See also Nadia Fava, "Tourism and the City Image: The Barcelona Olympic Case" (Universitat de Girona, Spain, 2012); COBI, "Barcelona: Urban Transformation and '92 Olympic Games," 2005 (http://www.mt.usi.ch/barcelona-123372.pdf); and London East Research Institute, "A Lasting Legacy for London?" (London, May 2007).

2. Sanchez and others, "Barcelona 1992," p. 21.

3. Of course, once the Olympic project was undertaken, the PGM was modified. It is also worth noting that Barcelona had a tradition of using mega-events to help transform the city. The 1929 World Exposition in Barcelona led to the construction of Parc Montjuic, and the 1888 International Expo led to the creation of the city's central park, Parc de la Ciutadella.

4. Ferran Brunet, "The Economic Impact of the Barcelona Olympic Games, 1986–2004," in *Barcelona: L'herencia deis Jocs,* ed. Miguel de Moragas and Miguel Botella (Barcelona: Centre d'Estudis Olimpics, 2002), p. 14. The percentages of private and public spending differ according to the source. The discrepancies are most likely a product of what investments are considered to be part of the Olympic effort. For example, Barcelona Holding Olímpic S.A. made the following expenditure calculations: 33.8 percent of total Olympic activities were financed by private sector investment and 66.2 percent of total Olympic activities were financed by public sector investment. See Barcelona Holding Olímpic S.A., "Los Juegos Olímpicos Como Generadores de Inversión (1986–1992)" (Barcelona, June 1992), p. 7. In any event, it is clear that the share of private funding was substantial.

5. John Gold and Margaret Gold, "Olympic Cities: Regeneration, City Rebranding and Changing Urban Agenda," *Geography Compass* 2, no. 1 (2008): 307.

6. Ferran Brunet, "An Economic Analysis of the Barcelona '92 Olympic Games" (Barcelona: Centre d'Estudis Olimpics, 1995).

7. European Tour Operators Association (ETOA), "Olympic Report," July 2005 (www.etoa.org), pp. 11–14.

8. Iris HIllier and Rafael Isun, "Barcelona: Before and after the '92 Olympic Games," February 2010 (www.insights.org.uk), p. 3.

9. Josep Maria Montaner, "The Barcelona Model Reviewed: Leading Up to the 1992 Olympic Games," lecture presented at the "Learning from Barcelona" conference, Birkbeck, Stratford, January 28, 2011, p. 5.

10. Unlike in other mega-events, however, there were no forced evictions in Barcelona, and those who did relocate were provided with other homes or housing subsidies. Unfortunately, many were relocated to distant areas, often compromising their employment situation. Sanchez and others, "Barcelona 1992," p. 29.

11. Ibid., p. 48.

12. Other criticisms of Barcelona's plan include the 40 kilometers of ring roads surrounding the city (which promoted personal car use at the expense of public transport and did little to alleviate inner-city traffic), the widespread use of migrant labor with long hours, and the high import component of building materials for the planned construction. See the LSE Study on Barcelona games, 2010; and Miguelez and Carrasquer, "The Repercussion of the Olympic Games on Labour" (Barcelona: Centre d'Estudis Olimpics, 1995).

13. See "2004 Universal Forum of Cultures" (en.wikipedia.org/wiki/2004_Universal_Forum_of_Cultures), p. 3.

14. Parks, Promenades & Planning: Brand Management with the 21st Century Urban Waterfront, "Barcelona: Event as Catalyst" (urbanwaterfront.blogspot.com), p. 6.

15. M. Müller, "State Dirigisme in Megaprojects: Governing the 2014 Winter Olympics in Sochi," *Environment and Planning A* 43, no. 9 (2011): 2091–108.

16. RT.com, February 4, 2013.

17. Jules Boykoff, "Celebration Capitalism and the Sochi 2014 Winter Olympics," *Olympika: The International Journal of Olympic Studies* 22 (2013): 54. A number of news reports put the price tag at $51 billion already in February 2013. For instance, see an Associated Press article of February 5, 2013, published in the *Washington Times* and elsewhere (www.washingtontimes.com/news/2013/feb/5/one-year-out-sochi-gearing-winter-olympics-spotlig/). These news reports appear to be based on the last official announcement in January 2013 of a price tag for the Sochi Olympics (at 1.526 trillion rubles—not including operational costs and security) by Sports Minister Vitaliy Mutko. No official figures have been made public since then. This lacuna also helps to explain speculations about a much higher price. See "Zatraty na podgotovku k Olimpijskim igram v Soči sostavjat 1,526 trln rublej," Gazeta.ru, January 2, 2013 (www.gazeta.ru/sport/2013/02/01/a_4949973.shtml).

18. Quoted in Boykoff, "Celebration Capitalism and the Sochi 2014 Winter Olympics," p. 39.

19. Boris Nemtsov, a former Russian deputy prime minister who was fatally gunned down on the streets of Moscow in February 2015, alleged that between $25 billion and $30 billion of the $50 billion-plus cost of the Sochi games was due to manipulated contracts and venality to the benefit of "oligarchs and companies close to Mr. Putin." Nataliya Vasilyeva, "Russian Oligarchs Foot Most of 2014 Sochi Olympics," Associated Press, May 20, 2013. See also *BBC News*, May 30, 2013, and *HBO Real Sports*, November 19, 2013.

20. Stephanie Baker and Ilya Arkhipov,"Rich Russians Sparring with Putin over $48 billion Olympics Bet," Bloomberg.com, November 26, 2013.

21. Thomas Grove, "Special Report: Russia's $50 billion Olympic Gamble," Reuters, February 21, 2013.

22. Ed Hula III, "Investment Bank Asks for Bailout on Sochi Losses," *Around the Rings,* July 7, 2014.

23. Human Rights Watch, "Race to the Bottom: Exploitation of Migrant Workers ahead of Russia's 2014 Winter Olympic Games in Sochi" (February 6, 2013).

24. Daniel Sandford, "Putin's Olympic Steamroller in Sochi," *BBC News Europe,* February 6, 2013.

25. Boykoff, "Celebration Capitalism and the Sochi 2014 Winter Olympics," p. 56.

26. Nikolas von Twickel, "Sochi Is a Hard Nut to Crack for PR Gurus," *Moscow Times,* February 7, 2013.

27. Steven Myers, "Putin's Olympic Fever Dream," *New York Times Magazine,* January 22, 2014.

28. Nataliya Vasilyeva, "Sochi Critics Get Terrorist Treatment," Associated Press, December 18, 2013.

29. M. Müller, "(Im-)Mobile Policies: Why Sustainability Went Wrong in the 2014 Olympics in Sochi," *European Urban and Regional Studies* 22 (2015): 13.

30. In the Soviet era, many workers' unions also had retreats in Sochi. Today Sochi is viewed as the patriotic place to go, and the Russian elite feel almost obligated to spend some time there on vacation.

31. Both quotations from Alexey Eremenko, "Can Sochi Become a World Class Resort after Olympics?," *Russia & India Report,* December 20, 2013 (indus.in/economics/2013/12/20).

32. Center for Security Analysis and Prevention, "Evaluation of the Investment Risks in the Field of Tourism Construction Industry in Sochi" (www.cbap.cz/?p=1253&lang=en#more-1253).

33. David Segal, "Now What? A City Fears a Flameout," *New York Times,* February 23, 2014 (www.nytimes.com/2014/02/24/sports/olympics/sochi-olympics-construction-weighs-on-citys-future.html).

34. Ibid.

35. Ibid.

36. Nick Butler, "Tax Breaks Announced for All Sochi 2014 Buildings in Bid to Reduce Financial Burden," *Inside the Games,* May 13, 2014 (insidethegames.com).

37. David Owen, "Sochi Unveils $261 Million Profit," *Inside the Games,* June 19, 2014 (insidethegames.com).

38. M. Müller and S. D. Wolfe, "World Cup Russia 2018: Already the Most Expensive Ever?," *Russian Analytical Digest* 150 (2014): 2–6.

Chapter 6

1. To be precise, economies of scale would apply to the double use of Maracanã Stadium or other facilities as well as to administrative savings where the work of preparing for the World Cup and for the Olympics is duplicative. Where the work for the two events is distinctive (they are considered separate products), then any administrative savings would be considered to be economies of scope.

2. Maracanã will be used for the opening and closing ceremonies, and for soccer matches, during the 2016 Olympics. The nearby João Havelange Stadium, which was built for the 2007 Pan American Games, after a very expensive renovation is scheduled to be used for track and field events in 2016.

3. Simon Romero, "Brazilians Go Back to Real Life," *New York Times,* July 13, 2014 (www.nytimes.com/2014/07/14/sports/worldcup/world-cup-2014-brazil-was-embarrassed-but-an-argentina-victory-would-have-been-intolerable.html).

4. Dom Phillips, "Brazilian Officials Are Giving Up on Some Unfinished World Cup Projects," *Washington Post,* May 7, 2014 (www.washingtonpost.com/world/the_americas/brazilian-officials-are-giving-up-on-some-unfinished-world-cup-projects/2014/05/07/cde52c2c-d17e-11e3-937f-d3026234b51c_story.html).

5. Emily Godard, "At Least Two Dead as Overpass Collapses in Brazil World Cup City," *Inside the Games,* July 3, 2014 (insidethegames.com).

6. Patricia Ray Mallen, "Brazil Skirts Organizational Disaster with the Most Expensive World Cup Ever," *International Business Times,* April 11, 2014 (ibtimes.com).

7. Quoted in "Brazilian Left Wanting by Flawed FIFA World Cup Investment," Reuters, May 19, 2014.

8. According to Christopher Gaffney, the government was originally contemplating using eighteen different cities and stadiums for the World Cup. See Gaffney, "Between Discourse and Reality: The Un-Sustainability of Mega-Event Planning," *Sustainability* 5 (2013): 3926–40.

9. M. Bastos and R. Mattos, "Esportes," *Folha de São Paulo,* São Paulo, May 19, 2011.

10. Ibid.

11. Dave Zirin, *Brazil's Dance with the Devil* (Chicago: Haymarket Books, 2014), p. 33.

12. Tony Manfred, "Brazil's World Cup Stadiums Are Becoming White Elephants a Year Later," *Business Insider*, May 13, 2015 (www.businessinsider.com/brazil-world-cup-stadiums-one-year-later-2015-5).

13. Zirin, *Brazil's Dance with the Devil*, p. 17.

14. Of course, most policies are likely to create winners and losers. The key is to understand the net welfare effect on a community. The experience of Maria Oliveira is not offered as definitive evidence that it was bad policy to build the stadium; rather, it is offered as evidence that often there are overlooked costs.

15. Juliet Macur, "When Dazzle of Stadiums Gives Way to Desolation," *New York Times*, June 29, 2014.

16. Tariq Panja, "Brazil's Flamengo Won't Make 'Stupid' Deal to Return to Maracanã," Bloomberg (www.bloomberg.com), June 18, 2013.

17. Brian Homewood, "Not Much Football to Look Forward to in Brasília," Reuters, July 7, 2014.

18. Manfred, "Brazil's World Cup Stadiums Are Becoming White Elephants a Year Later."

19. Bradley Brooks, "High Cost, Corruption Claims Mar Brazil World Cup," Associated Press, May 12, 2014.

20. Ibid.

21. Ibid.

22. The capacity of Morumbi stadium is over 80,000 and is the home field of Brazil's first division team, São Paulo FC. The stadium was built in 1952.

23. Tales Azzoni, "Brazil Holds Final Stadium Tests for World Cup," Associated Press, May 19, 2014.

24. Interview with Kfouri by Tulio Velho Barreto, *Colectiva* (www.colectiva.org), April–June 2012.

25. Some estimates for the renovation at Maracanã Stadium for the Pan American Games go above $200 million. According to Christopher Gaffney, the Pan American Games went ten times over budget. C. Gaffney, "Mega-Events and Socio-Spatial Dynamics in Rio de Janeiro, 1919–2016," *Journal of Latin American Geography* 9, no. 1 (2010).

26. Thêmis Aragão and Wolfgang Maennig, "Mega Sporting Events, Real Estate, and Urban Social Economics: The Case of Brazil, 2014/2016," Hamburg Contemporary Economic Discussions No. 47 (University of Hamburg, 2014). See also Zirin, *Brazil's Dance with the Devil*, chap. 1.

27. Dave Zirin, "Dispatches from Brazil's World Cup: 'No One Lives Here Anymore,' *The Nation*, June 15, 2014 (www.thenation.com/blog/180239/dispatches-brazils-world-cup-no-one-lives-here-anymore). For an interesting discussion of life in favelas, the threat of razing several of them for the World Cup or Olympics, and local movements to save them, see Zirin, *Brazil's Dance*

with the Devil, chap. 7. For historical background on the favelas and the recent eviction process, see Theresa Williamson and Mauricio Hora, "In the Name of the Future, Rio is Destroying Its Past," *New York Times*, August 12, 2012.

28. Batista is under investigation by the federal police for alleged financial wrongdoings. His $60 billion EBX empire, including interests in oil, mining, and logistics, crumbled in 2013. See *SportsPro Magazine*, June 2014, p. 31.

29. Panja, "Brazil's Flamengo Won't Make 'Stupid' Deal."

30. The Gini coefficient measures actual inequality relative to perfect equality. It ranges from 0 to 1, with lower numbers representing more equality.

31. Aragão and Maennig, "Mega Sporting Events," p. 18.

32. More precisely, the housing deficit was calculated by the João Pinheiro Foundation at 522,607 units in 2008. See Aragão and Maennig, "Mega Sporting Events," p. 12. On the callousness of the eviction process and its connection to private profit, see Williamson and Hora, "In the Name of the Future."

33. James Montague, "World Cup Only Benefits Outsiders, Say Brazil Protesters," CNN.com, June 18, 2013.

34. As of June 2013, the projected costs on infrastructure and stadiums for the 2014 World Cup were as follows: $5.8 billion for transportation, $2.9 billion for stadiums (likely to have ended up close to $5 billion), $2.8 billion for ports and airports, $2.3 billion for security and health, $1.9 billion for telecommunications and energy, and $900 million for new hotels in host cities. These items total to $16.6 billion and do not include future cost overruns and operational expenses during the games. *Sports Business Journal*, June 17–23, 2013, p. 19.

35. Cited in *Sports Business Daily Global*, February 24, 2014.

36. Quoted in Marina Amaral and Natalia Viana, "Why Are Brazilians Protesting the World Cup?," *The Nation*, June 21, 2013.

37. Facing the threat of additional layoffs, the transit workers in São Paulo agreed not to continue their strike on June 11, but workers at Rio's municipal and international airports declared a twenty-four-hour strike for the opening day of the World Cup, June 12. A court order required the union to maintain 80 percent staffing at each airport or face a heavy fine. Meanwhile, the hackers' group Anonymous claimed it "attacked a large number of websites associated with the World Cup, including Bank of Brazil's and that of the country's military police." There were also violent clashes between protesters and police in front of São Paulo's World Cup stadium before the opening match. See www.espnfc.us/fifa-world-cup/story/1874614/rio-de-janeiro-airport-workers-go-on-strike.

38. Vanessa Barbara, "Brazil vs. Brazil," *New York Times*, June 26, 2014.

39. Ricardo Sennes, "Will Brazil Get What It Expects from the World Cup?," Atlantic Council Policy Brief (Washington, June 2014).

40. By another accounting, Brazil's security forces were considerably more extensive. A special report in the magazine *Sport Pro* in July 2014 (p. 65) had the following to say: "The heart of Brazil's World Cup security operation across all 12 cities is the National Integration Command and Control Centre (CICCN),

located in the capital, Brasília. The giant control room there features 56 monitors connected up to key locations across the country. The CICCN is effectively a hub, gathering, processing and responding to information provided by 27 mobile command centres, 36 elevated observation links and 157,000 agents, including law enforcement officers and members of Brazil's armed forces. 57,000 members of the military . . . will be involved."

41. The London security bill included £514 million for venue-level security and £455 million for general security. Converted at the August 2012 pound/dollar exchange rate, this comes to $1.52 billion, not counting the security provided for the three months of the torch relay leading up to the games. National Audit Office, *The London 2012 Olympic Games*, report ordered by the House of Commons, December 2012, p. 24.

42. National Audit Office, "The London 2012 Olympic Games and Paralympic Games: Post-Games Review," Report by the Comptroller and Auditor General (London, December 5, 2012), p. 6. Reportedly, the United States was still concerned and sent 500 FBI agents to London to safeguard security. Jules Boykoff, "What Is the Real Price of the London Olympics?," *The Guardian,* April 4, 2012. Dave Zirin cites much higher estimates of London's security forces: "Forty-eight thousand security forces. Thirteen thousand five hundred troops. Surface-to-air missiles stationed on top of residential apartment buildings. A sonic weapon that disperses crowds by creating 'headsplitting pain.' Unmanned drones peering down from the skies. A safe zone cordoned off by an eleven-mile electrified fence, ringed with trained agents and fifty-five teams of attack dogs" (*Brazil's Dance with the Devil*, p. 164).

43. Interestingly, although FIFA took out withholding taxes on behalf of South Africa from the hundreds of millions of dollars in prize money paid to the thirty-two finalist country teams in the 2010 World Cup, in Brazil FIFA did not take out withholding taxes for the $576 million in prize money doled out in 2014. So, other than possible taxes on income earned by members of the Brazilian team, the Brazilian treasury did not earn tax revenue on the prize money generated during the 2014 World Cup. Personal communication with Sunil Gulati, FIFA Executive Committee member, July 21, 2014. See also Kelly Phillips Erb, "World Cup Mania: Figuring Out FIFA, Soccer & Tax," *Forbes,* June 16, 2014 (www.forbes.com/sites/kellyphillipserb/2014/06/16/world-cup-mania-figuring-out-fifa-soccer-tax/), and John Sinnott, "A Fair World Cup Deal for Brazil?," CNN.com, July 24, 2013 (http://edition.cnn.com/2013/06/24/sport/football/brazil-protests-fifa-tax/).

44. "Seeking a Silver Lining," *Pro Sports,* July 2014, p. 64.

45. "Brazil World Cup Workers Face Slave-Like Conditions," *BBC News,* October 10, 2013.

46. Some estimates have gone much higher. Dave Zirin cites an activist who claimed that 1.5 million families from favelas would be relocated by 2014. Zirin, *Brazil's Dance with the Devil,* p. 180.

47. Sennes, "Will Brazil Get What It Expects from the World Cup?"

48. Amaral and Viana, "Why Are Brazilians Protesting the World Cup?"

49. Simon Romero, "Slum Dwellers Are Defying Brazil's Grand Design for Olympics," *New York Times,* March 6, 2012.

50. Cited in *Sports Business Daily Global,* March 28, 2014.

51. See, for instance, the discussion in "Has Brazil Blown It?," *The Economist,* October 8, 2013.

52. According to an ESPN article, Brazil actually knew unofficially as early as back in March 2003 that it would be chosen as the 2014 host. Arguments within the Brazilian soccer federation and between the federation and local politicians thwarted the decisionmaking process. Making matters worse, the head of the federation and also of the local organizing committee for the World Cup, Ricardo Teixeira, was a compromised figure who, in March 2012, facing charges of ineptitude and corruption, was forced to resign his posts. See Tim Vickery, "Will Teixeira's Ouster Lead to Change?," ESPN.com, March 14, 2012. When the local organizing committee for the World Cup was formed with Teixeira at the helm, the committee consisted of his daughter, his lawyer, his press secretary, his personal secretary, a personal adviser, and an ex-president of the Bank of Brazil from the military era, but nobody from the government. Simon Kuper, "Game of Two Halves: The Ugly Side of Brazilian Football," *Financial Times,* May 9, 2014. According to Christopher Gaffney, "Between 2007 and 2009, the 2014 Organizing Committee conducted a competition among 18 cities, engendering a bidding war full of political intrigue in which host cities and states scrambled to outspend their competition on new stadiums, highways and airport terminals" ("Mega-Events and Socio-Spatial Dynamics in Rio de Janeiro, 1919–2016").

53. Tom Vickery, "Can Brazil Protests Be Traced Back to a 2003 FIFA Decision?," *BBC News,* June 24, 2013.

54. Ibid.

55. Gaffney, "Mega-Events and Socio-Spatial Dynamics in Rio de Janeiro, 1919–2016."

56. Nick Butler, "Construction Workers Vote to Continue Strikes in Yet Another Blow for Rio 2016," *Inside the Games,* April 15, 2004 (www.insidethegames.biz).

57. "Brazil Won't Meet Water Pollution Reduction Target before Olympics: Official," *Sports Business News,* May 18, 2014. Rio invited sailing teams to test the waters in Guanabara Bay in late July 2014. The results were not encouraging. An Austrian boat was damaged by garbage in the water and a member of the sailing team said that he saw a dead dog. Other sailors complained that the Bay "smells like a toilet because of raw sewage and trash that flow into [the Bay] on a daily basis." Tariq Panja, "Olympic Boast Damaged by Rio Bay Garbage as Sailors See Dead Dog," Bloomberg.com, July 29, 2014 (www.bloomberg.com/news/2014-07-29/olympic-sailors-boat-damaged-by-floating-garbage-in-rio-s-bay.html).

58. Interview with Kfouri by Barreto.

59. Mike Sheridan, "Racing to Get Ready: Rio 2016 Olympics," *Urbanland: The Magazine of the Urban Land Institute,* May 5, 2014.

60. The problem is that this was an emulation of form, but not content, of Barcelona's plan. More important, the political-economic context of the games in the two cities was entirely different.

61. "Construction of TransOlímpica Freeway for 2016 Rio Games to Displace 800 Families," *Sports Business Daily Global,* September 29, 2024.

62. The Brattle Group, *Analysis of the Boston 2024 Proposed Summer Olympic Plans.* Prepared for the Commonwealth of Massachusetts, Office of the Governor, President of the Senate and Speaker of the House. August 17, 2015, p. 104.

63. It is also noteworthy that, in a country where more than half the people identify themselves as black or of mixed race, the great majority of attendees at the World Cup matches were white and from Brazil's upper class. A Datafolha Polling Group survey published in the *Folha de São Paulo* newspaper said that at the June 28 Brazil-Chile match, 67 percent of attendees were white and 90 percent came from Brazil's top economic classes. *Yahoo Sports,* June 30, 2014.

64. See the blog post of Christopher Gaffney, "Hunting White Elephants / Caçando Elefantes Brancos," June 6, 2014. The *Wall Street Journal* quoted Daniela Ordonez, an economist at the financial firm Euler Hermes: "All the activity in consumpion and tourism [from the World Cup] was more or less offset by reduced productivity in other areas like construction and transportation. From an economic point of view, maybe it was not worth it." Ordonez also projected that hosting would raise the country's inflation rate. Vipal Monga and Emily Chasan, "When in Doubt, Blame It on the World Cup," *Wall Street Journal,* July 30, 2014.

65. Sennes, "Will Brazil Get What It Expects from the World Cup?"

66. Gaffney, "Between Discourse and Reality," p. 3931.

67. For a discussion of the Thames Gateway project, see Gavin Poynter, "From Beijing to Bow Bells: Measuring the Olympic Effect," London East Research Institute, Working Papers in Urban Studies (London, March 2006).

68. Iain MacRury and Gavin Poynter, "London's Olympic Legacy: A Thinkpiece Report Prepared for the OECD and Department for Communications and Local Government" (University of East London, November 2009), p. 96.

69. Stratford Mall was also planned prior to the Games' planning. Nonetheless, its construction is often pointed to as a positive outcome of hosting the Olympics.

70. Ari Shapiro, "Did London Get an Economic Boost from the Olympics?," *All Things Considered,* National Public Radio, February 4, 2014.

71. Anne Power, "The Olympic Investment in East London Has Barely Scratched the Surface of the Area's Needs," blog post, August 15, 2012 (http://

blogs.lse.ac.uk/politicsandpolicy/archives/2022); National Audit Office, "The London 2012 Olympic and Paralympic Games: Post-Games Review," Report by the Comptroller and Auditor General (London, December 5, 2012), p. 25.

72. Dan Brown and Stefan Szymanski, "The Employment Effects of London 2012," in *International Handbook on the Economics of Mega Sporting Events,* ed. Wolfgang Maennig and Andrew S. Zimbalist (Cheltenham, U.K.: Edward Elgar, 2012), pp. 546–70.

73. Cited in ibid.

74. Tim Hunt, "How Tax Avoidance Schemes Now Lie at the Heart of the Modern Olympic Games," *Ethical Consumer,* July 27, 2012 (www.ethical consumer.org).

75. Peter Woodman, "London Tourism Struggles during Olympics," *The Independent* (www.independent.co.uk/news/uk/home-news/london-tourism-struggles-during-olympics-7994159.html). See also "British Tourism Slumped during London Olympics," Associated Press, August 13, 2012.

76. The National Audit Report of December 5, 2012, stated, "The planning for venue security at the games did not go smoothly" (p. 6). The number of guards required was initially estimated at 10,000. The final number was over 20,000. One month before the games began, the company contracted to provide security informed LOCOG that it would not be able to provide the full number of guards in the contract. Ultimately the military was mobilized to do the job.

77. National Audit Office, "The London 2012 Olympic and Paralympic Games: Post-Games Review," p. 10.

78. Ibid., p. 24. This and other dollar cost figures are converted from British pounds at the rate of $1.69 to £1. This rate represents an average for the period 2005–12, the years that London was building to host the Olympics.

79. Tripp Mickle, "Panel at GE Event Addresses City Changes, Legacy of an Olympics," *Sports Business Daily,* July 31, 2012.

80. If all infrastructure expenditures are included, the total tab for London 2012 ran to $27.6 billion, according to a study done for the governor of Massachusetts by the Brattle Group. The Brattle Group, *Analysis of the Boston 2024 Proposed Summer Olympic Plans,* p. 90. It is also noteworthy that the initial plan called for 70 percent of all financing to be private. Over 80 percent ended up being public.

81. Jules Boykoff and Dave Zirin, "Protest Is Coming to the London Olympics," *The Nation,* May 21, 2012.

82. National Audit Office, "The London 2012 Olympic and Paralympic Games: Post-Games Review," p. 31.

83. Report by the Controller and Auditor General, *The Budget for the 2012 London Olympic and Paralympic Games* (www.nao.org.uk/wp-content/uploads/2007/07/0607612.pdf).

84. Quoted in Poynter, "From Beijing to Bow Bells," p. 23.

85. Gavin Poynter, "Afterword: A Postcard from Rio," in *London: Was It Good for Us?,* ed. Mark Perryman (London: Lawrence and Wishart, 2012), p. 4.

86. National Audit Office, "The London 2012 Olympic and Paralympic Games: Post-Games Review," p. 18.

87. "Olympic Challenge: How Do Host Cities Fare after the Games?," *CBS News,* February 24, 2014 (www.cbsnews.com). Matthew Saltmarsh, "Will the Olympics Save East London?," *New York Times,* July 28, 2011.

88. The original stadium cost a reported $706 million to build (www.dailymail.co.uk/sport/football/article-2741150/Cost-converting-Olympic-Stadium-use-West-Ham-rise-15m.html).

89. See www.bbc.com/sport/0/football/33780720.

90. Bill Carey, "Do Olympics Fulfill Economic Promises? A Look Back at London," *Sports Illustrated,* February 6, 2014.

91. Ibid.

92. Iain MacRury and Gavin Poynter, "London's Olympic Legacy: A Thinkpiece Report Prepared for the OCED and Department for Communications and Local Government" (University of East London, November 2009), p. 8. Oliver Wainwright, "London's Olympics Legacy Faces Early Disqualification," *The Guardian,* July 21, 2013.

93. "Other promises, like the Olympic Museum due to open this year, have simply been quietly dropped." Wainwright, "London's Olympics Legacy Faces Early Disqualification."

94. Boykoff, "What Is the Real Price of the London Olympics?"; National Audit Office, "The London 2012 Olympic Games and Paralympic Games," p. 25.

95. Poynter, "Afterword: A Postcard from Rio," p. 5.

96. Ibid., pp. 6–7.

97. Liam Morgan, "British Charity Blasts Government for Failure to Repay London 2012 Olympic Debt," Insidethegames.com, August 12, 2015.

98. Saltmarsh, "Will the Olympics Save East London?"

99. Robin Scott-Elliott, "Significantly Fewer People Now Playing Sport Regularly Than before Last Year's Olympic Games," *The Independent,* June 14, 2013.

100. See http://sportengland.org/research/who-plays-sport/.

101. Morgan, "British Charity Blasts Government. . ."

102. Quoted in www.parliament.uk/business/publications/research/key-issues-for-the-new-parliament/social-reform/2012-olympics-and-sporting-legacy/. See also www.publications.parliament.uk/pa/cm200607/cmselect/cmcu meds/69/69i.pdf, p. 37.

Chapter 7

1. R. A. Baade and V. Matheson, "Bidding for the Olympics: Fool's Gold?," in *Transatlantic Sport,* ed. Carlos Pestana Barros, Muradali Ibrahímo, and Stefan Szymanski (London: Edward Elgar, 2002), pp. 127–51.

2. Acreage estimates are from Judith Grant Long, "The Olympic Games and Urban Development Impacts," in P. Esteves and others, *BRICS e os Megaeventos Esportivos* (Rio de Janeiro: BRICS Policy Institute, forthcoming).

3. E. Cottle, ed., *South Africa's World Cup: A Legacy for Whom?* (University of KwaZulu-Natal Press, 2011).

4. However, cities and countries do not bid with dollar figures. Rather, they bid with fancy facilities, appealing infrastructure, and amenities. Since these have a price, their bids can be translated into dollar figures.

5. On the eve of its Islamic revolution, Tehran, Iran, was an early bidder for the 1984 games, but dropped out before the final selection was made in 1978.

6. And India, in the case of the 2010 Commonwealth Games. See, for instance, Nalin Mehta and Boria Majumdar, "For a Monsoon Wedding: Delhi and the Commonwealth Games," in *International Handbook on the Economics of Mega Sporting Events*, ed. Wolfgang Maennig and Andrew S. Zimbalist (Cheltenham, U.K.: Edward Elgar, 2012), pp. 504–26.

7. See, for example, Declan Hill and Jere Longman, "Fixed Soccer Matches Cast Shadow over World Cup," *New York Times*, May 31, 2014; Andrew Critchlow, "IoD Attacks Fifa in Wake of Qatar World Cup Scandal," *The Telegraph*, June 11, 2014; and Owen Gibson, "Qatar Hits Back at Allegations of Bribery over 2022 World Cup," *The Observer*, June 14, 2014.

8. See www.dezeen.com/2012/08/01/democracies-find-it-very-difficult-to-host-games-say-authors-of-olympic-cities-book/.

9. The *Washington Post*'s Catherine Rampell commented, "Norway's government looks likely to nix the bid later this year, since polls show only 36 percent of Norwegians are on board," *Washington Post*, July 11, 2014.

10. International Olympics Committee (IOC), "Olympic Agenda 2020: The Bid Experience" (Lausanne, June 2014), p. 4.

11. Duncan Mackay, "Paris Mayor Unenthusiastic about Bid for 2024 Olympics and Paralympics," *Inside the Games*, May 31, 2014 (www.insidethegames.biz/olympics). See also "Bill de Blasio Rules out NYC Bid," Associated Press, May 28, 2014.

12. Nick Butler, "Protests Held as Opposition Builds against New National Stadium in Tokyo," *Inside the Games*, July 5, 2014 (www.insidethegames.biz).

13. Duncan Mackay, "Exclusive: 'We Ask Too Much Too Early,'" *Inside the Games*, September 11, 2013 (www.insidethegames.biz).

14. See Duncan Mackay, "Changes to Olympic Bid Process on Way as IOC Members Debate Ideas," *Inside the Games*, February 5, 2014 (www.insidethegames.biz/olympics/1018223-changes-to-olympic-bid-process-on-way-as-ioc-members-debate-ideas).

15. Wolfgang Maennig and Andrew Zimbalist, "Future Challenges: Maximizing the Benefits and Minimizing the Costs," in Maennig and Zimbalist, *International Handbook on the Economics of Mega Sporting Events*, pp. 571–86.

16. "Tokyo to Reduce 2020 Olympic Bid Budget," GamesBids.com, December 2, 2011.

17. Jules Boykoff, professor of political science at Pacific University and prolific analyst of the Olympic Games, calls for the IOC to "create an independent body comprising respected sports economists, urban planners and political scholars who can objectively assess whether bids' construction plans fulfill longview development strategies." Jules Boykoff, "A Bid for a Better Olympics," *New York Times,* August 13, 2014.

18. Reportedly, there were IOC concerns about the weakness of Spain's economy. The Spanish economy was devastated by the post-2007 financial crisis in Europe and the United States and was indeed weak in 2013 (unemployment rates were over 25 percent). The Spanish economy, however, was already beginning to recover at the time of Tokyo's selection in 2013, and there was little basis for the IOC to condemn it to a recession seven years hence.

19. IOC, "Olympic Agenda 2020: The Bid Experience," p. 6.

20. Until the summer of 2014, FIFA rules provided for only twenty-four individuals to vote on the selection of the World Cup host. Many believed that with so few people involved, bribery was simpler and cheaper. Accordingly, in the wake of the Qatar vote-buying scandal, FIFA altered its voting procedures to include the entire 209-nation membership. Further democratizing reform in the voting procedure is proposed by Duncan O'Leary, "Football's Great Reform Act" (http://quarterly.demos.co.uk/aticle/issue-3/footballs-great-reform-act/).

21. See, for example, "FIFA Confirms Michael Garcia's World Cup Ethics Report Won't Be Made Public," *The Guardian,* July 21, 2014. FIFA did finally release a summary of the investigatory report in November 2014, but Michael Garcia promptly issued a denunciation, stating that the summary contained "numerous materially incomplete and erroneous representations of the facts and conclusions detailed in the investigatory chamber's report."

22. German Olympics expert Wolfgang Maennig called for Hamburg and Berlin to apply to host the 2024 Summer Games, but to do so with a twist: there should be no new permanent building, planning should be more participatory, and more music and art should accompany the athletic competitions, inter alia. Wolfgang Maennig, "Deutschland ist dran," *Frankfurter Allgemeine,* August 14, 2014. In early September 2014, both Berlin and Hamburg announced their preliminary bid plans for the 2024 Games. In both cases the initial plans were rather modest and scaled back, emphasizing the use of existing facilities, though Hamburg's plans became considerably more elaborate by the time it was selected over Berlin to be the German entry. See "Berlin, Hamburg Reveal Olympic Concepts for Potential 2024 Summer Games Bid," *Sports Business Daily Global,* September 2, 2014, p. 1.

23. Jim Armstrong, "Tokyo Governor Defends 2020 Olympics Venue Relocation Plans," July 1, 2014 (http://wintergames.ap.org/article/tokyo-governor-defends-venue-relocation-plans).

Postscipt

1. For a fascinating, detailed account of the inner workings and machinations of FIFA, see Heidi Blake and Jonathan Calvert, *The Ugly Game: The Qatari Plot to Buy the World Cup* (New York: Simon and Schuster, 2015). A discussion of Blatter's manipulations to win the 1998 and 2002 elections appears in Chapter One of this book

2. Claire Newell and others, "Qatar World Cup 2022 Investigation," *The Telegraph*, March 17, 2014.

3. As I write in late August 2015, Blatter has only once traveled outside of Switzerland, to St. Petersburg, Russia. Switzerland's longstanding policy has been not to extradite its own citizens. It remains to be seen if Blatter will travel to a western democracy, as he continues to declare his innocence.

4. The reality is actually still worse because the women's World Cup is part of the 2015–18 quadrennium, which benefits from higher television rights fees and sponsorship revenue than the 2011–14 quadrennium, and, other things equal, would have higher levels of prize money.

5. Stephen Eisenhammer, "500 Days Out, Rio Risks Olympic Cost Surge as Building Lags," Associated Press, May 8, 2015.

6. Stephen Wade, "Olympic Organizers Counting on Rio," Associated Press, July 29, 2015. In *Dancing with the Devil in the City of God* (New York: Simon and Schuster, 2015), Juliana Barbassa describes these condominium units as follows (p. 163): "The Sunday paper carried a full-page advertisement for Riserva Golf, the condominium that would rise by the Rio 2016 golf course. The super-deluxe, marble-and-glass-skinned high-rises had apartments that were 'suspended mansions,' the ad said, costing between $2.3 million and $23 million each."

7. See Simon Romero, "In Run-Up to Olympics, Rio's Property Market Already Looks Hung Over," *New York Times*, November 12, 2015.

8. For an excellent discussion of this process, see Barbassa, *Dancing with the Devil in the City of God.*

9. Brad Brooks and Jenny Barchfield, "AP Investigation: Olympics Athletes to Swim, Boat in Rio's Filth," Associated Press, July 30, 2015.

10. See, for instance, "Brazil's Economy: Desperate Times, Desperate Moves," *The Economist*, September 5, 2015, p. 39.

11. For a penetrating discussion of Rio's perilous political and economic situation, see Barbassa, *Dancing with the Devil in the City of God.*

12. To be sure, there are bound to be a variety of inconveniences. For instance, there is woefully inadequate parking for buses at many venues, which will lead to severe traffic snarls, the special VIP and BRT lanes notwithstanding. Travelers will encounter off-the-chart hotel prices with first-class rooms going for $1,000 and up nightly with twenty-one-day minimum stays. Although the Brazilian currency has been plummeting in value, hotels are setting their prices

in dollars and euros. See Ben Fisher, "Rio Presents Serious Logistical Challenges," *Sports Business Journal*, August 3–9, 2015, p. 20.

13. Duncan Mackay, "Pyeongchang 2018 Audit Reveals Big Shortfall in Sponsorship Revenues," *Inside the Games*, December 27, 2014.

14. "Five Politicians May Face Probe over Pyeongchang Olympics," *Korea Times*, May 5, 2015.

15. "Turmoil in Tokyo as Cost of City's National Stadium Soars," *London Times*, June 16, 2015.

16. "Tokyo Olympic Stadium Designer Strikes Back at Critics," Associated Press, July 28, 2015.

17. Duncan Mackay, "Japanese Government under Pressure over Costs of Olympic Stadium in Tokyo 2020," *Inside the Games*, July 15, 2015 (insidethegames.com).

18. Jules Boykoff, "Beijing and Almaty Contest Winter Olympics in Human Rights Nightmare," *The Guardian*, July 30, 2015.

19. Ibid.

20. Ibid.

21. Bach made this remark in Moscow in late July 2015. See http://chinadigitaltimes.net/2015/07/rights-advocates-oppose-beijings-2022-winter-olympics-bid/.

22. It is claimed that the rail will cut the time to travel between Beijing and Zhangjiakov from more than three hours to less than one hour. "Olympics: Smooth Piste for Beijing's 2022 Bid," Lenovo.com, July 29, 2015.

23. While the geographical water distribution imbalance is acute, China has a nationwide water shortage with 21 percent of the world's population and only 6 percent of the global water resources. It is estimated that more than 300 million people in China drink contaminated water on a daily basis. See World Bank, World Development Indicators, "Renewable internal freshwater resources per capita" (http://data.worldbank.org/indicator/ER.H2O.INTR.PC) and Shannon Tiezzi, "China's Looming Water Shortage," *The Diplomat*, November 30, 2014 (http://thediplomat.com/2014/11/chinas-looming-water-shortage/).

24. China launched a $60 billion water diversion program from the south before the 2008 summer Olympics. Zhangjiakou, the site of Nordic skiing, only gets eight inches of snow per year and will require copious water supplies for artificial snow making. See Lily Kuo, "Hosting the Winter Olympics in Beijing Is a Terrible Idea," Reuters, April 1, 2015. Also see www.nytimes.com/2015/07/30/sports/olympics/2022-winter-games-vote.

25. ADM Capital Foundation, "China Water Risk" (http://chinawaterrisk.org/notices/north-china-plain-groundwater-70-unfit-for-human-touch/). This source reports on a 2013 survey showing that the North China Plain suffers from severe groundwater pollution with over 70 percent of overall groundwater quality classified as Grade IV+—in other words, unfit for human touch.

26. See, for one, Claire Topal and Yeasol Chung, "Interview with Daniel K. Gardner," China's Off-the-Chart Air Pollution: Why It Matters (and Not

Only to the Chinese), Part I, National Bureau of Asian Research (www.nbr.org/research/activity.aspx?id=394).

27. Toronto, having hosted the Pan American games during the summer of 2015 at a cost of over $2 billion, was actively considering a bid for the 2024 summer Olympics. The Canadian Olympic Committee was promoting it strongly. But on the last day to submit a bid, September 15, 2015, Toronto mayor John Tory decided against it. Tory faced a lack of corporate support, criticism from the city council, reluctance from the provincial government, and increasing public skepticism.

28. Casey Wasserman, who has headed up the Los Angeles 2024 bid, explained to a meeting of the Los Angeles City Council why Boston was originally chosen. Part of his answer was: "There are a bunch of athletes based in Boston on that [USOC] board, and a couple of executives on the board, and Boston in their mind was a new, fresh city." A similar explanation was provided to me by a longstanding member of the USOC. On the Boston 2024 bid, Wasserman also asserted: "The bid book that they put forward wasn't a bid book that was defensible." Ben Fischer, "Wasserman Offers Insights into 2024 Bid Choice," *Sports Business Daily*, August 28, 2015.

29. Katherine Seelye, "Details Uncovered in Boston 2024 Olympic Bid May Put It in Jeopardy," *New York Times*, May 30, 2015.

30. For these and all other venues, Boston 2024's 2.0 plan used a contingency fund of only 5 percent. The Brattle Group's analysis of the plan asserted that a typical contingency for a construction project at the conceptual stage is between 20 and 30 percent. Los Angeles has replaced Boston as the U.S. bid city, and in its initial bid book, it employs a contingency fund of only 10 percent. London 2012 used a contingency fund of 41.7 percent of the base budget. Using contingency funds below the industry standard, of course, only further increases the risk of eventual cost overruns. See The Brattle Group, *Analysis of the Boston 2024 Proposed Summer Olympic Plans*. Prepared for the Commonwealth of Massachusetts Office of the Governor, President of the Senate, and Speaker of the House, August 17, 2015, pp. 14, 49.

31. This estimate is based on a 2015 rate of $29.20 per $1,000 of assessed value, and an assessed value of $1,662,785,388.

32. According to the 2.0 plan, in the 2050s the developer would pay 50 percent of the normal property tax and in the 2060s, 75 percent. At Columbia Point, the developer would pay 20 percent of the normal rate from the 2030s through the 2060s.

33. This estimate is based on (a) the cost of the deck per acre at Hudson Yards in New York City and (b) an email communication from Chris Dempsey. Plan 1.0 referred to a deck and platform at Widett Circle of 36 acres. Dempsey used Google Maps and the drawings of plan 2.0 to estimate that the deck would be at least 20 acres. See Michael Levenson, "T Repair Facilities Pose Challenges to Olympic Stadium," *Boston Globe*, April 29, 2015 (www.bostonglobe.

com/metro/2015/04/28/repair-facilities-pose-challenges-olympic-stadium/mx-ek9RNT5hfghPFDFv9oWJ/story.html).

34. Interestingly, one of the most vocal supporters of Boston 2024 was USOC member Dan Doctoroff, who headed the New York 2012 bid. When he led the New York City bid, back in 2004, Doctoroff supported legislation passed by the state legislature that would have limited the state's financial liability to $250 million for cost overruns. Yet Doctoroff refused to endorse a limit to Boston's or the state's financial liability for 2024, despite the IOC's Agenda 2020 that purports to be host friendly. See N.Y. Code—Article 16: Olympic Games Facilitation Act (http://codes.lp.findlaw.com/nycode/COM/16). It is also noteworthy that the Los Angeles City Council would only give its endorsement to a Los Angeles bid for 2024 if its joinder agreement with the USOC contained a specific provision that allowed the city council to veto any financial arrangement between the city and the USOC or the IOC. Thomas Bach, apparently, was so keen on having a U.S. city in the race (to boost the PR effort of Agenda 2020) that he was willing to overlook this facial flouting of an ironclad IOC requirement, that is, a full and unequivocal financial backstop offer from the host city.

35. To be sure, beyond playing the finals at the TD Boston Garden, the 2.0 plan regarding the location of the volleyball competition in the Northeast corridor was left vague, though it was clear that there was no plan to play any volleyball games in Holyoke. Baseball, basketball, and, perhaps, rugby were targeted for large arenas in the Northeast.

36. "IOC President Thomas Bach Hits out at Boston for Aborted 2024 Olympics Bid," Reuters, July 29, 2015.

37. Hayden Bird, "Mayor Walsh's Response to Criticism from the IOC President over Boston 2024" (http://bostinno.streetwise.co/2015/07/29/mayor-walsh-responds-to-ioc-president-thomas-bachs-boston-2024-olympic-comments/).

Index

Tables are indicated by "t" following page numbers.

ABC (TV network), 16
Advertising, 45, 49
AECOM (consultants), 96
AEG (construction company), 100
Afghanistan, Russian occupation of, 18
African boycott of Montreal 1976 Summer Games, 17
Agenda 2020 of IOC, 151, 155–58
Ahmad Al-Fahad Al-Sabah (Kuwaiti prince), 4
Albert II (prince of Liechtenstein), 4
Albertville 1992 Winter Games, 63, 66
Aldeia Maracanā indigenous community (Brazil), 68
Alevras, Athanasios, 71
Ali bin Al-Hussein (Jordanian prince), 4
Almaty (Kazakhstan) as candidate for 2022 Winter Games, 155–58
Amateurism, era of, 9–10, 12–13, 22
Ancient Greece, 9–10
Andrade Gutierrez (construction company), 100
Anne (British princess), 4

Antwerp 1920 Olympic Games, 11–12
Around the Rings on Sochi 2014 Winter Games, 85–86
Associated Press: on Brazil 2014 World Cup, 100; on protests over Sochi 2014 Winter Games, 88; on Rio 2016 Summer Games preparations, 152
Athens: 2004 Summer Games, 43, 54, 59, 60, 64, 70–71, 134, 144; business disruption, 45; as historic site of Olympic Games, 9, 10–11, 129; proposed as permanent site of Summer Games, 140; security issues, 46
Athleticism, benefits of, 9, 123
Atlanta 1996 Summer Olympics, 54, 60, 72, 134, 144
Atlanta Braves (baseball team), 72
Atlantic Council, 112
Authoritarian countries as hosts, 130, 134–35

Bach, Thomas, 6, 26, 136, 138–39, 140, 151, 156, 163

Baker, Charlie, 158–59

Barcelona 1992 Summer Games, 75–82; compared to Sochi 2014 Winter Games, 92–93; competition for hosting, 22; construction effect on employment and output, 77; factors contributing to success of, 77; General Metropolitan Plan (PGM) for city, 76, 128; historical background, 75–76, 128; land use, 82, 130; as model for future Games, 96, 128, 144; private funding, 77, 144; real estate prices, 81–82; stadium issues, 72, 76; tourism generally vs. Olympic effect, 62, 78–81, 80*t*

Barcelona 2004 Universal Forum of Cultures, 82

Baseball, 163

Batista, Eike, 101–02

Beijing 2008 Summer Games: Bird's Nest stadium, 69–70; budget, 43; cost of hosting, 2, 26, 134; land use and central complex design, 130, 144; opening ceremony costs, 44–45; political repression, effect on, 156; tourism during, 38, 54, 60

Beijing as candidate for 2022 Winter Games, 155–58

Beijing Guo'an soccer team, 70

Benefits of hosting. *See* Hosting benefits

Berlin 1936 Olympic Games, 13–14, 129

Bidding: for 2022 Winter Olympics, 134–35, 142, 151, 155–58; for 2024 Summer Olympics, 137, 138, 151, 158–64; corruption in bid awards, 23–24, 142; costs of, 5–6, 44, 137, 141; effect on possible gains, 131–32; effect on trade and investment, 64; number of cities bidding, 6, 22, 26, 27*t*, 134–35;

reform proposals, 139–40, 142; since 1984, 129

bin Hammam, Mohamed, 32–33, 145, 147

Blatter, Sepp, 3, 4, 32, 33, 106, 136, 145–46, 148–51

Boston 2024 (private group), 158–62

Boston as candidate for 2024 Summer Games, 158–64; bid documents for, 158–59; commission for study on, xiii–xiv; development and financing, 159–63; loss of bid, 163–64; Plan 2.0 and temporary venues, 160–61; public discussion on, ix

Boycotts: African boycott of Montreal 1976 Summer Games, 17; of Los Angeles 1984 Summer Games, 20; of Moscow 1980 Summer Games, 18–19

Boykoff, Jules, 87, 155

Bradley, Thomas, 19

Brasiliense (football team), 99–100

Brazil: 1950 World Cup, 101; 2013 Confederations Cup, 2–3, 103, 104; complex political system in, 112; education budget, 103; inflation and unemployment, 153–54; as major economic player, 107, 112. *See also* Brazil 2014 World Cup; BRICS; Rio 2016 Summer Games

Brazil 2014 World Cup, 96–108; bidding for, 31, 106–07, 136–37; Blatter and Valcke in attendance at, 149; cost of, 26, 43, 98, 100, 134; discrimination, effect on, 68, 113; effect of event revenues on national GDP, 40–42; effect on productivity, 111–12; effect on public morale, 51; FIFA covering operating expenses of, 33; forced relocations, 105–06; infrastructure investment, 50–51, 67–68, 74, 96–97, 106–07; local attendees and revenues, 39; migrant labor, use of, 105; private funding, 97–98, 107; prize money distribution, 150; protests against, 2–3, 16, 48, 103–04, 105, 136; public opinion on hosting, 107; real estate pricing, 102–03; relocations, 101, 105–06; stadiums, 95, 97–100, 101–02, 109–10; tourism during, 39, 55–56, 60, 62, 111; transportation, 67, 96–97, 103, 130; white elephants, 102

Brazilian Airline Association, 55

Brazilian Football Confederation, 97

BRICS (Brazil, Russia, India, China, and South Africa), 4, 25–27, 134

Britain: bid for 2018 World Cup, 146–47; boycott contemplated of Moscow 1980 Summer Games, 18–19; Culture, Media and Sport Committee (Parliament), 123; educational system, 9. *See also* London 2012 Summer Games

Broadway (New York City), xii, xiii

Brown, Dan, 116

Brundage, Avery, 11, 14, 16

Bruning, Heinrich, 13

Budgets, 49–50

Business disruption, 45

Business elite as benefiting from hosting, 130–31

Calgary 1988 Winter Games, 60, 63

Canada, 2015 women's World Cup, 149–50

Carlos, John, 17

Carter, Jimmy, 18–19

CBS (TV network), 14

CBS News on Beijing stadium, 70

Center for Security Analysis and Prevention report, 85

Charter of Olympic Games, 10–11, 66, 86

Chechen terrorists, 88

Chicago's failed bid for 2016 Summer Games, 44, 137

China, People's Republic of: boycott of 1980 Moscow Summer Games, 19; recognition of, 17; water resources as issue for 2022 Winter Games, 156–57. *See also* Beijing 2008 Summer Games; BRICS

Circus Maximus (ancient Rome), xiv–xv

Civil rights. *See* Inequality

Clean Games, 105

Closing ceremonies, 44–45

Coates, John, 24, 110, 136

Coe, Sebastian, 125

Colectiva (magazine), 109

Commercialization and end of amateurism, 20–24

Communications technology, 68

Competition to host Games, 1–2, 22. *See also* Bidding

Confederations Cup. *See* Brazil

Consórcio Maracanã (construction group), 101–02

Construction: effect on employment and output, 51–53, 77, 131; overrun costs to meet deadlines, 47–48; profits of construction companies, 130–31; strikes, 108, 136. *See also* Sports venues and nonsport infrastructure

Corporate sponsorships, 20, 25, 162–63

Corruption: in bid awards, 23–24, 142; costs of, 49; in hosting costs, 26; in World Cup and FIFA activities, 30–31, 73, 99–100, 145–48

Cost overruns, 46–48, 47*t*, 162

Costs of hosting. *See* Hosting costs

Coubertin, Pierre de Frédy, baron de, 9–10, 13

Crime rates, 66

Culture, Media and Sport Committee (British Parliament), 123

Czech Center for Security Analysis and Prevention, 90

Dentsu Institute for Human Studies, 35
Denver, withdrawing from hosting 1976 Winter Games, 17
Deripaska, Oleg, 84, 85
Developing countries, 2, 16, 134. *See also* BRICS
Directory of Social Change (DSC), British charity, 122
Discrimination. *See* Inequality
Dmitriev, Vladimir, 86
Doctoroff, Dan, ix, xii, xiii
Dodd, Moya, 4
Drapeau, Jean, 18
Drug testing of athletes, 18. *See also* World Anti-Doping Agency (WADA)
Dutch report on authoritarian countries as hosts, 135

Earth Summit (Rio de Janeiro), 66
East Germany: boycott of 1984 Los Angeles Games, 20; dominance in certain sports, 18
Economic impact: cycles of leverage, 133–37; difficulty in calculating, 37, 127–31; ex ante studies, 35–39; ex post studies, 40–43; hosting benefits, xi, 50–56, 59–69; hosting costs, 2, 44–50, 69–77; input-output models, 36–37; insurance for capital replacement, 162; long-run, 57–74; modest positive effect (7 cases), 40, 41–42*t*; negative effect (3 cases), 40, 41–42*t*; no positive effect (16 cases), 40, 41–42*t*; reforms from above, 137–43; reforms from below, 143–44; revenues from Games, 14, 15*t*, 24–25, 27–29, 40–42, 127, 141, 162–63; short-run, 26, 35–56, 41–42*t*. *See*

also Hosting benefits; Hosting costs
El Salvador and World Cup participation, 29–30
Employment. *See* Labor market; Migrant labor
Ender, Kornelia, 18
England, as possible choice to host 2018 World Cup, 146
Environmental issues. *See* Pollution and environmental issues
Environmental Watch on North Caucasus, 87
European Economic Community, 77
European Tour Operators Association (ETOA), 46, 54, 59, 60, 61, 78, 79
European Union, 77

Fédération Internationale de Football Association (FIFA), xv, 29–34, 145–51; Blatter reelection (2015), 145–46; changes in procedures, 136–37; country selection process, 146–47; on environmental issues, 68; executive compensation, 3–4; history of founding, 13; internal struggles of, 30–33; prize money distribution, 150; reform, need for, 150–51; special tax treatment of, 104–05; on stadiums, 73, 97, 100, 140–41, 149; Sub-Committee on Compensation, 3; UEFA's (European soccer organization), competition from, 149; women's vs. men's World Cup policies, 149–50. *See also* World Cup
Feel-good effects, 51, 66
Feisal bin Al Hussein (Jordanian prince), 4
Ferreira, Marília Sueli, 98–99
FIFA. *See* Fédération Internationale de Football Association
Financial Times on Brazil 2014 World Cup, 106

Financing: of Olympic Games, 27–29, 28*t*, 122; of World Cup, 33–34. *See also* Private funding

Flamengo (Brazilian soccer team), 101–02

Forced relocations, 51, 66, 69, 86–87, 101, 105–06, 110, 111, 116, 152–53

Forman, Lance, 120

Fortaleza International Airport (Brazil), 97

FOX television, 148

France 1998 World Cup, 34

Franco, Francisco, 75

Frederik (Crown Prince of Denmark), 4

French educational system, 9

Gaffney, Christopher, 68, 106, 113

Galeão International Airport (Rio de Janeiro), 97

Garcia, Michael J., 148

Gazprom, 87

Germany: 1936 Olympic Games, 13–14; 2006 World Cup, 34. *See also* East Germany

Giesecke, James, 62

Gleeson, Brian, 91

Globe and Mail (Toronto) on Athens Olympics, 70

Goodwill Games, 139

Grant Thornton reports, 35, 115, 125

Greenpeace, 87

Gryzlov, Boris, 84

Guardian (London) on Qatar construction labor, 53

Gulati, Sunil, 4

Hamburg as candidate for 2024 Summer Games, 158

Havelange, Joao, 149

Haya Bint Al Hussein (Jordanian princess), 4

Hidalgo, Anne, 135–36

History of Olympic Games: BRICS, effect of, 25–27; commercialization and end of amateurism, 20–24; development of Olympic brand, 12–20; era of amateurism, 9–10; new Olympic movement, 10–12; sharing the revenues, 14, 15*t*, 24–25, 27–29

Hitler, Adolf, 13

Hoitsma, Jan-Marten, 98

Honduras and World Cup participation, 29

Hospitality issues: hotel capacity requirements, 55, 63, 64, 142; Sochi 2014 Winter Games, 89, 90

Hosting benefits: business elite as benefiting, 130–31; construction effect on employment and output, 51–53; feel-good effects, 51; higher real estate prices, 51; long-run (legacy), 26, 59–69; overcoming political gridlock, 50–51; qualitative benefits, 66–69; short-run, 26, 50–56; tourism, 53–56, 59–64; trade and investment, 65

Hosting costs, 2; bidding, 44; budgets for, 49–50, 154, 157; business disruption, 45; cost overruns, 46–48, 47*t*, 162; human costs, 49; land use as, 82, 120–21, 124–25, 129–31, 144; long-run, 69–77; long-term debt, 51–52, 74; opening and closing ceremonies, 44–45; opportunity costs, 49, 52, 74, 129; other costs, 49–50; Qatar 2022 World Cup, 146; revenues unable to match, 127; security costs, 46; short-run, 44–50; Sochi 2014 Winter Games, 2; sports venues and nonsport infrastructure, 45, 130; white elephant venues, 34, 69–73, 102, 127, 160

Human costs, 49, 147

Human rights, 146–47, 156

Human Rights Watch, 86, 87, 156

Image issues, 17–19

IMG (consultants), 96

IMX (construction company), 101–02

India. *See* BRICS

Indigenous Cultural Center (Rio de Janeiro), 101

Inequality: black athletes from U.S. and, 14, 17; Brazil 2014 World Cup and, 69, 102–03, 113; FIFA administration and, 31; German 1936 Games and, 14; in host countries, 4–5, 82; of IOC members who select winning cities, 143; London 2012 Summer Games and, 124–25; Sochi 2014 Winter Games, 86–87; in South Africa, 16; Thorpe's loss of medals and, 11; upper class benefiting from Games, 10, 12; women participants, 11–12

Inflation, 46, 47, 102, 153–54

Infrastructure investment: Beijing 2018 Winter Games bid, 156–57; Boston 2024 Summer Games bid, 159, 161–63; Brazil 2014 World Cup, 50–51, 67–68, 74, 96–97, 106; budget for, 49–50; sports venues and nonsport infrastructure, 45. *See also* Construction

Innsbruck 1976 Winter Games, 63

Inside the Rings (newsletter), 138

Insurance for cost overruns, 162

International Basketball Federation, 109

International Federations (IFs) of each sport, 15, 22, 109

International Handbook on the Economics of Mega Sporting Events (Zimbalist & Maennig), xiii

International Olympic Committee (IOC), xiii, 1, 151–64; Agenda 21 and environmental policy, 66; Agenda 2020 reforms, 151, 155–58; on amateurism, 13; applicants' fees, 5; board members as elites, 3; brand protection policy, 45; changes in procedures, 136; change under Samaranch's leadership, 23; compensation of members, 4, 23–24; image issues of, 17–19; on legacy benefits, 57–58; on professional athletes' participation, 22; sharing in TV rights revenues, 14–15, 15*t*, 24–25; stadium requirements, 140, 142; on sustainability, 68. *See also* Bidding; Olympic Games; *specific locations of games*

International Trade Union Confederation, 147

InterVISTAS Consulting, 35

Investment and trade, 26, 37, 65

Italy 1934 World Cup, 13–14

Japan: 2002 World Cup, 33, 34, 35, 72, 136; 2020 Summer Games, 136, 154–55; boycott of 1980 Moscow Summer Games, 19. *See also* Nagano 1998 Winter Games; Tokyo

Japan-U.S. 2015 women's World Cup, 150

Javits Convention Center (New York City), 50

Jews, 14

Justice Department, U.S., 146, 148, 150–51

Kasyanov, Mikhail, 85

Kazakhstan as candidate for 2022 Winter Games, 155–58

Kfouri, Juca, 100–01, 109–10

Kickbacks. *See* Corruption

Killanin, Michael Morris, 3rd Baron of, 19

Knight Frank Global House Price Index, 102

Labor market: construction-related, 51–53, 131; London 2012 Summer

Games, 116; Sochi 2014 Winter Games, 86–87; tourism-related, 55. *See also* Migrant labor

Legacy benefits. *See* Long-run (legacy) benefits

Legacy costs. *See* Long-run (legacy) costs

Lend Lease (Australian developer), 121

Lillehammer 1994 Winter Games, 63

Local economy of host city, 28–29, 38–39. *See also* Tourism

Local organizing committees for the Olympic Games (OCOGs), 15–16, 15t

London: 1908 Olympic Games, 11; 1948 Olympic Games, 14

London 2012 Summer Games, 114–25; budget and operating costs, 43, 117–18, 160–61; business disruption, 45; choice of London, xiii, 25; estimate of short-run economic impact, 35; land use and complex design, 120–21, 124–25, 130, 144; legacy effects, 114–15, 118–25; physical activity level of general public after, 123; security costs, 104; short-run effects, 115–18; size of, 129; sources of revenue, 27; stadium renovation after Games, 119; tourism during, 38, 54, 60–61, 117; transportation, 115, 117

London Docklands Development Corporation, 114

Long, Judith Grant, xiv

Long Island Railroad, xii

Long-run (legacy) benefits, 59–69; IOC list of, 57–58; as payoff for hosting, 127; qualitative and other benefits, 66–69; tourism, 59–65; trade and investment, 26, 65

Long-run (legacy) costs: debt and opportunity costs, 74; London 2012 Summer Games, 118–25; white elephants, 69–73

Long-term debt, 17–18, 51–52, 74, 131

Los Angeles 1932 Games, 1, 13

Los Angeles 1984 Summer Games: boycott of, 20; financial success of, 20, 40, 129; as model for future Games, 144; private funding, 19–20, 129; revenue sharing of television rights, 16; as sole bidder, 1; taxation, 19–20; televised, 20

Los Angeles as candidate for 2024 Summer Games, 158

Los Angeles Times on Rio protests (2014), 48

Lottery, diverting funds from, 122

Lula da Silva, Luiz Inácio, 107

Lviv as candidate for 2022 Winter Games, 155

Macur, Juliet, 72

Madden, John, 62

Madrid's failed bid for 2020 Summer Games, 140, 154

Maennig,Wolfgang, xiii, 65

Major League Baseball (MLB), 163

Maklyarovsky, Alexander, 89

Market power or leverage, 133–37

Masuzoe, Yoichi, 143

Matheson, Victor, xiv

Mazitelli, David, 63

MBTA (Boston public transportation system), 161–62

McKinsey (consultants), 96

Medvedev, Dmitry, 86, 91

Melbourne 1956 Olympic Games, 14

Melo, Carlos, 106

Mexico City 1968 Games, 1, 16–17, 59–60

Meyers, Steven, 88

Migrant labor, 53, 86–87, 105, 131, 147

Montaner, Josep Maria, 81

Montreal 1976 Summer Games, 1, 17–18, 60

Morale effects, 51, 66
Moscow 1980 Summer Games, 18–19
Moscow Times on Sochi 2014 Winter
    Games, 87–88
Müller, Martin, 88, 91
Munich 1972 Summer Games, 1, 17, 60
Mussolini, Benito, 13–14

Nagano 1998 Winter Games, 23–24,
    45, 71–72
National Audit Report (UK), 118, 119
National Football League, 148
National Olympic Committees
    (NOCs), 5, 14–15, 15*t*, 24–25; of
    Austria, Germany, Sweden, and
    Switzerland, report by (2014), 135,
    141–42
Nawaf Faisal Fahd Abdulaziz (Saudi
    prince), 4
NBC and television rights, 137
Nedelko, Olga, 89
Netherlands and 2028 Summer
    Games, 44
New York City's bid for 2012 Olympic
    Games, xii, 50, 137
New York Jets (football team), xii, xiii
New York Times: on Brazil 2014
    World Cup, 96, 104; on London
    2012 Summer Games, 123; on
    Sochi 2014 Winter Games, 88, 91;
    on South Africa 2010 World Cup,
    72; on Vancouver 2010 Winter
    Games, 74
New Zealand, 17, 55
NHK (Japanese broadcaster), 155
Nikolaev, Igor, 83
Nippon Professional Baseball (Japan),
    72
Nonprofit companies, 122
Nora (princess of Liechtenstein), 4

Odebrecht consortium (construction
    company), 100
Office for National Statistics (UK), 54

Oliveira, Maria Ivanilde, 98
Olympic Delivery Authority (London),
    121
Olympic Games: change of schedule
    to alternate Winter and Summer
    Games, 22; Charter, 10–11, 66,
    86; compared to World Cup, 30,
    61–62, 108; elimination of certain
    sports, 25, 163; revenues, 141. *See
    also* Economic impact; History
    of Olympic Games; International
    Olympic Committee (IOC); *spe-
    cific locations of games*
Olympstroi (Russian construction
    firm), 87
Opening and closing ceremonies,
    44–45
Operating budgets, 49–50
Opportunity costs, 49, 52, 74, 129
Organization of American States, 30
Oslo as candidate for 2022 Winter
    Games, 134, 155
Owens, Jesse, 14

Pagliuca, Steve, ix
Pan American Games (2007), 101, 109
Papandreou, George, 71
Paris: 1900 Games, 11; Exposition
    (1900), 11; not bidding for 2024
    Summer Games, 135–36
Patino, George, 48
Patrick, Deval, xiii–xiv, 159
Payoffs. *See* Corruption
Peace, promotion of, 10, 29
Pew Research Center, 104
Physical activity, Olympic Games'
    effect on level of participation of
    general public in, 123
Platini, Michel, 33
Political gridlock, 50–51
Pollution and environmental issues:
    Beijing as candidate for 2022
    Winter Games and, 156–58; Brazil
    2014 World Cup, 67–68; London

2012 Summer Games, 122–23; Mexico City 1968 Games, 60; Pyeongchang 2018 Winter Games, 154; Rio 2016 Summer Games, 108–09, 110–11, 153; Sochi 2014 Winter Games, 87–88; South Africa 2010 World Cup, 67

Portinho, Carlos Francisco, 108

Potanin, Vladimir, 84, 85

Power, Anne, 116

Poynter, Gavin, 121, 123–24

Premier Soccer League (South Africa), 72

Press Freedom Index, 156

Private funding: Barcelona 1992 Summer Games, 77, 144; Boston 2024 Summer Games bid, 159–61; Brazil 2014 World Cup, 97–98, 107; London 2012 Summer Games, 124; Los Angeles 1984 Summer Games, 19–20, 129; Sochi 2014 Winter Games, 84–86

Probst, Larry, 137

Professional athletes, 22

Protests: in Brazil, 2–3, 16, 48, 103–04, 105–06, 136; in Japan, 155; in Mexico, 16, 17, 60; in Sochi, 88; in South Korea, 154

Public opinion on hosting, 107, 135, 141–42, 158, 163

Public-private partnerships, 97–98

Pujol Barcelona Architects, 96

Putin, Vladimir, 32, 83–84, 88, 91, 92, 112

Pyeongchang (South Korea) 2018 Winter Olympics, 154

Qatar 2022 World Cup, 2, 32–33, 45, 53, 134, 142, 146–48

Quinn Emanuel Urquhart & Sullivan (law firm), 148

Racism. *See* Inequality

Rainha, Renato, 100

Real estate prices, 48, 51, 66, 81–82, 102–03, 121–22, 152

Rebelo, Aldo, 108–09

Reform proposals, 137–44

Relocations, 51, 66, 69, 81, 86–87, 101, 105–06, 110, 111, 116, 152–53

Renewable energy, 123

Reporters without Borders, 156

Reuters: on Brazil 2014 World Cup, 97; on Sochi 2014 Winter Games, 87

Revenues from Games. *See* Economic impact

Rhodesian exclusion from 1968 Games, 16

Richter, Felix, 65

Rio 2016 Summer Games, 108–13; compared to 2014 World Cup, 108; construction plans, 110–11; construction strike, 108, 136; consultants to design strategy, 96; cost of hosting, 26; economic impact likely, 111–13; environmental issues, 108–09, 110–11, 153; forced relocations, 110, 111; golf course construction, 67–68, 108, 110; IOC involvement in preparation, 108, 110; modeled on Barcelona 1992 Summer Games, 96, 144; preparation problems, 152–53; protests, 152; real estate prices and overbuilding, 152–53; stadiums and housing, 95–96, 110–11; transportation, 110

Ritchie, J. R. Brent, 60

Rogge, Jacques, 59, 139

Romário de Souza Faria, 104–05, 107

Rome 1960 Olympic Games, 14

Romney, Mitt, xiii

Rose, Andrew K., 65

Rosenberg, Stan, xiv

Rousseff, Dilma, 111, 153

RTLnews (Netherlands), 44

Russia: 2018 World Cup bidding, 32, 146–47, 148–49. *See also* BRICS; Sochi 2014 Winter Games; Soviet Union

St. Louis: 1904 Games, 11; World Fair in, 11
Sakorafa, Sofia, 71
Salt Lake City: 2002 Winter Games, 54, 143; bid to host 1998 Winter Games, 23–24
Samaranch, Juan Antonio, 20, 22–24
Saunders, Doug, 70
Schmemann, Serge, xv
Schoenfeld, Gerry, xi, xii–xiii
Security costs, 26, 46; Brazil 2014 World Cup, 104; Sochi 2014 Winter Games, 88
Segal, David, 91
Sennes, Ricardo, 112
Shapiro, Ari, 115–16
Shubert Organization, xii–xiii
Silva, Orlando, 107–08
Sinaenco (Brazilian trade group), 97
Skiba, Tatiana, 86–87
Sky News on renovation of London stadium after 2012 Summer Games, 119–20
Smith, Brian H., 60
Smith, Tommie, 17
Soares, Marcos, 99
Soccer: at Athens Games (1896), 11; exclusion from Olympics, 13; promotion in United States, 32; use of term, xv. *See also* World Cup
Sochi 2014 Winter Games, 83–93; budget and financing, 43, 83–84; business disruption, 45; civil rights, worker exploitation, and forced relocations, 86–87; compared to Barcelona 1992 Summer Games, 92–93; construction problems, 112; cost of hosting, 2, 26, 83, 134; hospitality and

venue issues, 89; pollution, 87–88; private funding from Russian oligarchs, 84–86; terrorism during, 83, 88; tourism, 60, 90–93; weather issues, 89
Sochi 2018 World Cup, 83, 92
Son, Kitei, 14
South Africa: 2006 World Cup bid, 106; 2010 World Cup, 2, 33–34, 35, 43, 67, 72–73, 131, 134, 136, 148; African boycott of Montreal 1976 Summer Games over New Zealand's relationship with, 17; business disruption, 45; exclusion from participating in Olympics, 16–17; Premier Soccer League, 72. *See also* BRICS
South Korea 2002 World Cup, 33, 34, 54, 72, 136
South Korea 2018 Winter Olympics, 154
Soviet Union: boycott of 1984 Los Angeles Games, 20; Five-Year Plan (1928–32), 84; hosting 1980 Games, 18, 60; and Sochi development, 83
Spiegel, Mark M., 65
Sport England, 123
Sports Illustrated on community rehabilitation related to London 2012 Summer Games, 120
Sports venues and nonsport infrastructure: costs of construction or renovation, 45, 130; IOC stadium requirements, 140, 142, 155; precluding use of land for other reasons, 127–28, 129–30; temporary, 160–61; white elephant venues, 34, 69–73, 102, 127, 160; World Cup stadium requirements, 34, 97, 100, 140–41, 149
Stadiums. *See* Construction; Sports venues and nonsport infrastructure
Stockholm 1912 Olympic Games, 11

Straus, Bill, 159
Straw, Jack, 118–19
Substitution effect and mega-sporting events, xi, 28–29, 42–43. *See also* Tourism
Sunday Times (London), 3, 33
Sustainability, 66–68, 87–88, 142, 151
Sydney 2000 Summer Games, 24, 54–55, 62–63, 134, 144
The Sydney Olympics: Seven Years On (Giesecke & Madden), 62
Szymanski, Stefan, 115–16

Taiwanese team, Canada refusing entry to for 1970 Games, 17
Tamim Bin Hamad Al Thani (emir of Qatar), 4
Taxation: Boston bid for 2024 games, 159–62; development subsidies and abatements, 161–62; FIFA's demands for special tax treatment, 104–05; London 2012 Summer Games, 116–17; Los Angeles 1984 Summer Games, 19–20; raising taxes to pay for construction, 52
Technical Manual on Brand Protection (IOC), 116
Teigland, Jon, 63–64
The Telegraph (London) on Athens Olympics, 71
Television rights: 2015 women's World Cup, 150; buying, 14; history of, 21, 21*t*; history of revenue distribution, 14–16, 15*t*, 24–25; long-term benefits for tourism from, 59; Los Angeles 1984 Summer Games, 20; Qatar 2022 World Cup, 148; revenue as source of financing for Games, 27–28, 28*t*; United States as choice to host and, 137
Terrorism: Munich 1972 Summer Games, 1, 17; Sochi 2014 Winter Games, 88

Thatcher, Margaret, 19
Thornton, Grant, 125
Thorpe, Jim, 11
Ticket prices, 162–63
Tokyo: 1964 Summer Games, 14, 129; 2020 Summer Games, 140, 143, 154–55; failed bid to host 2016 Summer Games, 44, 140; protests against 2020 Summer Games, 136
Tourism: additional tourist taxes and, 19–20; Barcelona from 1990 to 2009, 78–81, 80*t*; Beijing 2008 Summer Games, 38, 54, 60; Brazil 2014 World Cup, 39, 55, 60, 62, 111; decline in or no additional revenues at time of Games, 38–39; economic impacts, 48; European cities, 79, 80*t*; London 2012 Summer Games, 38, 54, 60; long-term benefits, 59–64; Salt Lake City during 2001–02 Olympic year, 54; short-term benefits, 53–56; Sochi 2014 Winter Games, 60, 90–93; South Africa 2010 World Cup, 43; substitution effect and, xi, 28–29, 42–43
Trade and investment, 26, 37, 65
Transparency, 142
Transportation: Barcelona General Metropolitan Plan and, 76; Boston 2024 Summer Games bid, 161–62; Brazil 2014 World Cup, 67, 96–97, 103; Brazilian economy and, 74; London 2012 Summer Games, 115, 117; Rio 2016 Summer Games, 110; South Africa 2010 World Cup, 67
Turner, Ted, 139

Ueberroth, Peter, 1, 20–21, 129
UEFA (European soccer organization), 149
United Nations: Environment Program, 88; Security Council, 16

United States: 1994 World Cup and, 2, 32, 34, 147; 2022 World Cup choice and, 146–47; black athletes from, 17; boycott of Moscow 1980 Summer Games and, 18–19; Dream Team at Barcelona 1992 Summer Games, 22; future bids for Games and, 137; macroeconomic models of economy of, 37. *See also specific cities*

United States Olympic Committee (USOC), xiii, 18, 24–25, 137, 158, 163

Universal Forum of Cultures (Barcelona 2004), 82

Uruguay, 1930 World Cup in, 13

Valcke, Jerome, 33, 103, 148

Vancouver 2010 Winter Games, 35, 55, 72, 74

VEB (Russian development bank), 86

Venue budgets, 49–50

Walsh, Mary, 158, 163–64

Warner, Jack, 147

Weather issues: Beijing 2018 Winter Games bid, 157; for Qatar 2022 World Cup, 147–48; for Sochi 2014 Winter Games, 89

West Germany's boycott of Moscow 1980 Summer Games, 19

West Ham United (soccer team), 119–20

Wilkinson Eyre Architects, 96

Women: 2015 women's World Cup, 149–50; as East German medal winners, 18; as Olympic participants, 11–12

World Anti-Doping Agency (WADA), 18, 105

World Baseball Classic, 163

World Cup, xiv–xv, 29–34; compared to Olympics, 30, 61–62, 108; competing with NFL, 148; continental rotation of hosting, 30–31, 106, 136–37; cost of hosting, 2, 146; economic impact of, 37–43, 41–42t; financing of, 33–34; history of, 13, 29; national animosities and, 29–30; revenues, 141; stadium requirements, 34, 97, 100, 140–41; tourism and, 61–62. *See also* Fédération Internationale de Football Association (FIFA); *specific locations of games*

World Health Organization, 109

World Rugby Championship 2019, 155

World War I, 11–12

World War II, 14

World Wildlife Fund, 87

Yamaguchi, Sumikazu, 24

Zhemukhov, Sufian, 91

Zhukov, Alexander, 84

Zirin, Dave, 98, 101